History of St. Mary's Parish, Barrie

History of St. Mary's Parish, Barrie

A Sure and Certain Hope

BY

FRANCIS V. MCDEVITT

RNU PRESS

This edition published by RNU Press
I-12 Commerce Park Drive
Barrie, ON, L4N 8W8
www.rnupress.com

RNU PRESS

ISBN: 978-0-9877784-5-1

This book is printed on acid-free paper.
This book is a work of non-fiction. Places, events, and situations in this book are true.

For Tenie, who promised that after infatuation there is love and showed it by her sixty seven years of monastic life.

Contents

Introduction

THE reluctance of a religious community to explore its history is often a fear that imperfection and limitations will become obvious or worse choose to tell the story as if all was perfection. We each of us live imperfection and limitations, and either in faith, or in response to some essential ideal embrace a sure and certain hope that calls us forward.

This is a time when religion and history live in almost exclusive separation from each other. To strive to understand the human story without religion, is as facile as striving to understand the human story while ignoring economics or politics.

St. Mary's offers some desirable advantages for the study of people and their religious identity. The parish is singular in its relationship with the area. It is not one of many Catholic parishes vying for the loyalty of the people. Barrie's second Catholic parish was not founded until 1957.

To understand the foundation of St. Mary's we must go back before 1855 to see how ministry was done before parishes were formed. The first brief chapter reminds us that history has its share of broken lines and the second chapter explores church life in the county in the earliest times of European settlement.

From its creation in 1855, the parish allows us to observe the evolution of Catholic church life. To study the Catholics of the Barrie area is not just to look at the life of those who share a common religion, but to strive to understand their relationship in a larger community where they lived the paradox of integration and separation.

A couple of comments before we proceed. This is not a work of genealogy. The life of St. Mary's Parish is dependant on the lives of a great army of people who strove to live the Catholic faith in Barrie and district. I have not consciously avoided naming names, but I certainly have not went out of my way to include litanies of committees and association memberships. When the narrative thread was to be lost without the inclusion of names they were included. I am conscious that for some who may pick up this book, your attachment to St. Mary's is very much tied to the lives of those in your family that preceded you and you may clearly have a desire to see them memorialized in this history.

I have included a number of blank pages at the back and I invite you to take the time and write your own short history of you and your families connection to St. Mary's for posterity.

Not everything I was told has been included in the book. Much of that should be included on the back pages of personal copies.

Throughout the writing of this book I was tempted by the strictly academic form of writing and veered away since the book has not been written with academics in mind. Quotations, and there are a lot of them, have been given proper citation for they may lead others on a quest and verifies where the statement in the book was garnered. In the case of quotes from announcement books, the quotations have been been formed to make greater sense, especially when the announcement was written simply in point form. I have corrected egregious errors in correspondence, but have tried to maintain the quaint turn of phrase.

This undertaking began in 2004, when St. Mary's was moving towards its sesquicentennial. It has been given active attention over many periods of time and ignored for equally if not longer periods, including one full year.

I have been greatly supported by the interest and energy of a number of good people. The final product is a reflection of their support. Any omissions or mistakes are a reflection of my own frailties.

F. V. McDevitt

Acknowledgments

I am indebted to:

The late John D'Ambrosio for his computer expertise and patience with one who is not an expert and the late John Brennan for his deep well of knowledge of all things Barrie.

To Valerie and Guy Hachey who translated a number of early letters from French and Marg Mullen for her translation of other early papers of the parish.

To those who read the manuscript to rein in my steadily deteriorating grammar and spelling in this age of information technology.

I am indebted to the following institutions:
(The Acronyms of the most frequently used sources precede their title)

All Hallows College Archivies, Dublin
ARCAT - The Archives of the Archdiocese of Toronto and their archivist, Marc Lerman, Toronto
AO - The Archives of the Province of Ontario, Toronto
The Archives of the Sisters of St. Joseph and their archivist, Linda Wicks, Toronto
The Archives of the Redemptorist Order and their archivist, M. C. Havey, Toronto
BPL - The Barrie Public Library for their efficient and friendly service.
Jesuit Archives in Canada, Montreal
MTRL - Metro Toronto Reference Library
National Archives of Canada, Ottawa
Regis College Library, Toronto
SMPA - St. Mary's Parish Archives
SCA - The Simcoe County Archives, especially Ellen Millar whose enthusiasm is not only infectious but generously leads the researchers to new paths of exploration.

The First Christian Moment

People stood on the heights above Kempenfelt Bay and observed the changing seasons and the evolving story of humanity for thousands of years before any European even imagined the existence of this part of the world. From 1615, when Fr. Joseph Le Caron and Champlain sojourned at Cahiague, near the present day Village of Warminster, the Christian message was introduced to the native communities which lived around the shores of Georgian Bay, Lake Couchiching and Lake Simcoe. The early development of the Christian mission came to full flower under the Jesuits at St. Marie Among the Hurons in the 1640's. Aboriginal people who had been baptized by the Jesuit missionaries in the mid 1600's and French adventurers who spread out across North America in service of profit and the crown carried with them the Christian faith. Not only among the Hurons were converts found, but among the Iroquois and Neutrals over the many years of missionary endeavours.

This first Christian moment was intimately entwined with the 1635 to1649 mission to the Huron nation. Huronia did not embrace the present area of Barrie. It was the northern part of Simcoe County as far south as Orr Lake and the lower reaches of the Town of Orillia.

The Hurons were successful traders with other tribes and it was this aspect of their society which was to be both the cause of their early connection with Europeans and also their demise as a nation at the hands of the Iroquois.

French contact with the Hurons was first initiated in the interest of trade and therefore French sovereignty, but also for the purpose of evangelization and Catholic sovereignty.

Furs were desired by the European market and the technologies that Europeans could introduce to the natives were equally desired in return. The aboriginal people wanted iron tools for domestic use and to expedite trapping.

This was not an ambivalent dance of vastly different people, but an eager coming together of two cultures concerned to secure the advantages for themselves before competing interests. On the part of the French these competing interests were the other European traders present in North America and on the part of the Hurons the other nations eager to trade with the Europeans.

When a frontier presents itself, human culture will rush up against it in any number of ways. Though we are less likely to critique economics or social mores, we need to accept that with these ideologies the ideas of faith will likewise wash against the new frontier.

The destruction of the Huron nation during the era of the French missionaries was the work of the Iroquois who were motivated by a desire to clear out the Hurons to gain the advantage in trade. Throughout these raids the Jesuit missionaries fell victim to the Iroquois raiding parties at various points throughout Huronia.

Were the missionaries ever in the Barrie area? This is hard to know. Archaeological research has found extensive proof of French trade goods well within the confines of Barrie and the surrounding townships. If the trade goods were carried to Barrie, surely the ideas prevalent among the French were carried into this area too.

As Lake Simcoe became an established source of transportation, the head of Kempenfelt Bay was in particular an attractive landing point for traders heading across The Nine Mile Portage to the Nottawasaga River.

They would also have in this time of perpetual motion lived their Catholic identity with conviction or ambivalence on the trade routes through the Barrie area. Among those who would have passed below the hill on which St. Mary's stands today would have been the great explorer LaSalle on his way with his thirty Frenchmen and one hundred Indians, 'all who could use guns', on their course of discovery in the west.[1]

Long before Europeans set down permanent roots there were those of Christian faith who travelled the length of Kempenfelt Bay below the heights on which St. Mary's now stands. We can well imagine as the Christian message was carried among the native people, it was discussed and debated, with gentleness and with rancour as they shouldered their burdens or unloaded them at the beginning or the end of the portage. How often did a native walk that nine miles carrying a canoe while his mate on the other end of the burden questioned him about his Christian faith and invited him to return to the ancient beliefs of the elders? How often did they in the end agree to disagree as they dipped their paddles in the water of the bay as they set their course for the south of the lake and The Carrying Place which would lead them to Lake Ontario?

We know that long before we begin our story of the Catholic faith in the Barrie area that the rituals and prayers of the faithful laymen, both aboriginal and European, had been expressed with quiet conviction along the shores of

---

1. Andrew Hunter, *History of Simcoe County*, page 9.

Kempenfelt Bay and on the portage across our parish.

And yet, this first moment is, in the end, not where the roots of Catholic life are to be found, rather, in the beginning of settlement, the creation of European communities and the establishing of the frameworks of faith.

Persevering Zeal in the Advancement of our Holy Religion

When nine-year-old Napoleon Caisse fell from the dock of his father's hotel, The Queen's Arms Inn, and drowned, "while amusing himself fishing," in the spring of 1848, the *Barrie Magnet* paid homage to the deceased, "as an interesting little fellow."[1]

In our present age in a much larger community, the same story would galvanize the population.

Life on the frontier was difficult. Few could claim the luxury of effusive grief. One wonders how the Kenny Family of Vespra Township could survive the death of seven of their children in 1838, in a matter of weeks, from eating poisonous mushrooms.[2]

For those extended the opportunity of coming to Upper Canada whether they arrived with wealth and connections or were striking out into the unknown to establish life in a new land, the challenges on the frontier were demanding.

The majority of the Catholic settlers who were in the area that was to be established as St. Mary's Parish, were Irish. There was a significant French speaking presence at Penetanguishene from early in the nineteenth century as there would be at New Lowell, Brentwood and Bell Ewart in the second half of the century.

Settlement of Simcoe County.

This chapter will look at church life in Simcoe County leading to the establishment of St. Mary's Parish in 1855. Though we will spend some time on the shores of Kempenfelt Bay, we will also find ourselves on the shores of Georgian

1. BPL, *Barrie Magnet*, April 28, 1848. The Queen's Arms was on the north side of Dunlop St. where the Queen's Hotel now stands. At the time the shoreline was much closer to Dunlop St. and The Queen's Arms owned a wharf on the waterfront.

2. The grave marker for the Kenny children is on the left of the center driveway of St. Mary's Cemetery not far from the front. The Kenny Family prospered in Vespra and Myles Kenny the father of the family went on to become the first reeve of Vespra Township.

Bay and in many places in between where early settlements were created.

The initial development of Simcoe County was centred on the importance of water for military defense and as a source of transportation.

Kempenfelt Bay verged on perfection in these early endeavours. A sheltered bay of such length provided great opportunity for military and domestic needs. Robert Pilkington notes its excellence, in passing, on his map drawn in 1793, to show, "The Route from the Town of York to Penetanguisheen." He mentions that Kempenfelt Bay is reported to be twelve miles deep.[3]

Settlement around Penetanguishene by military personnel began in 1814, in response to the deficits in defense, during the War of 1812. The Penetanguishene Road which connected Lake Simcoe at Kempenfelt Bay to Georgian Bay at Penetanguishene was surveyed by Samuel Wilmot in 1811. Samuel Wilmot had first surveyed the area of Penetanguishene in 1808 and on completion of the survey of Penetanguishene Road in 1812, laid out town plots at Penetanguishene and Kempenfelt Village.[4] In 1814, the Penetanguishene Road was cleared by the military under the direction of William 'Tiger' Dunlop. The road itself was constructed in 1818.[5]

The Village of Kempenfelt never realized its original promise. Located further east of Barrie, at the present time it is found south of Blake Street on the Shanty Bay Road. There is a historical plaque that notes where the Penetanguishene Road began.

Barrie began to grow, but citizens with an interest in promoting the cause of Kempenfelt Village continued to assert its preferred status. In the 1830's they were still advocating for their interests.

Francis Hewson in 1833, states that he had purchased lots at Kempenfelt and made improvements with a view to building a store. The government had altered the plan of encouraging a town there and had laid out another town within one and a half miles of the proposed Town of Kempenfelt, called Barrie, whereby the property in the former place has suffered in value. Hewson hoped to be granted lots in Barrie in compensation so he could build a dock. He was told that he would need to buy the lots.[6]

---

3 MTRL, Baldwin Room, Pilkington, Robert, Sketch of the Route from York Town to the Harbour of Penetanguisheen on Lake Huron, JRR Map 912.713.P38. The same map identifies Cowan's Trading House, though on the wrong side of the river and the ruins of the Church of St. Mary's where St. Marie Among the Hurons now stands.

4. Ladell, John L., *They Left Their Mark*, Dundurn Press, 1993, page 108. Highway 93 runs more or less the same course as the original Penetanguishene Road.

5. AO, *Upper Canada Sundries*, December 13, 1817, p. 16461, D 23.

6. AO, *Upper Canada Sundries*, September 30, 1833, p. 73515, D. 23.

Three years later a petition of the citizens of the Penetanguishene Road and their descendants took up the cause of Kempenfelt, since many of them had purchased lots around the town and one thousand acres had been set aside for public buildings as far back as 1814.

They framed their argument in the most emphatic way, "we must further observe that it is not likely any persons of respectability would ever make Barrie their choice of residence at any season of the year as close to the S. W. of it there is a swamp of some extent fully as low as the lake, which said, prevents a possibility of its being ever drained and with a S. W. wind a noxious vapour will be frequently hovering over Barrie."[7]

Whatever the hope there was for Kempenfelt, time favoured Barrie.

The Nine Mile Portage was to become the seed that gave original sustenance to Barrie. The portage began in what is now downtown. It provided a more direct route to Georgian Bay by way of an overland route to the Willow Creek and the Nottawasaga River.

George Head, the commissary for the construction of the establishment at Penetanguishene, sojourned on the shore of Kempenfelt Bay in the spring and summer of 1815 and actively promoted the head of the bay and Nine Mile Portage as the more efficient route of transportation.[8]

His preference was so fully accepted that the project at Penetanguishene Harbour was abandoned in favour of a military depot on the Nottawasaga River, called Schooner Town. This experiment in the end proved problematic as the shifting sands at the mouth of the Nottawasaga River made the creation of an effective harbor impossible and in 1818 Penetanguishene was re-established as the preferred terminus on Georgian Bay by way of the Penetanguishene Road which was constructed that year.[9] Twelve years later when Penetanguishene was established as a parish, Barrie was one of its missions.

The Earliest Catholic Community in Simcoe County.

In the earliest times of settlement the transitory nature of life caused people to come into an area and then move on in search of greater opportunities. There are those for whom we have a clearer picture of their life, because of the role they played in the community. Four families will be highlighted here.

7. AO, *Upper Canada Sundries*, October 1836, p. 93525, D23.

8. At the present time if one was to draw a line from the cenotaph on Fred Grant Square past Victoria Village and on past Good Shepherd School, you would be creating more or less the course of the Nine Mile Portage.

9. Murdoch et al, *Beautiful Barrie*, 2007, page 23.

They reflect the spectrum of adherence to religious life and how it was embraced or lost on the frontier.

The Bergins.

Settlement began on the Penetanguishene Road in 1819. Among the early settlers were Michael Bergin and his wife, Catherine Lodge. They took up their claim at lot 19 on the Oro Township side of the road.[10] James and Francis Lodge, Catherine's father and brother, located across the road in Vespra Township at lot 20, sometime later.

Michael Bergin and his wife had left the Parish of Clonenagh, in Queen's (Offaly) County, Ireland in 1818. They came to Canada by way of New York City. In September of 1819, Michael petitioned the government for land assuring them that he would accept whatever, "your excellency may deem meet." He asserted further that he would have means to improve the land.[11]

From the Bergins, threads spread out connecting many of the Catholic households of the earliest times in Simcoe County. Michael Bergin's sister, Ann, was married to Israel Mundy of Penetanguishene.[12] Israel Mundy's mother, Marguerite (Cornelier) Vallieres had originally been employed at the Royalist French settlement on Yonge Street at the present day site of Oak Ridges. Marguerite and her husband, Jean Baptiste Vallieres, had come to Upper Canada in 1798 from Lower Canada. Jean Baptiste died in 1800 and a year later Marguerite married Asher Mundy.

Her connection with Simcoe began when she established a shop at Schooner Town at the mouth of the Nottawasaga River in 1816. They moved to Penetanguishene in 1818 when the military establishment relocated. Asher Mundy transported goods on Georgian Bay and in later life, he was the lighthouse keeper near Penetanguishene. Their son, Israel, later assumed this duty. Marguerite's daughter, Elizabeth Vallieres, the child of her first marriage, married George Cowan.

George Cowan had been captured by the French during the war of 1758 and 1759 and had adopted the language and culture of the French, using the name Georges Constant. He established himself at a trading post on Matchedash Bay, in behind the present day Village of Coldwater, and traded

10. Simoro Golf Course is now located on the Bergin Farm. The Bergins eventually owned, as well, the farm directly across the road. The Lodges farm was on the Vespra side just above the twentieth side road.

11. AO, *Land Petition*, September 22, 1819, Michael Bergin, RG 1,C1625-Vol. 43, B 177.

12. ARCAT, *Sacramental Records*, St. Anne's, Penetanguishene.

and farmed there from the later part of the 1770's, until his accidental death in 1810.[13]

In an interesting document from July 1829, citizens along the Penetanguishene Road and in the Village of Penetanguishene petitioned Sir John Colborne to consider making Michael Bergin a magistrate. The four petitioners were Asher Mundy, Israel Mundy, Francis Lodge and James Lodge. Obviously, since all of the petitioners were related to Bergin in some way, we cannot ignore the self interest, but there was also a real problem on the frontier as asserted in their petition. "We, the undersigned inhabitants on the Penetanguishene Road, on behalf of ourselves and neighbours, beg leave to represent to your Excellency that owing to there being no magistrate on any part of the road nearer than Newmarket in West Gwillimborough or Big Bay Point, whenever any little difference arises or that there is even only a settlement duty to be certified it requires we labour under very great inconvenience and are at considerable expense in order to have our affairs settled. We hope your excellency will be pleased to take our case into consideration and appoint some person to the commission of the peace amongst us. We at the same time beg leave to recommend Mr. Michael McDonnell and Mr. Michael Bergin as most competent to act in that capacity."[14]

There is no indication to suggest that Colborne acquiesced to their petition.

Church life for these very earliest of settlers was exclusively dependant on the missionary priests that made their way through the area.

Michael Bergin was to have a place of prominence in the early development of church life at Barrie. This was in part because of the location of the Bergin farm on Penetanguishene Road.

In 1840, Fr. James Quinlan[15] acknowledges in a letter to Bishop Gaulin, at Kingston, that Bergin will commit himself to the advancement of Catholic ministry. "He (Bergin), it is true, has a welcome for a priest, so far as a cursory visit, but to have a constant boarder he would not condescend, he candidly assigns his reason, that those people coming on business to the priest, and their horses would be an extraordinary trespass, and that I know."[16]

Michael Bergin died early in 1852. After his death, it appears that Catherine remained on the farm across from her father and brother. When her

13. Hunter, *History of Simcoe County*, page 21. ff.

14. AO, *Upper Canada Sundries*, July 13, 1829, pp 52976, D23.

15. ordained 1834.

16. AO, *Diocese of Kingston Papers*, James Quinlan to Bishop Remigius Gaulin, October 29, 1840. BB16-01.

father, James Lodge, died in 1857, Catherine and her brother Francis gave the land they held on either side of Pentanguishene Road, a total of three hundred acres to the Sisters of St. Joseph at Toronto.

In spite of the risk of getting out of chronological order it may be useful to conclude the story of the Bergins and the Lodges.

Francis Lodge died, in Toronto, in November 1863.

In noting, in the *Canadian Freeman*, a paper that served the Irish Catholic community, that a mass on the one month anniversary of Lodge's death had been celebrated at St. Paul's Church in Toronto, they also gave some impression of the man himself. "On Thursday last a solemn requiem mass was celebrated in St. Paul's Church in this city by the Rev. J. B. Proulx for the repose of the soul of the late Mr. Francis Lodge who died about a month ago. The Very Rev. J. F. Jamot, Rev. Messrs. Rooney, Flannery and Gribbin were present in the sanctuary. The deceased lived and died an exemplary practical Catholic, most of his time was spent in the church in adoration and prayer before the Blessed Sacrament. About seven years ago he made over a farm of a hundred acres of land in the Township of Vespra together with the buildings, chattels and all to the Sisters of St. Joseph for the benefit of the poor of The House of Providence in which situation he spent the last years of his life. As the orphans and those able to walk attended the funeral obsequies and followed the remains a considerable distance toward their last resting place, so they were present at the month's mind to offer up their heartfelt prayers for the repose of the soul of their kind benefactor."[17]

Catherine Bergin, like her brother, had become a boarder at the House of Providence with the Sisters of St. Joseph and lived an extraordinarily long life. She died in 1894. As the annals of the order report on November 12th of that year, "Mrs. Bergin, an old, old, old lady, who has boarded with the sisters for years is very low; her death is daily expected."

Death came the next day and *The Annals of the Sisters of St. Joseph* on the fifteenth of the same month report on her funeral, "Poor old soul, she has gone to rejoin her loved ones, gone before. She was a most devout old person and doubtless she is now receiving the reward of her many good deeds."[18,19]

---

17. AO, *Canadian Freeman*, December 17, 1863.

18. Sisters of St. Joseph of Toronto Archives, *Annals of Sisters of St. Joseph*, Toronto, November 12, 1894.

19. AO, *Catholic Register*, November 22, 1894. Her obituary may be somewhat fanciful, it states that she was 102, but also relates that her father lived to be 106 and her brother 103.

The McDonalds.

Another early settler on the Penetanguishene Road was John le Borgne McDonald who had been chief factor of the Northwest Company. He settled at lot 5 of the Penetanguishene Road with his wife Marie Poitras in 1827.[20] McDonald had been born in Scotland in 1770 and at the age of sixteen immigrated to Glengarry County, in eastern Ontario, with his family. Marie was Metis having been born in the west.

The Northwest Company was set up in competition with the Hudson Bay Company. This competition resulted in violent clashes, the most extreme being the Seven Oaks Massacre. In June 1816, the Hudson Bay Company clashed with the Northwest Company and their Metis allies at Seven Oaks, which is now part of the city of Winnipeg. The Hudson Bay Company lost twenty-one men and the Northwest Company, one. Among those killed was the governor of the Red River settlement, Robert Semple. McDonald, as well as others, were implicated in the mayhem.

The crime, in such a remote part of the country allowed the judicial proceedings to drag on as the location of the trial in Quebec or Upper Canada was hammered out. By 1818, McDonald and others were indicted for, "treason, conspiracy and as an accessory in the murder of Robert Semple and to divers other murders, robberies and felonies in the course of May and June 1816." As time wore on and the unification of the contending fur trading companies took place, the charges were dropped.[21]

When the Northwest Company and Hudson Bay Company amalgamated in 1821, McDonald became a chief factor. The development of the fur trade pushed for the opening of secure routes free of border incursions from the south. Its active participation in the promotion of the development of the Penetanguishene Road as an advantage for the fur trade had lead to the company's desire for land grants at Kempenfelt and Penetanguishene. Two thousand acres were granted to the chief factor, William McGillivray, along the Penetanguishene Road. When McGillivray died, the land passed into the hands of John McDonald, the new chief factor. He made his home on one of the lots.

Though little of his correspondence still exists, what does exist, give us a window into the life of a man who lived on the furthest reaches of European influence in western Canada. Some of this correspondence relates to oversee-

---

20. There are other sources that suggest that McDonald settled just above the Crown Hill Swamp.

21. AO, *Upper Canada Sundries*, Indictment, February 7, 1818, p. 17811ff, D23.

ing the care and education of his children by his brother James in Glengarry County. As much as they were united by their common roots, they were a contentious family.

In 1819, James has custody of John and Marie's children and John includes a letter with a shipment of furs and others things for the use of those in Glengarry. "I forward, directed to your care, a Pack of Skins and which you will dispose of as follows: There are three buffalo robes sent by their mother to the boys, but if they do not want them, keep one for the house, give one to Malcolm and the other to my sister Catherine. There are two garnished capot, the largest for yourself and other for Angus. Each of the boys has seven pairs of shoes and each of the little girls seven. There are besides thirteen pairs of garnished shoes and five pairs not garnished . . . mother will dispose of them as she thinks proper amongst the family . . . also a bundle in the pack marked and directed for the Rev. Alexander Macdonell[22] containing six dressed skins which you will have the goodness to deliver to him.

Tell the little boys that the cinctures their mother sent them were left by mistake at some place on the way out, but others will be sent to them next year. I hope they will be good boys obedient and attentive to their superiors. They must break themselves of the propensity for playing and bind their minds on their education. If so, they will find I will discharge my duty toward them giving them every support according to their merit."[23]

Unfortunately, the arrangement seems to have floundered after a number of years. John explains his discontent with James' custodial care at the end of August in 1825, "Respecting my ordering my children, from under your protection, it was a necessary step and I am only sorry that it was not done five years sooner. If so, I should not have the mortification to hear them branded as vagabonds. They were as promising children as ever left this country when they went down. Had I then placed them with strangers, as others did, they would have turned out otherwise than other children in similar situations, but they are not the only ones when placed with their relatives who turned out in the same manner "[24]

McDonald was a legendary character. In the historian of Simcoe County, Andrew Hunter's archival notes, one of his informants told him that McDonald married his wife, because she had saved his life. The Indians were going to

---

22. born 1762, ordained (priest)1787, ordained (bishop) 1820, died 1840.

23. AO, John McDonald Files, John McDonald to James McDonald, August 6, 1819. Mu 2201, box 6, file 2. The cintures that McDonald refers to would have been the belts worn over pants and shirt which would have been part of a young Metis' boys dress.

24. Ibid., John McDonald to James McDonald, August 27,1825. Mu 2201, box 6, file 2.

kill him and she threw herself on the prisoner to prevent this. "It was something like Pocahontas and Captain John Smith."[25] This is a fanciful story, for in fact, Marie and John were not married until near the end of their life. Another correspondent of Hunter's stated that McDonald had seven sons and that some of them were nearly seven feet tall. The same correspondent notes that the sons, "lawed with their youngest sister, Catherine, for the property, but she beat them."[26]

This story of 'lawing' is substantially true, because in fact, John and Marie McDonald had been married according to the custom of the country and raised a large family only marrying legally before the birth of the last child in 1825. After the death of the John and Marie McDonald only the youngest of their large family, three year old Catherine, was entitled to inherit the estate as she was the only one who was born after the marriage was solemnized.

It was, in fact, not her brothers that held up the probation of the estate but her uncles, Finan and James, who felt they had claims against the estate. Extensive probation in 1839 achieved little, it was only in 1850, twenty-two years after McDonald's death that the estate was settled in Catherine's favour.[27]

McDonald was well immersed in his Highland Catholicism and his wife, Marie, would have likewise been formed by her Metis Catholic culture.

John writes his brother about the death of their "ever lamented" nephew whose body was conveyed to the church at St. Raphael's in Glengarry County. "He was interred immediately after mass . . . we ought to be thankful and resigned to the will of the Omnipotent dispenser of all our pleasures and sorrows. What consolation to his poor afflicted mother and relations to have the body interred where they can daily kneel by his grave and shed a parental tear to his memory."[28]

McDonald reports on another nephew that has been sent out to the west to be under John's tutelage. Apparently he felt the potential for the boy did not suggest a life on the trap lines as he reports, "He (Finan) sent one of his boys across to me last year and I had him placed in the Catholic Bishops School in Red River. He lives at the Bishop's house and is a great favourite with him and the priests. He is a fine boy. It is he who serves at mass. He knows all the responses already and promises to be a good French and Latin

25. SCA, *Andrew Hunter Papers*, Sibald to Hunter. 971-57.
26. Ibid., box 8, envelope 5, page 6.
27. AO, Estate files, 638-Reel 56, McDonald.
28. AO, McDonald Files, McDonald to McDonald, June 19, 1819, MU2201, box 6, file 2.

Scholar, but knows not a word of English."[29]

McDonald and his wife, Marie Poitras, both died in 1828, Marie during child birth in January and McDonald himself the following month. One of his neighbours, John Spencer, a fellow fur trader, noted at his passing, that he died depriving us of a gentleman that so many looked up to as nearly the father of the flock."[30]

For want of a cemetery in Barrie, they were both buried at the public cemetery in Newmarket.[31] Tradition states that the grave marker on the McDonald's grave was provided by Lady Franklin, the wife of Sir John Franklin, in appreciation for his support of her husband during his 1825 trip in search of the Northwest passage.[32]

After the death of her parents, Catherine was raised in the home of her uncle, Finan. Catherine married Angus Grant, a Scottish immigrant and carpenter, and settled in Tay Township, keeping a store at Wyevale.[33]

By the time that the census was taken in 1861, she had three sons and a daughter being raised in the Church of Scotland, but was still identifying herself as a Roman Catholic.[34]

The Baxters.

Samuel Baxter a native of County Tyrone, Ireland and his wife Mary Anne Bennis of County Limerick, Ireland came to Barrie about the year 1830. Samuel had originally been attached to the military, as a tailor, and no doubt on his arrival in Canada made his living in this trade. The family arrived with a number of children. Samuel was received into the Catholic Church, his wife's faith, with all of his children at Barrie. The family took the commitment to faith and religious practice very seriously. The Baxters had been given a land grant on the sixth line of Vespra Townships at lot 14. Though some effort was made to clear the land and a house was built, by 1858 it seems they had lost the grant for lack of completing settlement duties, which would have included clearing a specific number of acres.

---

29. AO., McDonald File, John McDonald to James McDonald, August 27, 1825, box 6, file 2, MU2201.

30. Archives Canada website. *Dictionary of Canadian Biography*, John (le Borgne) MacDonald.

31. The cemetary founded in 1820 did not become an Anglican cemetary till the 1860's. It is found on Eagle Street, east of Yonge and south of Davis. The marker is no longer there.

32. Ibid.

33. Hunter, *History of Simcoe County*, p. 27.

34. BPL, 1861 Census of Tiny and Tay Township.

The Baxters, like most families, came to Barrie, raised their family and disappeared into history. Essentially this is true for the Baxters except for their son Richard who was nine when they came to Barrie.

Richard Baxter, in his youth, was sent away to study first in Toronto and later in the Sulpician Seminary in Montreal. At the same time, the Jesuits were reestablishing themselves in Canada. Richard entered the Jesuit novitiate in 1845. He was the first English speaking Jesuit in Canada. He persevered and was ordained a priest in 1854. His early work was in education and pastoral ministry in the United States. In 1863, he was sent as a missionary to northern Ontario.[35]

Fr. Baxter's reputation rested on his size and physical prowess and on his forthrightness in conversation.

His first mission was at Sault Ste. Marie and around the shores of Lake Michigan. He, with a lay brother, dug the foundations of the Church of the Sacred Heart at the Sault when Bishop Jamot sought to establish a parish there.[36]

After a short hiatus in the south, Fr. Baxter was sent to Port Arthur in 1872, where he oversaw the establishment of St. Andrew's Parish.

The towns of the north were being connected during this time by railways. Fr. Baxter made it his particular ministry to travel to the men working on the railroads. In this work his fame spread as a missionary priest. Not only did he bring his priestly ministry but was active in providing proper nutrition for the workers who often developed scurvy. Later during the construction of the Canadian Pacific Railway, Baxter was assigned solely to the pastoral care of the workers. His ministry along the railway lines continued until the early 1890's. During his train ministry he was instrumental in forming parishes at White River and Schreiber. He eventually returned to parish ministry and in his declining years returned to Montreal where he died in 1904.

We can trace the family's continued presence in Barrie up until the beginning of the twentieth century. The family is present in the 1861 census, though by then Samuel is dead. His wife, Mary Ann, was buried at St. Mary's Cemetery in 1878, having lived to a great age. The son, Samuel Jr., died in 1890.

The final connection between this family and Barrie was severed with the death of the youngest daughter Mary Ann in 1916. After a career as a teacher in private schools, she made her living making lace and fancy goods. As the

35. Regis College Library, *Canadian Messenger*, vol 15, # 6, Obituray of Richard Baxter S. J., p. 259 ff.

36. Ibid.

Barrie Examiner reported, "Miss Ann Baxter died in Toronto on Saturday, February 12 following a decline in health caused by advancing years. The body was brought to Barrie for interment. Rev. Dean O'Malley officiated at the requiem high mass. Miss Baxter was 88 years of age and will be remembered by many of the older residents of the town, she having been a school teacher here many years ago. Of an exceedingly religious character, Miss Baxter was somewhat of a recluse in later life devoting herself almost entirely to the attainment of a higher life. Her niece accompanied the remains from Toronto."[37]

THE HEWSONS.

A student of the early history of Barrie would be familiar with the Hewsons. Francis has appeared a few pages earlier as the petitioner for lands in Barrie as compensation for the loss of value on his lands at Kempenfelt.

Francis Hewson and his second wife, Anne Hutchinson, settled at Big Bay Point in 1820, the first settlers in that area. They brought to the wilderness a growing family. We have a view into this family through the correspondence of Bishop Macdonell.

Francis Hewson was well connected with influential people, including Duke of Richmond for whom he served as an aide.[38] He had sufficient status to solicit the assistance, in Upper Canada, of Colonel Fitzgibbon one of the heroes of the War of 1812.

He also garnered the support of Thomas Cardinal Weld.[39] Cardinal Weld was raised at Lulworth Castle in Dorset, the oldest son of an aristocratic family. He had married and after the death of his wife had become a priest. He was ordained a bishop and was made coadjutor to Bishop Macdonell of Upper Canada. A coadjutor bishop assists the present incumbent and succeeds the incumbent on his death. Weld never made it to Upper Canada because of his daughter's ill health and his own fragile condition. He resigned as bishop for Upper Canada in 1830 and was raised to the College of Cardinals at the same time. This honour would have been bestowed in part because of his connections with the upper classes in Britain and as an acknowledgment that the Weld Family had given tremendous service to the refugees from many religious houses that were fleeing the revolution in France.[40] Until his death in 1837

37. BPL, *Barrie Examiner*, Feb 17, 1916.

38. Various genealogical sites on line.

39. born 1773, ordained (priest) 1821, ordained (bishop) 1826, raised to College of Cardinals 1830, died 1837.

40. Wikipedia, on line, Thomas Weld.

Weld maintained a keen interest in church affairs in Upper Canada.

Most people looking back on the Hewsons would understand them as Protestant. In fact, Francis was. His wife, on the other hand, was Catholic. Hewson approached Bishop Macdonell in 1828 to register his two sons in the seminary at Montreal. This was no doubt for a classical education and not with a view to priestly ordination.[41]

Weld's first enquiries regarding Hewson were not responded to by Bishop Macdonell, in the most pastoral of ways. Macdonell explained, "After writing repeatedly for information respecting the Hewson Family of Lake Simcoe I have been told by a clergyman who visits that neighbourhood that the father is a bigoted Protestant and the mother a renegade from the Catholic religion. I wrote, however, to the father that he should take his sons to the nearest Catholic clergyman who would report to me on their disposition and qualifications."[42]

By the spring, Bishop Macdonell had tempered his thoughts doubtless in part due to the influence of powerful men. He communicates to Cardinal Weld, "I wrote to Mr. Hewson of Lake Simcoe that I would most cheerfully recommend one of his sons for admission to the seminary of Montreal,....I also wrote to the superior of the seminary of Montreal to put him in mind of his promise to your Lordship. . . . The last post brought me a letter from Mr. Hewson saying that he would be down one of these days with two of his boys to get them into the seminary."[43]

The Hewson's continued to be very present in the public life of the county and to serve in various capacities. Overtime any expressed connection to the Catholic community dwindled away.

The Mission at Coldwater and Georgian Bay.

People would generally recognize that the first European incursion into Simcoe County by the Jesuit missionaries focused on the native people of the area. It can be somewhat less obvious that with the coming of Europeans at the end of the eighteenth century and the beginning of the nineteenth century that once again the native people were very much a central concern of the church. At the heart of the undertaking is one of the most interesting and active Catholic layman of the earliest times; the great catechist Assiginack, also known as Blackbird. He is honoured for many reasons. He is remembered

41. AO, *Macdonell Letter Books*, Macdonell to Hewson, no date, order of the letter suggests fall 1828, p. 504, MS709.

42. AO, *Macdonell's Letter Books*, Macdonell to Weld, November 26, 1828. p. 508. MS 709.

43. Ibid., March 29, 1829, p. 571, Ms 709.

for his leadership of the native community, his war record with the British in 1812 and many years as an effective bridge between the Native and European communities.[44]

Jean Baptiste Assiginack was of the Ottawa tribe having been born at L'Arbe Croche (Bent Tree) in the present state of Michigan and educated by the Sulpicians at Lake of Two Mountains on the Ottawa River.[45] Assiginack had a distinguished career as a translator and diplomat. He provides a portrait of an aboriginal Catholic layman whose Christian faith and Catholic tradition was not accidental or happenstance, but a very clear expression of who he was.

In 1829, Bishop Macdonell, the first Catholic bishop of Upper Canada, wrote to Fr. O'Grady at York, to remind him to be proactive in getting the mission to the natives at Penetanguishene on a good footing as the government will provide a pension for the Catholic missionary and land for a school. Macdonell also hopes this same missionary will be responsible for the shores of Lake Simcoe and as far east as Fenelon.[46]

The earliest Catholic pastoral work in Simcoe County was tempered by a tension between the far-flung clergy and the government agent, Thomas Anderson, who was given responsibility to manage the integration of the native community.

Thomas Gummersal Anderson had a long career in the civil administration. Among those he worked with most closely as an agent of the crown was Assiginack. Anderson was an ardent Anglican and Assiginack an ardent Catholic.

Anderson espoused evangelical Anglicanism. In private correspondence with his daughter, Sophie, he relates that a native woman, the wife of a trader for the Hudson Bay Company was advocating for the Catholic Indians at Manitoulin or as he put it, "for the worship of idols" and further acknowledges, his resistance to Catholic expectations with the rhetorical question, "when will this dark cloud pass?"[47]

In an 1849 diary of a trip to Fort William to meet with native leaders, Anderson notes his misgiving with the Jesuits. "Breakfasted at 9 and shortly after the Indians began to assemble, about 25 were all that could be mustered.

---

44. Curiously not only is Assiginack remembered for his leadership but also his carvings which are included in the collection of the National Art Gallery of Canada in Ottawa. In Barrie there is public school named in his honour.

45. Smith, *Sacred Feathers*, p. 107.

46. AO, *Macdonell's Letter Books*, Macdonell to O'Grady, October 26, 1829, p. 64, MS 709.

47. MTRL, Baldwin Room, *Anderson Papers*, letters 71 &72.

They were accompanied by a Jesuit named Frimeault and finding he meddled with our business, I could not forgo the pleasure of informing him he had no business to interfere . . . he did not move his body though his tongue was less busy. The Jesuits here, as well as elsewhere, try to influence the Indians way of thinking not only as regard his erroneous creed, but also as regards our mission not because he is familiar with our object but because he fancies he can direct the Indians and thus influence the government into what he considers a good bargain for the natives and ultimately he might get their cash for the exclusive benefit of his priest craft, but this government must be on their guard."[48]

John Bell, a Catholic layman, of Metis origin, who served as an interpreter for the government also served as the eyes and the ears of the bishop on the shores of Georgian Bay. He relates to Macdonell, Anderson's efforts shortly after Macdonell visited Drummond Island in 1827," These lines will inform you that shortly after your departure from this place, Mr. Anderson called a meeting of the inhabitants of this island and that the purpose of the meeting was to appoint a president, vice president, secretary and committee to take measure to memorialize (write) the Commander of the Forces for a Protestant missionary with an allowance of 50 pounds per annum . . . (they) succeeded in getting the greater part of the Canadians and half breeds to agree to the same, at the same time, not informing them that it was a Protestant clergyman they were about to apply for and bring their children up in the tenets of the Protestant faith which is the full intent of the memorial and to do away with the Catholic religion, if possible, which is so happily begun on this island.

I beg leave further to state I waited on Mr. Assiginack who requested of me to be kindly remembered to your Lordship and inform your Lordship that it is not Mr. Anderson nor all the men of the island who will ever turn him or any of the Christian Indians from the faith they now enjoy as they have already promised to stand firm against any attempt that may be made to turn them."

Bell further stated that Mr. Anderson held a council of the Indians on the same day, telling them he was going to apply to the government for a school the same as they have at Michelmascanak (sic) and if a missionary should be sent to them that they should accept him as their guide saying if they received the present of a coat from their father they were not to ask what colour it was but receive what was given them.[49]

In 1829, Sir John Colborne envisioned the settlement of three of the Ojibway tribes on the land that stretched from the Narrows at Orillia to Coldwater.

---

48. MTRL, Baldwin Room, *Anderson Papers*, Diary, part b, September 24, 1849.

49. AO, *Mcdonell's Letter Books*, Bell to Macdonell, July 24, 1827, p. 295, MS 709.

He put Anderson in charge of this undertaking in which Coldwater was to be the centre of commerce and administration.

In 1832, Assiginack came to Coldwater. From the outset, there was a controversy between the Catholics who were opposing the use of scriptures in the school and Anderson. The disagreement was causing the Catholics to remove their children from the school when devotions were undertaken.

Fr. Bennet[50] on his missionary journey in 1832, reports back to Bishop Macdonell in a way that clearly shows the confidence that Assiginack was held. "I afterwards spoke to one of the Indian women who had two or three children with her and asked her what the reason was that she did not send them to the school. She told me there was no person to teach them their prayers or catechism.

In order to do away with that excuse I waited on Captain Anderson to know if he would permit one of the Indians themselves to teach the Catholic children morning and evening their prayers in their own language. He promised to do so and seemed pleased with the proposal. The person he thought most suitable for that purpose was Siginook or Blackbird who seemed a particular favorite with the captain. It was my intention to request of Captain Anderson a place where the Catholic Indians might assemble on the Sunday to say their prayers, but he anticipated my wishes by offering an apartment for that purpose in a new frame building while it could be spared by the government."[51]

The conflict over scripture was not so easily resolved. Their lack of cooperation resulted in Anderson limiting their access to government facilities almost as quickly as he offered it. "They remove their children during prayer and their daughters all together from the school.

I feel it my duty to withdraw the promise I had made of allowing them to occupy a room in the frame building for their devotions during the winter as such abominable conduct flying in the face of and daring to oppose the Government that is raising them from a life of misery and destruction to one of happiness."[52]

The controversy over the accommodation of Catholic worship had been going on throughout the year. Earlier in the summer two of the congregation wrote to Fr. O'Grady at York in the summer that the native people feel

50. born ca 1801, ord 1832, died 1843

51. AO, *Macdonell's Letter Books*, Bennet to Macdonell, no date 1832, p. 1126, Reel Ms 228-1. The date would be late in the year as Fr. Bennet was given his directive for his missionary journey on October 15, 1832. This will be highlighted later in the chapter.

52. AO, *Diocese of Kingston Papaers*, Andersen to Bennett. November. 5, 1832, ACO7-11.

they are being pressured by other denominations. "There was a building put up here for the purpose of educating us all and to assemble on Sunday for the purpose of prayers which we did on one Sunday in the forenoon and never since for there was a Methodist preacher waiting until we had our prayers finished . . . we have built a house of bark which would do us very well if we had only a clergyman."[53]

Jean Baptiste Tauguinni wrote the Bishop about the structure the Catholics are using for worship noting that it is a very poor one for winter.[54] That is why Bennett considered asking Anderson for accommodation, for Anderson recognized the unfairness of what the Catholics were using for worship, when closed in buildings were available.

Henry Solomon, the translator for the government, wrote Bishop Macdonell in December to state that the people were satisfied to have Blackbird as the catechist for the community. His reputation is obviously an advantage for the Catholic community. Solomon notes that four Indians and three women have traveled 1,100 miles to be at Coldwater to be Catholics.[55]

Assiginack quickly became the leading Catholic layman of the area. His reputation as a preacher and as leader allowed him to convert, at Coldwater, in 1832, John Aisance the hereditary chief from Methodism to Catholicism.[56]

The ongoing tension between Catholics, Anglicans and Methodists is unremitting. John Bell wrote to Macdonell at the beginning of the summer 1833, "send a priest, even if for a few weeks, the greater part of the traders who have been out for twelve months have returned to stop a short time making ready their outfits for another year and no doubt he will have many marriages as well as christenings to perform with their other duties incumbent upon them."[57]

The distrust of Anderson by the Catholic clergy continued unabated. In August 1833, Anderson wrote to the Lieutenant Governor from Coldwater, "I have been called off while writing the above to receive a visit of a priest from York who after very short introductory compliments took upon himself to say, "you are cramming religious principles down the throats of the children and instilling into their minds doctrines contrary to their religious

53. AO, *Diocese Of Kingston Papers*,Tauguinini and Louis Tebasikgeneault to O'Grady, July 10, 1832. ACO7-10.

54. Ibid.

55. AO, *Diocese of Kingston Papers*, Solomon to Macdonell, December 19, 1832. ACO7-03.

56. AO, *Diocese of Kingston Papers*, John Bell to Macdonell, October 2, 1832, AC14-05.

57. AO, *Diocese of Kingston Papers*, Bell to Macdonell, June 18, 1833. AC14-06.

feelings. I could not on being thus assailed avoid saying that I did not cram down the throats of the children any particular principles that the children were simply taught to read and write and that the testament was of course among the books read. That book he replied, The Bible, is a book in which I do not believe, it is not to be read to Catholic children, if this be the case they shall not remain in the school.

It may be observed that every visit made to this establishment by the Catholic instructors has left an excitement of discontent on the minds of the Indians prejudicial to its prosperity. I challenged this priest whose name I do not know, but he is an Irishman, to bring forward one of his followers to prove that I had ever attempted to prosletyse them but this he knew was not necessary. It is reported that he told some of the Methodist Indians that he would make them all Catholic which has made them fear and hate him"[58]

This less than pastoral priest was Fr. Dempsey whom we will spend some time with in a few pages.

The experiment of striving to settle the natives on the land between Lake Couchiching and Matchedash Bay lasted from 1830 to 1836. The goal had been to form the aboriginal people into farmers and village dwellers. The arrival of settlers hungry for land made this undertaking less practical in the eyes of the Upper Canadian authorities and the land was sold to benefit the native groups.

Chief Yellowhead and his band purchased land at Rama, Chief Aisance and his band settled at Christian Island and Chief Snake's people went to Snake and later Georgina Island in Lake Simcoe. [59]

John Bell infers that Chief Aisance and the Catholics had begun moving to Christian Island in 1834 as they felt they were under pressure to convert.[60]

The Lieutenant Governor's experiment in which religious life became a particular source of tension was soon to be replaced by a new challenge for the church; the care of the far-flung settlers who were beginning to open the wilderness to European settlement.

---

58. AO, Anderson to the Lieutenant Governor, *Macdonell's Letter Books,* August 2, 1833, MS. 709, p. 1267. The controversy about scripture is somewhat confusing, especially when it is played out in the correspondence of the time. The issue would not so much be the use of scripture, but the translation used and it was no doubt the King James Version which would be an issue for the Catholic congregation. The visiting priest would hardly have said he does not believe in the Bible.

59. Murdoch et al, *Beautiful Barrie,* 2007, p. *24.*

60. AO, *Diocese of Kingston Papers,* Bell to Macdonell, April 8, 1834. AC16-01.

The Coming of the Irish.

If the first impetus for the settlement of the Simcoe area was water, the second was land.

The future members of St. Mary's Parish arrived in Vespra and the surrounding townships in significant numbers in the 1820's and 1830's.

The great Irish famine of 1847 was such a central moment in the creation of the Irish community in North America that it is easy to miss the fact that in Canada, the Irish who first settled the rural heartland of Ontario came long before that national disaster in their native country. They came with some material resources, but saw that their future was not to be tied to Ireland with its burgeoning population and ever scarcer opportunity for agricultural success.

In 1690, when King William of Orange prevailed at the Boyne, and defeated King James the Second, he put an end to any hope of toleration of Catholicism in Ireland. The penal laws which were imposed over time effectively brought about the denigration of Irish Catholic power in Ireland. These laws reached into all aspects of life of the Catholic majority. They prevented Catholics from buying land and all Catholic children were to equally inherit land on the death of a parent except where one of the children converted to Established Church (Anglican) and was therefore entitled to inherit the whole of the property. Catholics had access to land through leases which were set at a period of thirty-one years.

The practice of Catholicism was restricted. Unregistered priests caught saying mass were to be exiled. If they returned, they were to be hanged. All bishops were banished.[61] The penal laws were not directed only at Catholics. They were in place for the firming up the place of the Anglican Church and were therefore directed against Presbyterians and other Protestant groups, though with less rigour.

As brutish and extreme as the penal laws were, their strict enforcement was not all that common. Many conscientious Anglicans dissented from the laws and aided their Catholic neighbours and family members. What was created, however, was a milieu where the Catholic majority was vulnerable to the whims of a non-Catholic minority in Ireland.

When Catholicism was given toleration in 1829, it was found that a serious lack of clergy had deeply influenced the way that people practiced their faith. These early Irish immigrants were not the products so much of a piety that was centred on the church, but of a profoundly religious people, absolute

---

61. Connolly, P*riests and People in Pre-Famine Ireland*, p. 35-36.

in their identification with Catholicism, but living a religion which was heavily influenced by Celtic spirituality. Where the Irish language persisted, traditions and folkways emphasized the presence of the divine in the ordinary order of life and nature. Much of this spiritual orientation came to be perceived as superstition.

For many of the early Irish Catholic immigrants who came to Canada full religious practice was not as pressing an issue as we might think. To be initiated into the church and to leave this world in the bosom of the church was of the first importance. How one mediated religious life between initiation through baptism and the final rites at the end of life was very much left to one's own discretion.

It was a source of anxiety for Bishop Macdonell that his diocese was receiving so many Irish immigrants. In describing his need to educate Irish priests it is so they may, "administer the bread of life to the many thousand of their countrymen that have been cast in a state of destitution on the shores of these provinces."[62]

Bishop Macdonell wrote to Lieutenant Governor Maitland at the end of the winter of 1826 to plead the cause of his church, but in a particular way to advocate for the Irish. "I have been so completely knocked up by the fatigues of the long and painful journey in which I had the honour of accompanying Your Excellency through the new settlements of Irish immigrants and other parts of this province that I could not, till this day, forward this communication which Your Excellency was pleased to authorize me to make on the subject of Catholic education and religious instruction. . . . I consider it a most fortunate circumstance that Your Excellency should have so good an opportunity of witnessing the loyal principles and good impression of the Irish emigrants, and of the Catholics in general, through every part of your route. . . . There are no inhabitants of this province more loyal to their sovereign or more attached to Your Excellency's person and administration than the Roman Catholics who already form a large proportion and who are likely to form in a short time the majority of the population of Upper Canada. . . . The loyalty of the Catholics whose religious principles are interwoven with a monarchical form of government and obedience to the authority of superiors hold out the strongest pledge for the allegiance of these colonies to the mother country. But in order to secure this loyalty the Catholic should be afforded the means of knowing his religion and the important duties it imposes on those that possess it and,

62. AO, *Diocese of Kingston Papers*, Macdonell to Wm. Peter MacDonald, July 8, 1831. AA02-05.

this is the more necessary, as it is a notorious fact that an ignorant and wicked Catholic is of all others the worst subject and that when from worldly motives he forsakes his own he never can be sincerely attached to any other religion."[63]

The Irish who had slowly increased in numbers from the 1820's onwards, became a source of supreme anxiety in 1847. Famine in Ireland resulted in the transportation of hundreds of thousands of starving and diseased people to Upper Canada. If some had been in a general way ambivalent to the Irish; the onslaught of the famine Irish turned their ambivalence to hostility. In 1847, alone, 38,000 Irish immigrants arrived in Toronto of which 2,000 settled there.[64]

We find Judge James Gowan of Barrie in June 1847, in a letter to John Beverly Robinson, at Toronto, inviting him to consider sending immigrants to Barrie, "If you could only pass up a few of the Emigrants who have sure little means to begin with or who would be willing to work at a reasonable rate we of Lake Simcoe would thank you. I fear that they will suffer much before they can be settled in situations."[65]

The first Barrie newspaper, the *Barrie Magnet*, began in 1847. There is generous evidence in the Magnet of their rising alarm and general ambivalence to the Irish immigrants. Reports on immigration noted with concern the increase of immigrants in 1847, when the number of immigrants doubled.[66]

Reports from Grosse Isle were a regular feature of the paper. Grosse Isle located in the St. Lawrence River was set up as a station for arriving ships to stop and have their passengers checked for cholera. Those with the disease were to remain at Grosse Isle until recovered. *The Magnet* informed its readers that during the week of August 8th to the 14th three hundred and twenty two people died at Grosse Isle. The patients at the station numbered 2,264.[67]

The Magnet acknowledged the efforts being made to raise funds for those suffering through the famine. It, however, reported as well on a petition made by the Catholic clergy in Ireland. The *Magnet* described the Catholic Church as the church "that enforces views so bigoted." The petition of the clergy directed responsibility for the famine to the Protestant leadership of the country with a warning that famine would increase in the winter of '47 and '48. *The Magnet* reported, "Lord Clarendon replied with one of his admirable lectures

---

63. AO, *Upper Canada Sundries*, Macdonell to Maitland, March 9, 1826, p. 41131, D23.

64. Clarke, Brian, Piety and Nationalism, page 16.

65. SCA, *Gowan Letter Books*, Gowan to John B. Robinson, June 29, 1847, E5 B1 R5B Sh. 4, All of this part of the letter is crossed out.

66. BPL, *Barrie Magnet*, August 20, 1847.

67. Ibid., August 27, 1847.

on the duties of social order, industry and self reliance."[68] Obviously the vision of Lord Clarendon did not reflect the core reality. During the famine years one quarter of the population of Ireland disappeared either into the grave or the migrant ships.

Private thoughts on some level are more important than public. William Hunter set sail for Canada in 1849, from his native Scotland. Hunter was not to rise to prominence, though his son Andrew F. Hunter was a Barrie newspaper editor and historian whose work is still foundational in the study of Simcoe County.[69]

What William Hunter did leave was a diary and his ambivalence to the Irish shines through. He holds the sensibilities which were likely shared with many who were seeking to make Canada their home. He writes, "I heard today that we had 414 passengers on board and mostly Irish; no Scotch in the ship, but about 10. Toward evening I lost track of the airts (directions). I thought the sun was setting in the north east. There is such a noise and stir that it is impossible to read, and as difficult to collect my thoughts to think of anything that concerns the immortal soul. We have some very decent people on board, but for the most part they are very wild and regardless. May God look on us in mercy."[70]

Two days later, Hunter relates one of his last encounters with the Irish in their own territory. "Toward evening a boat came along side and sold a good deal of fish to the crew and passengers. They were real Paddies from Cork, a set of poor naked wretches."[71]

A disparaging attitude to the Irish was fully validated by the press. Barrie's *Magnet* ran an ongoing series of fictional letters from Biddy O'Toole back to her husband Jerry, the spalpeen, which represented the Irish as crude, unlettered and violent.

A paper which published letters condemning the use of alcohol on the Sabbath and pigs roaming the streets of Barrie could happily include the following bit of entertainment. "A Son of the Emerald Isle meeting a country man whose face was not perfectly remembered after saluting him most cordially inquired of his name. "Walsh" was the answer. "Walsh, Walsh," responded Paddy, "Are ye not from Dublin? I knew two ould maids there of that name . . . was either

68. Ibid., December 3, 1847.

69. If William is somewhat narrow in his views, it is also worth noting that among the interesting aspects of his son Andrew Hunter is his total benignity toward the Irish and Catholics in Simcoe County whom he includes in his historical narrative.

70. AO, *Andrew Hunter Papers*, William Hunter's Diary, May 9, 1849, F 1084, MU 7824-2.

71. Ibid., May 11, 1849.

of them yer mother?"[72]

James Gowan and the Little Family Compact.

The narrowness of some was easily balanced by the broad mindedness of others. James Gowan appears in this history from time to time as one of those effective leaders who strove to create an inclusive society. Gowan was judge, senator, leading activist in the creation of Barrie and confidant of Canada's first prime minister.

James Gowan was born in Ireland. His father who was a man of property was heavily impacted during the Irish Rebellion of 1798.

Gowan immigrated to Canada as a youth with his parents settling in Albion Township northwest of Toronto. He studied law, with John King at Toronto, and after a short career as a lawyer was appointed a judge in Barrie at the age of 27.

As a young man, James wrote to his sister Ann about her religious responsibilities, "You ought to above all think to attend to religious duties, that is a thing above all others that should not be disregarded. It is not like other things temporary and flitting. Eternity, never-ending eternity, is dreadful yet pleasing, though dreadful indeed to forever be in endless torment and misery looking up for a drop of water to cool your tongue and again on the other part delightful. How pleasing it is spending a never-ending state of bliss in the bosom of your creator."[73]

Ann at this time was working as a governess away from her family. When James became the judge for Simcoe in 1843, his parents as well as his sisters were eventually drawn to Barrie. Ann married one of the sons of Samuel Ardagh, the Anglican minister at Trinity.

The Ardaghs, the Gowans, the Strathys and other families were of the same religious sensibility. They were all evangelical Anglicans, highly suspicious of anything that veered off the path of an austere Protestantism. The movement to high Anglicanism with its commitment to ritual, music and regalia was perceived as "Catholic" or as it was expressed at the time"popish."

The second half of the eighteen hundreds was a time of a particularly volatile interaction within the Anglican communion. The Oxford Movement within Anglicanism was emphasizing the use of crucifixes, a return of confessionals and other rituals which carried a 'Catholic' hue.

---

72. BPL, *Barrie Magnet*, September 9, 1851.

73. AO, F28, *Gowan-Ardagh Papers*, James Gowan to Ann, April 15, 1834.

This does not at the same time suggest these Evangelical Anglicans were ready to put their lot in with a generalized Protestant tradition. Whatever misgivings they may have had with Roman Catholicism, their ambivalence to the Methodists was equal if not stronger. The Methodists with their camp meetings and appeal to one and all were quite perplexing to those who clearly saw themselves as part of the established church, that is the Church of England.

Gowan received a letter from his mother when she was still on the farm in Albion where she mentions the local news including, "Mrs Stern went to the camp meeting at Shincousy on Friday evening with Mrs. McDougall. I suppose for a bit of amusement."[74]

Evangelical Anglicanism was deeply committed to the Word of God and the individual's response to it. Strip away all decoration and all excesses and meet God in his Word.

James Gowan was to be strongly identified with a schism at Trinity Anglican Church in Barrie in the later part of the nineteenth century. As the history of Trinity Anglican states it, "One Sunday in 1876, Judge Gowan, a man with an Irish temper, saw the lovely stone font that he had donated some years before, not only decorated with flowers of a gaudy hue, but surrounded with a colored hanging of some kind. He dashed to the front, threw the flowers on the floor, tore down the Babylonish garment and said, "This is a Protestant Church."[75] This was the breaking point that lead a significant part of the community to leave and join together as a Reformed Episcopal congregation, which built its church across from Trinity. The break away parish functioned until 1916 when the two churches were reunited.

In spite of these strong personal views Gowan could see his way clear to not only accommodate the Catholic community, but to also endorse their place in Upper Canada. And though it may seem contradictory it also caused him and those in his circle to hold a rather dim view of the Orange movement.

Shortly after his appointment to Barrie as a judge, he wrote to Robert Baldwin about his early connection to the Orange movement which was emphatically opposed to anything that suggested accommodation of the Catholics. "I feel annoyed that I could ever have been such an ass as to submit to be the tool of anyone and be made godfather of things that I neither examined nor understood, but such things are useful to Orangemen."[76]

---

74. AO, *Gowan-Ardagh Papers*, Elizabeth Gowan to James, June 7, 1835. F 28. Shincousy is actually the Township of Chinguacousy. Elizabeth in 1835 is spelling it as the locals say it.

75. *Trinity Anglican Church*, 1835-1985, p. 26.

76. SCA, *Gowan Letters*, Gowan to Baldwin, November 29, 1843.

His cousin, Ogle Gowan, was of a radically different perspective in this matter. Ogle Gowan is fairly called the father of Orangeism in Canada. There was a poorly organized set of structures in place and a few scattered lodges when he arrived in 1829. Through his efforts the Orange movement became a force to be reckoned with. James was in his youth drawn to the Orange Order and served in various capacities including grand secretary.

In his own political evolution James broke his ties with the Orange Order. In a very telling letter James Gowan lays out, apparently for a second time, his feelings about the Orange Lodge, to his cousin Ogle, "My Dear Ogle, I have received your notification to attend a meeting of the Grand Orange Lodge at Kingston on 1st Nov, next.

I thought you had been aware of my having for some time past withdrawn from the institution and if I do not forget, in a former letter, I gave you my reasons several months since. What I have since observed confirms me in this determination. I write that my name should not appear as in any way connected with an association which I consider has so decidedly failed to carry out the objects it professes and is too often presented as brought to bear for the worst purposes. It was at one time my intention to address myself to the members throughout the province giving them my views and urging the total dissolution of the body. For certain reasons I abandoned this cause.

You may recollect it was at your insistence I became a member (at a time when I was not very capable of thinking for myself.) I now deeply regret it–I know not what is the object you have in view in calling the meeting. I sincerely desire it may be to dissolve the Institution which I believe at this moment would have a most useful effect.

Remember me most kindly to Mrs. G. and the family.

I believe we are your affectionate cousin."[77]

In 1842, Edward O'Brien wrote his cousin Samuel Ardagh, an Anglican minister, to come to Canada to undertake ministry here. His description of the religious and social state of Barrie though not reflecting the most liberal views is not particularly concerned about Catholics, in fact, less so than Methodists. He writes, "Difficulties and disappointments are increased by the unsettled religious habits of the people as are to be found elsewhere; English, Irish, Scotch, Canadians, (thank God, no Yankees), Church of England, Presbyterians, Papists, Methodists, nondescript and nothing at all are pretty well mixed up together - the feelings and character are decidedly loyal and essentially British.

Indeed, it may be taken generally through the country that from want

---

77. SCA, *Gowan Papers,* Gowan to Gowan, October 27, 1841.

of religious instruction sects of many varied names and character are found among whom the Methodists are the most mischievous, but many good people join them in the feeling that some description of joint worship is better than none."[78]

O'Brien may have been in part seeking to temper the narrow religious views of Ardagh even before he left Ireland, where he had employed his time in the Church's mission society, trying to convert Roman Catholics to the Church of Ireland. Ardagh's memoirs recount the rancour that was caused by this undertaking in his native country.

Ardagh came to Canada and was instrumental in creating the foundations of Anglican church life in the Barrie area. In his memoir he recalls that during his early ministry in Shanty Bay and district he was called to a Catholic home. "I went to visit a sick man, whose whole family were Romanists. I found him deplorably ignorant of the way of salvation. I read the third chapter of St. John's Gospel and explained that the way for a sinner to be saved and concluded with prayers in which the rest of the family joined. He was most anxious to receive Holy Communion but I declined to administer it as I saw he thought it would save him."[79]

By1890, James Gowan, had reached a great age. In his private family notes on genealogical matters, he includes a comment on the Rebellion of 1798 in Ireland, "I know that there was a dreadful state of things, before, as well as after the Rebellion of 1798, and I quite understand its demoralizing influences. Yet, with all, I must think the Irish Protestant gentry were guilty of a great injustice in not recognizing, when it could have been safely done, that Roman Catholics and Protestants were entitled to equal rights before the law. On the contrary some of them, I think, would even have desired to perpetuate, if not enlarge the unjust penal laws under which Roman Catholics suffered, and I may say were degraded."[80]

Divisions.

Divisions were not solely Protestant and Catholic, they were equally to be found between the French and Irish within Upper Canadian Catholicism.

---

78. MTRL, Baldwin Room, *O'Brien Papers*, Wm. O'Brien to S. B. Ardagh, January 12, 1842. O'Brien had settled at Shanty Bay with his wife, Mary, who is remembered for her diaries which were published in the last century.

79. Ardagh, *Brief Memoir of Samuel Ardagh*, 1874, p. 36.

80. AO, *Gowan Papers*, Genealogy Notes, September 9, 1890, F 28, MU 447.

The *Toronto Mirror*, noted in November of 1837, when Bishop Gaulin[81] was leaving St. Raphael's in eastern Ontario, to live at York that the parishioners offered an address expressing their thanksgiving, "This is a very happy instance, they noted, of attachment to a good man, without reference to origin."[82]

In 1840, Fr. James Quinlan, had been made pastor of Newmarket, which included the care of the Barrie area. Previously the French priests stationed at Penetanguishene had served the area. In his initial report to Bishop Gaulin, who was French Canadian, he was not hesitant to mention that, "the people of each station I made, poured forth their fervent prayers and blessing on behalf of your Lordship for your favour in sending a missionary amongst them whose dialect and language suit them better than the former, tho, inferior in other points, in my opinion."[83]

In the 1850's, the fact that Bishop Charbonnel[84] was actively recruiting priests from France found an opportune forum for Irishmen to direct their discontent to ethnicity as a foundational cause of whatever was their complaint.

One issue which caused constant consternation in the early years of the church was pew rent which was seen as a natural way to draw funds out of the faithful. The suggested rent was to represent one hours wages for the head of the household and if the funds were not at hand, the family would be given a pauper's ticket. This issue created opposition for the embarrassment it may cause the poor, but it was seen as a natural segue into the discontents of a vocal part of the Irish community. The debate regarding the pew rent was carried on in the Catholic press of the time and through handbills, which were widely distributed amongst the Irish Catholic community, which in one case referred to Bishop Charbonnel as, "the giddy headed Frenchman."

The same handbill went on to encourage a petition to the Pope requesting the replacement of the French clergy with those of the British Isles. The case was made that the lack of connection between the priests and their Irish parishioners was at the core of the high rate of drunkenness and incarceration among the Irish.[85] It was needless to say, a rather simplistic argument for serious problems.

This tension was to carry on over the years ahead. The first pastor of St.

---

81. born 1787, ordained (priest) 1811, ordained (bishop) 1833, died 1857.

82. AO, *The Toronto Mirror,* November, 18, 1837. It is interesting to note that this comment also came at the time of the Upper Canadian Rebellion.

83. ARCAT, *Diocese of Kingston Papers*, Quinlan to Gaulin, October 29, 1840. BB 16-01. Among those who preceded Quinlan were Proulx, Charest and Marivaux..

84. born 1802, ordained (priest) 1825, ordained (bishop) 1850, died 1891.

85. Moir, *Church and Society*, pp. 28, 29.

Mary's Parish seemed to have little but positive comments for the men who assisted him. The only exception was a curate who had been reported to him as having been out and about in the parish making comments about, "these French priests," which the pastor took great exception to.[86]

Religious tensions were a constant feature of life in Upper Canada. Exacerbated by the Orange Order and large population of poor Irish immigrants, the sectarian tensions were always just under the surface. In 1853, in the lead up to July 12, the traditional marching day of the Orange Order, Bishop Charbonnel gave clear directives to the Catholic population of his diocese. He first acknowledges that it was a poisonous environment which he had himself experienced. "How could we be astonished at our having been hissed at in a public place, where we went by courtesy? At our having received shavings thrown at our back?...At our having been called "jackass" by students in their full dress, "devil" by many others, and often sent with him to Hell? Sneers, curses, railleries, and mimicries are not better proofs than lies and calumnies of one being in the right; but unquestionably they proceed neither from extended information, nor from charitable and heavenly inspirations.

Yet must we add, for our comfort, that the proceedings of a great many Protestants towards us, have made, and continually make ample compensation of the mentioned vulgarities."

Then Charbonnel directs the pastors to speak to their congregations before July 12th recommending them to "temperance, work, Christian forbearance, and no interference with what is not their business . . . Were Catholics of our diocese to forget those principles of true Christianity and caused any disturbance on the occasion of the 12th of July he shall be deprived of receiving Holy Communion for a length of time according to the degree of the scandal; and if he dies a victim of his disobedience to this present ordinance his corpse shall be deprived of Ecclesiastical burial."[87]

Pastoral Care in the Earliest Times.

Bishop Walsh,[88] on a visit to Barrie in 1890, recalled his early memories of Barrie and Simcoe County. The first sermon he ever preached after being ordained a priest, in 1854, was preached at St. Mary's Church. He also shared

86. ARCAT, *St. Mary's Files*, Correspondence, Jamot to Lynch, March 2, 1863.

87. Moir, *Church and Society*, page 210-11. The reference to 'shavings' refers to wood shavings which were used as bedding in horse stalls.

88. born 1830, ordained (priest) 1854, ordained (bishop) 1867, died 1898.

that he narrowly escaped becoming Barrie's parish priest. He recounted some missionary journeys during his brief stay in the fall of 1854. "In going to Penetanguishene, the driver of the sorry team which was used, went into every tavern along the road which were as close together as milestones. He reached Penetanguishene at about eleven o'clock at night thoroughly fagged out and half famished.

In going into Nottawasaga to give spiritual comfort to Catholic settlers there, he had to go through the bush by the aid of a blazed path and guided by an English Protestant who volunteered his assistance."[89]

By the time the newly ordained John Walsh was sent out in 1854, there had already been 35 years of pastoral care undertaken in the vast wilderness of Simcoe County.

In 1828, Bishop Macdonell wrote to one of his priests, Fr. Fluet,[90] who was obviously asking for clarification of how to proceed in the pastoral field. The bishop gave the following advice, "I also grant you permission to offer up the holy sacrifice of the mass in private houses provided they are clean and decent and that the temporary altar you erect be perfectly firm and solid and not liable to shaking or falling down and that no children or dogs be allowed to run about the house, or go near the altar. With regard to baptizing, preaching and catechizing in private houses there can be no difficulty whatever."[91]

The pastoral care of the Catholic settlers of Simcoe County was fraught with problems. The number of clergy was insignificant and the settlers lived in relative isolation. When settlers arrived in Vespra and the other surrounding townships, Barrie was part of the Diocese of Kingston. It was not until 1842 that Toronto became a separate diocese.

Settlement itself was in the earliest times undertaken in a tenuous way. The infrastructure of roads and emigrant sheds were often non-existent. The isolation of many of the communities had a profound impact on their progress.

Nottawasaga Township is an interesting example for which sufficient records exist that can help us understand these early struggles. In 1833, the Sunnidale Road was opened and a bridge built across the Nottawasaga River. The extension of roads opened areas to settlement in a scattered way. The settlement of Nottawasaga Township involved a curious initiative of sending indigent settlers to the township and providing them with five acres per family to maintain themselves, but with the expectation they would invest their time

89. BPL, *Northern Advance*, May 29, 1890.

90. born 1801, ordained 1826, died 1831.

91. AO, *Macdonell Papers*, Macdonell to Fluet, May 26, 1828, p. 446.

in clearing land for "a better class of settler." The original plan was to send fifty families, many who were German, though only thirty-six actually went.[93]

The program was a limited success. There were constant suspicions of dubious practices on the part of the agents who were to provide supplies to these settlers in such a remote part of the county. In 1835, Patrick Bertles, who later figured prominently in establishing Catholic life in Nottawasaga challenged the undertaking of the local agent. He alleged that if the settlers did not sign a chit stating they had received more supplies than they in fact did, they would be starved out by the agent whom Bertles called, "The Nottawasaga Nero."[94]

Four years later the citizens of Nottawasaga had coalesced sufficiently to make common protest in light of their ongoing isolation. At the very end of December in 1839 they wrote to the Lieutenant Governor about the state of their settlement. "The petition of the undersigned inhabitants of the Township of Nottawasaga, County Simcoe, Home District, humbly sheweth, that no houses of public worship, schools, stores, post office, a market for grain or other produce is at less distance from us than 40 miles (Barrie), the road thither being of the very worst description. That from Mr. Bowerman's on Hurontario Street southward the roads are equally bad without a human dwelling on 40 miles save 3 or 4, owing chiefly to absenteeism. The inhabitants of this infant settlement are loyal, orderly and industrious being absolutely free from crime, quarrel or lawsuit and we call on your excellency to observe that we are doubly taxed for the purpose of erecting a gaol and court house in Barrie. A tax which we feel unable to furnish (the population being chiefly composed of indigent immigrants located on five acre lots . . .) That in this state of bad roads and scarcity in the money market we ask . . . your excellencies serious consideration of these statements and that your excellency would be graciously pleased to appropriate the said taxes for repairing our roads which we humbly believe would much improve the country and our own condition."[95]

Bishop Alexander Macdonell visited the settlements around Lake Simcoe early in 1827. In May of the same year, Macdonell assigned his nephew, Fr. Angus Macdonell[96] as pastor at York. As the pastor of York he had charge of all of Simcoe County. When an Irish priest appeared on the scene in the person of William O'Grady[97] in 1828, he was offered the York parish as the vast majority

93. AO, *Upper Canada Sundries,* March 14, 1835, p. 14835 & June 8, 1835, p. 84299.

94. AO, *Upper Canada Sundries,* August 17, 1835, p. 85609.

95. AO, *Upper Canada Sundries,* December 28, 1839, p. 129021.

96. born 1799, ordained 1922, died 1875.

97. ordained 1816, died 1840.

of the congregation was Irish.

On leaving York, Fr. Angus hoped to invest his ministry in the region east of Lake Simcoe where there was extensive Scottish settlement from Glengarry which Fr. Angus himself had been a strong supporter of. This was not to be so as he was soon transferred to Bytown.[98]

In June 1828, O'Grady had come to Upper Canada from Cork, Ireland, by way of Brazil where he had served as the chaplain of a mercenary group lead by Connell Baldwin. O'Grady's solution to the problems of the many missions attached to his parish at York was to seek a second priest who could serve the townships.

Edward Gordon,[99] the missionary priest, to the townships above York, served the area of Durham, Simcoe, Peel, and Halton from 1830 to 1833. In that time he visited the Lake Simcoe district as his sacramental register proves.[100]

Others were sent out from York with the view to assist with the care of the scattered communities especially those at the greatest distance. The following instruction in 1832 to Fr. Bennett shows the magnitude of the undertaken by these early missionaries. We see, too, the continuing concern for the aboriginal population. "Mr. Bennett on his arrival at Newmarket will give notice to the Catholics of that place if he finds any number of them disposed to come to the Sacraments. He will give them confession and mass in the morning before setting out for the landing place. On arriving at the Narrows he will enquire if there be any Catholics there and will give religious assistance to such as may apply to him. Should the steamboat call at the Little Talbot or at any other part of the shores of Lake Simcoe, Mr. Bennet will give notice that he will return that way and mention the time he may expect to return. He will remain at Coldwater until he confesses and instructs the Catholic Indians of that place. From there he will proceed to Penetanguishene where he will remain as along as he may find necessary. He will bless the church and the cemetery and keep a register of christenings and marriages and of all communicants in every place he visits. On his return he will go by way of Thora, Brock and Georgina and he will make the Catholics carry his baggage wherever he goes. He will enquire on his route the most central place to make his stations and send notice before him and give people time to convene.

---

98. *Kelly*, p. 50-51.

99. bn. November. 1, 1791, ord. January 29, 1829, d. October. 15, 1870.

100. McDevitt, *Father Gordon's Records*, various pages, chronological record. The baptisms were for Theodore Matt and Margaret Pilkington, October 10, 1830, Owen Raynes, June 21, 1831, Margaret McDonnell, January 4, 1833 at the Narrows. (Orillia).

Let them defray his expenses from place to place and he may inform them that on their doing so depends their getting another opportunity of the same kind. Mr. Bennett will not fail to procure a correct list of all the Catholics in the townships through which he travels and in the adjoining townships as far as he can get the information respecting Catholics that can be of interest for the good of religion especially the best stations for building churches and the possibility of the people being able to build them and their willingness to defray the expense of the priest that might visit from time to time."[101]

Bennett's pilgrimage began well enough, but when at Coldwater where he gave instruction and celebrated Eucharist in an "open sort of wigwam, he caught a severe cold which caused him to end the trip prematurely.[102] This was the structure previously described as the place of worship utilized by the aboriginal Catholics at Coldwater when they were refused the use of the government buildings.

Throughout Upper Canada, in these earliest of times, a tension existed between the church and the Catholic people in the matter of establishing parishes and locating priests among them. This was in part resistance to a financial strain that would be placed on them, but it seems the ambivalence on the part of many was also the sense that the establishment of parishes and missions was hardly necessary. The transient priest who would baptize and make himself available to the dying was sufficient.

The other sacraments and ministries of the church would be received if and when available. This was a people who had living memories of an Ireland where mass was celebrated in the open air and whose religious commitment had endured in spite of much in the way of oppression. They were often unclear of the value of the structures which the church was encouraging.

This historical root of the transient priest continued in a tenuous way in Ontario through the practice of the keeping of stations. A station was a home that would open itself to the celebration of mass for those in the immediate district.

The practice of stations continued in St. Mary's Parish as late as 1919 when stations were kept at Utopia, Midhurst, Oro and Vespra with a view to parishioners fulfilling their Easter duty.[103]

There were also, of course, Catholics who like their bishop, Alexander Mac-

101. AO, *Macdonell Letter Books,* Macdonell to Bennett, October 15, 1832, p. 1108.

102. AO, *Upper Canada Sundries*, 1832, p. 139039.

103. SMPA, *Announcement Books*, April 16, 1919, Easter duty is the expectation placed on all Catholics to go to confession and receive communion at least once between the beginning of Lent and end of the Easter season.

donell, saw the need for the establishment of parishes and institutions as the best way to most effectively integrate the Catholic population into the larger population. Many activist laymen would not have shared the bishop's Tory politics and sympathy for the Family Compact, but they saw their personal progress in part in the progress of the church. The establishment of the church reflected well on their establishment as Catholic farmers and tradesmen. It also gave clearer structure to the Catholic community that gathered in worship.

The Short Unsettled Ministry of Fr. Lawrence Dempsey.

Lawrence Dempsey[104] was ordained by Bishop Macdonell in 1831. He had been trained in the seminary at St. Raphael's in Glengarry County. His first assignment was to assist Fr. O'Grady in Toronto. Macdonell sent him on his way to York where Fr. O'Grady had been advised, "I could wish you keep Dempsey under your own immediate eye for sometime till he gets perfectly acquainted with the admonition of the sacrament and ceremonies of the altar. Mr. Dempsey is full of zeal and piety, and altho of a warm temper, will prove I hope a laborious and useful missionary."[105]

Fr. Lawrence Dempsey, was assigned to Penetanguishene in 1832, as the first resident pastor. At that time the parish included the Village of Barrie and surrounding district. His was a short and difficult pastorate. Fr. Dempsey found the work in the isolated missions arduous and less than rewarding.

When he came to Penetanguishene, he found himself at odds with Captain Anderson, the Indian agent, who was introduced earlier in this chapter. Dempsey felt the Catholics natives were being given an uneven consideration by Anderson's administration.

Dempsey's 'warm temper' could get the best of him. The Lieutenant Governor was informed of Dempsey's poor judgement by someone who attended mass at Penetanguishene. It seems that Dempsey was reacting to Captain Anderson's letter to the Lieutenant Governor that arose out of their confrontation about the school at Coldwater, where Dempsey had challenged Captain Anderson on the use of The Bible in the school. The report to the Lieutenant Governor stated, "About four weeks ago, as near as I can recollect, I attended the Catholic Church for the purposes of hearing Mr. Dempsey preach. When he had got about half way through the service he got up from praying and said, I have another thing to mention to you and commenced abusing Captain

104. bn. August. 1804, ord. 1831, d. October 9, 1833.

105. AO, *Macdonell's Letter Books*, Macdonell to O'Grady, June 25, 1831, p. 899.

Anderson in the most shameful manner. Talking abt. Capt. A. he called him a person of Coldwater who has charge of the affairs there and who is called a Captain. How he came by that title no person knows and like another Judas offered to do anything for me, when leaving him, that lay in his power, but no sooner had I left him that he set down and writes a parcel of lies to the Governor. Or words having the same tendency and at same time comparing Capt. A. to a baboon or monkey. And a great many more expressions of the same nature. Expressions which the lowest blackguard of the place would be hesitant to make use of in a common bar room and would certainly would blush at the thought of using them in a place of public worship."[106]

Dempsey was be a bit of a whirlwind of discontent, frustrated with the civil authority and church authority too.

In a telling letter from Edward Gordon, who was Dempsey's classmate at the seminary, in a spirit of friendship cautions Dempsey to remain quiet and wait to see how the new bishop, Remigius Gaulin, "who is a Canadian" fares compared to Macdonell. "Perhaps the new bishop will put things in order, keep to yourself till you hear how affairs are likely to turn out. Indeed they cannot be much for the worse with respect to you and I at all events."[107]

Dempsey placed great store by his Irish identity in a place where the Irish were perceived as a group needing a great deal of care because of their destitute state.

Dempsey received a letter from Macdonell at the end of November 1832 in which Macdonell acknowledges the charge that he never writes. "I am sorry to acknowledge that you are not the only one that has cause to complain of me as a bad correspondent. The truth is that since you left this place my time has been so much taken up in attending the committees for widows and orphans and writing tickets and recommendation for provisions and clothing for distressed Irish emigrants that I have not a moment of time at my own command and am therefore obliged to neglect some of the most important part of my own duty."[108]

Dempsey states within a year of his ordination that he intends to return to Ireland. He is discontent with his work in Upper Canada. He states again and again that he is sick and believes that he is dying. He would very much like Macdonell to come to his area to see the progress that is being made and

---

106. AO, *Diocese of Kingston Papers*, AB10-04, Angus Anderson to Lieutenant Governor, undated.

107. AO, *Diocese of Kingston Papers*, AB25-07, Gordon to Dempsey, September 18, 1833.

108. AO, *Macdonell Letter Books*, Macdonell to Dempsey, November 26, 1832, Page 1116.

to accept whatever punishment that is fair if he has not fulfilled his duties well. He concludes that, "If no fault be found, I wish to depart free of the infamous brand that others received, and afterwards were preferred to me, and received I may say my talent."[109]

Macdonell reminds him that he was rejected by the seminary in Yamaska, Quebec and that he had presumed that Dempsey's desire was to serve his destitute countrymen. "If by the advice of evil and designing persons you violate all those sacred ties and leave many thousands of your countrymen to perish for want of the spiritual food which the Almighty appointed you to administer to them, then indeed will you run the risk of undergoing the punishment of the unprofitable servant."[110]

Dempsey died on a return trip to Penetanguishene from York. Even in death, Dempsey was to be a source of debate and discussion. The *Canadian Correspondent* noted his passing. The *Correspondent* the paper edited by William Lyon MacKenzie was no friend of Bishop Macdonell. Any opportunity to place the bishop in a bad light was welcomed. Their death notice was as follows, "We had not space in our last to insert the following communication from Penetanguishene of November 12, 1833. The Reverend Laurence Dempsey, a native of Ireland, departed this life on the 9th instant, at 5 o'clock a. m. on the Penetanguishene Rd., where he had been detained in consequence of illness while on his return from York to this place. He was universally respected and esteemed by all who had the pleasure of his acquaintance at this place and the poor of this place, in him have lost a kind friend, benevolent benefactor and a most devout pastor. Long will his little flock mourn his loss. His remains were brought up on the evening by his parishioners and will be interred tomorrow in the R. C. burial ground.

Thus has one of the most exemplary, pious and zealous ministers of religion been permitted to die neglected and without the common necessaries of life in a miserable hovel on his way to his mission. He begged and prayed his Bishop to allow him a respite of a few days in this town to recruit his health, and offered to produce a certificate of ill health given him by his medical adviser.—No excuse would be taken. The Bishop was inexorable, and the unfortunate Demspsey sunk under his infirmity, and a victim of the Bishop's tyranny. Whether such conduct be in accordance with the dictates of Chris-

---

109. AO, *Diocese of Kingston Papers*, AB 1001, Dempsey to Macdonell, November 20, 1832. p. 50-51.

110. Ibid., Both Dempsey and Macdonell refer to the parable of Jesus where servants are given talents to invest.

tianity or the true apostolic spirit, we will leave the public to judge. We have been told by persons upon whose word we place every reliance that the last words which Mr. Dempsey spoke to the Bishop were, "Remember, my Lord, now that you are forcing me out on the mission that I will lay my death at your door." Whatever qualms of conscience his Lordship may have respecting Mr. Dempsey's death he must accuse himself of having persecuted the unfortunate man even unto death."[111]

Dempsey on leaving Toronto, would have made his way to Holland Landing and traveled by boat to Kempenfelt. His form of transportation then is unclear, but he only made it as far as Michael and Catherine Bergin's home. There he lingered a number of days before dying.

The highly editorialized, announcement of his death did not sit well with his parishioners in Penetanguishene. The following letter was published in the *Correspondent* in the next month. "Sir: The manner of announcing the decease of the Rev. L. Dempsey which appeared in your paper of the 23rd ultimo, was not in accordance with the sentiments of the body over who he had been assigned to preside but also with all in this neighbourhood with whom he had been acquainted.

The purpose of the present letter is elicited from what appears in editorial remarks viz.: that the deceased was left in a miserable hovel without the comforts or necessaries of life. Now sir in duty to the worthy family in whose house the death of our esteemed pastor took place, we do state that every comfort and attendance was furnished and it will be consolatory to his friends to know that medical aid was procured and every thing was sent from this place that could in any wise contribute to sooth his last moments."[112]

The Mission of Barrie.

With Dempsey's demise the Penetanguishene parish was left unmanned for a period.

When Remigius Gaulin was appointed coadjutor bishop to Macdonell in October 1833, one of the tasks that Gaulin was given was to seek out priests in Quebec.

In September of 1835, Gaulin himself went on an extensive tour of his diocese and while at Pentanguishene baptized thirty-two children.[113]

111. AO, *Canadian Correspondent,* November 23, 1833.

112. Ibid., December 21, 1833.

113. ARCAT, St. Anne's Sacramental Records.

He recruited Jean-Baptiste Proulx[114] who was assigned to Penetanguishene in the fall of 1835, the same year as his ordination. He served the area from 1835 to 1838 which would have included regular visits to Barrie and the townships.

The opportunity arose in 1834 to build a church in Medonte at Mount St. Louis. The faithful communicated with the bishop that, "At a meeting of this and the adjoining townships it was resolved that a block of ten acres of land should be purchased to erect a chapel upon. All of us are desirous to contribute to the utmost that our means will permit, but this being quite a new settlement the inhabitants are not sufficiently wealthy to carry this object in effect unless they receive some assistance from beyond."[115]

The extent of the work of Fr. Proulx is extraordinary. The baptism records of St. Anne's include baptisms as far away as Owen Sound and many in Nottawasaga. The ministry was also to the aboriginal people along the Georgian Bay coastline. In fact, in 1838, when Fr. Amable Charest[116] came to Penetanguishene, Fr. Proulx made ministry to the native people his sole occupation. Late in life he served various parishes in the southern part of the diocese.

Fr. Proulx returned to Medonte for a banquet when the construction of the second church at Mount St. Louis in 1861. His presence at the occasion afforded the chairman of the event to acknowledge and honour him for his service to the church in Simcoe County. As it was recorded for the paper of the day, "In the course of his remarks, he pointed to the venerable Father Proulx, the patriarch missionary of the diocese, the pioneer of Christianity amid the forest beneath the shadow of whose leafy plumes we are now assembled. He depicted the labour and trials that Fr. Proulx must have been subjected to thirty years ago, when laden with the heavy trunk that contained his altar and sacred vestment. He was traversing the unopened and trackless forest of north Simcoe or he braved the fury of the temptuous lakes that surround us in his frail canoe in order to administer the consolation of religion to the dying Indians."[117]

Fr. Amable Charest served Penetanguishene from 1838 until 1854. His care of Barrie ended when the mission was transferred to the care of Newmarket in 1840.

---

114. born 1808, ordained 1835, died 1881.

115. AO, *Diocese of Kingston Papers*, AC11-01, Faithful of Medonte to Bishop Gaulin, March 6, 1839.

116. born 1808, ordained 1837, died 1872.

117. AO, *Canadian Freeman*, February 21, 1861.

Charest reports in January of 1839 that there are eight hundred souls in Penetang and seventy families scattered throughout Flos, Oro and Medonte. In the same letter he is asked about the names of the different churches he serves. He states that Penetang is dedicated to St. Anne, Medonte to St. Louis, Barrie to Sacre Coeur de Marie, Orillia to St. Patrick and that Nottawasaga has no saint. He also states that on the first Sunday of the month he is in Barrie, the second in Medonte and on the third and fourth in Penetang."[118]

Fr. Quinlan, stationed at Newmarket took up the care of Barrie which he visited on a regular though hardly a weekly basis.[119] He was also taking responsibility for the parish in Medonte and striving to improve the material situation of the church in each of these places. As he noted in 1841, "I have the pleasure to inform your Lordship that I have succeeded this season to bring the church in Medonte to a pretty good state of repair and built an altar in it without any expense to that congregation."[120]

Before There was a Church at Barrie.

"I officiated in Barrie last Sunday where I had a pretty congregation."[121] This was the optimistic note struck by Fr. Quinlan to the bishop at Kingston in the fall of 1840.

The first building other than a private home used by the Catholic community in the Barrie area for the celebration of the Eucharist was offered through the hospitality of Charles Thompson.

Thompson was, by any standards, a successful entrepreneur in the early life of Upper Canada. His home was on Yonge St., at Summerhill. Thompson developed the stage coach lines that traveled Yonge Street and carried the mail to the northern reaches of settlement. In 1833, he purchased the steamer, The Sir John Colborne, which had been built at Holland Landing by half pay soldiers in 1831. It was purchased to travel Lake Simcoe from Holland Landing, the northern terminus of Yonge St. to various ports around the lake. In 1844 he purchased a half interest in "The Beaver" which plied the same waters. "Steamboat" Thompson was essentially the sole provider of transportation from Lake

---

118. AO, *Diocese of Kingston Papers*, AC 16-05 and AC 16-06, Charest to Macdonell, January 31, 1839.

119. The priests at Newmarket who came to Barrie were: Nightingale (before records kept), James Quinlan: January 1849-1852, Marivinault: February 1852- July 1852, O'Loughlin: June 1852- October 1854, McNulty: October 1854 - 1855.

120. AO, *Diocese of Kingston Papers*, BB16-02, Quinlan To Gaulin, November 4, 1841.

121. AO, *Diocese of Kingston Papers*, BB16-01, Quinlan to Gaulin, October 29, 1840.

Ontario north to Barrie and beyond until 1850.[122] Thompson's other business was construction. He was the builder of the original court house at Barrie in 1842.[123] He also built the Barrie Jail which has been a prominent landmark for the city throughout its history. He signed the contract for its construction in May of 1840.[124] For the construction of the jail he had the wherewithal because of his extensive transportation network to bring down the distinctive white limestone from Longford on the far side of Lake Couchiching.

It states in the memoriam of the parish, "After some time a Protestant named Charles Thompson gave the Catholics the use of his large stable for a church and mass was offered up there for some time as the building gave ample room for the congregation."[125] These notes were written about a half a century after the fact. The idea that the building was a stable in truth seems unlikely. Stables as the refuge of animals are by their nature messy places and it seems unimaginable that the Catholics would opt to use a stable for Eucharist. We have already read Bishop Macdonnel's advice that in homes in which mass is to be said should not have dogs running loose. It is safe to assume that there would be equal concern about barn animals. Charles Thompson's extensive entrepreneurial interests, would suggest that the building may have been more likely a warehouse of some sort, particularly because of his extensive interest in shipping. It could have also have been an immigrant shed, where newly arrived settlers could store their personal effects until progress had been made at clearing their land and building a house. It is not clear where this building was located, but the best speculation would have placed it somewhere on the water's edge. Thompson would have been clearly aware that the immigrants arriving to take up land in the townships would have made their way to Barrie on his transportation. To look after those who look after you is quite simply good business.

By 1837, the Catholics of the Barrie district were ready to seek the consideration of the government in promoting the cause of their church in the district. On November 2, 1837, a petition was made for land in Barrie. "To his Excellency Sir Francis Bond Head , knight commander of the Royal Hanoverian Guelphic Order, and of the Prussian Military order of Merit, Lieutenant Governor of Upper Canada.

---

122. Hunter, 1948, page 71. With the coming of the railroad, Thompson was ruined financially.

123. Ibid., page 248.

124. Ibid., page 249.

125. SMPA, Registrum Memoriam, page 1.

126. AO, *Diocese of Kingston Papers*, Land Petition, November 2, 1837.

May it please your Excellency, that we the undersigned, Inhabitants of the Township of Vespra, Barrie, and Penetanguishene Road, most humbly sheweth your Excellency the many advantages we are deprived of for some time past in not having a small portion of ground granted us (comprising one acre) for the purpose of a proper place of Interment and in order to erect a Roman Catholic Church thereon for the clergyman where at any time he would visit us . . .

We therefore confidently anticipate from that fervent zeal which your Excellency had always manifested in promoting the welfare of this province that your Excellency will be graciously pleased to grant the above-mentioned quantity of ground in the Town of Barrie as being the center and most advantageous place for the adjoining neighbourhoods. And we as in duty bound will ever pray. With the humblest confidence we will await your Excellencies reply."[126]

The first petition was recommended in council and the Catholics were given one acre composed of lots 127 and 128 on McDonald Street on which to build a church and to establish a cemetery.

Nothing succeeds like success and so we find the people of Barrie writing again, ten months later, "The Petition of the Roman Catholics of the County Simcoe and Others, Humbly Sheweth that whereas grants of land have been made to Roman Catholics as sites for churches in different parts of the province and patents issued to most in trust for the use of and benefit of said churches. Your petitioners humbly pray your Excellency would grant a deed of the under petitioned lots with conveyance in the Town of Barry in the County of Simcoe to the trustees (who shall be elected by the members) and to their successors in order to there erect a church thereon. By having a church in said Town of Barry would be an encouragement to settle in said town and vicinity."[127]

This second request is for lots 125 through to lot 129 on McDonald St. as well as a grant of two hundred acres at lot 10 of concession four of Vespra Township as a means of support for the clergy. This petition includes 344 names and 6 magistrates as well as one member of parliament. On November 9, 1838, the government reminds them that have been granted lots 127 and 128. Lot 129, in fact, belonged to the Anglican Church and land requested in Vespra was a clergy reserve. The lot at 126 was purchased from the government by James Gowan five years later.[128]

When Fr. Quinlan, pastor of Newmarket, reported on his mission at Barrie in the fall of 1840, he noted that he had a number of men clearing the lot in Barrie. "They are to attend one day in every two weeks until it is clear and

---

127. AO, *Diocese of Kingston Papers*, Land Petition, September 21, 1838.
128. SCA, *Gowan's Letter Books*, Gowan to Alexander, September 28, 1843.

piled." [129]

By the fall of 1841, Fr.Quinlan is reporting that the lot is ready at Barrie, "as far as manual labour can go, which is the only assistance that most of that congregation can afford."[130]

The problem is lack of money, which Quinlan believes he may have a solution to as he explains to Bishop Gaulin. "I am invited, My Lord, to make a private collection in Toronto for our church in Barrie, by Protestants as well as Catholics, many of whom have extensive properties in the limits of Barrie and will be liberal."[131]

It is intriguing to speculate who these benefactors may be and if in fact, the collection did go ahead. We can well presume that James Gowan and Charles Thompson may have been among the advocates of the campaign. It may in fact not have in the end been undertaken for it was almost seven year before work began on building a church.

The administrator of the diocese, after the death of Bishop Power and before the installation of Bishop Charbonnel, Fr. J. Hay,[132] received a letter on Feb. 2, 1849 from Fr. Levesques discussing the state of the church in Barrie. Levesques believes that Barrie would be the ideal site for the creation of a parish. He writes, "Flos Township which is only 10 miles from Barrie and 20 miles from Penetanguishene still has no chapel because of the small number of families. It seems reasonable that they be attached to the mission of Barrie, if possible, which has only fifty families. The twenty families from Flos would be a big help in building a decent chapel in a prominent place, in an area which will be an important place soon . . . A church had been a consideration at Barrie for some years. Fr. Quinlan stationed at Newmarket and caring for the Barrie area had wanted it at Flos but even he doubts that there are enough people to count on building a chapel at this time. I propose to follow the old plans of Fr. Quinlan which are very good but to shorten the building by 20 feet. There would still be about 50 feet left."[133]

---

129. AO, *Diocese of Kingston Papers*, BB16-01, Quinlan to Gaulin, October 29, 1840.

130. AO, *Diocese of Kingston Papers*, BB16-02. Quinlan to Gaulin, November. 4, 1841.

131. SMPA, Quinlan to Gaulin, February 5, 1842.

132. AO, Diocese of Kingston, AA01, *Reminiscences of the Rt. Rev. Alex Macdonell-W. J. Macdonell*, Williamson & Co. Tor, 1888. p. 24. In the realm of trivia it is worth noting that Fr. Hay who was the administrator of the diocese on Bishop Power's death was born with twelve fingers. One from each hand required amputation before ordination as hands deformed or with serious injury were an obstacle to having permission to celebrate mass.

133. ARCAT, *St. Mary 's Parish Files*, Levesques to Hay, February 2, 1849.

First Initiatives of the Catholic Community at Barrie.

In these early times when priests were scarce the oversight of the life of the church in a material sense was in the hands of trustees, not unlike trustees who take responsibility for a school system.

On Christmas night 1867, ten minutes before the stroke of midnight, Leon Caisse lay dying in his Peterborough home. In the presence of the parish priest and his doctor he communicated verbally his last will and testament, leaving his property to his wife and large family. He lingered throughout the Feast of St. Stephen and died on morning of December 27th.[134] He was eulogized in the local papers as a highly esteemed owner of Caisse's Hotel.[135]

Leon Caisse before making his mark in Peterborough had been in Barrie where he leased the Queen's Hotel from John Bingham in 1846.[136]

He was in charge of the construction and it appears took a significant role in financing the first Catholic church in Barrie. A native of Berthier, Quebec, his French Canadian roots would no doubt have connected him well with Fr. Levesques, who was overseeing the area.

His presiding over the most well known hotel in Barrie would make him an excellent candidate to be a trustee for these initial undertakings of the local church.

Leon Caisse left Barrie in 1853.[137] Still, at the end of the decade he wrote to Bishop Charbonnel regarding an outstanding loan. He maintains that he has written Fr. Jamot three times regarding the outstanding expenses owed him for the erection of the church. He has received 27 pounds but there is still 13 pounds outstanding. He makes it clear that he will be happy with the 13 pounds and will make a gift of the interest owing.[138] His pleas did not fall on deaf ears as the parish did have a special collection in 1859 to pay Caisse what he was owed.[139]

The construction of the first church made of timber began in 1849 and was completed in 1850. This church fronted on McDonald Street on the lot that

---

134. AO, Estate Records, Will of Leon Caisse, GS 1-182, Will 1868, #179.

135. AO, *Peterborough Review*, December 27, 1867.

136. Henry O'Brien of the O'Brien's of Shanty Bay mentions in passing that a trip back to Shanty Bay that he arrived at Barrie late and stayed at Caisse's. Henry O'Brien Diary, December 6, 1853. MTRL, Baldwin Room, O'Brien Papers,. Also, Samuel Peter Jarvis' diary of a trip to Penetanguishene notes that he stayed at Case's Hotel with Charles Thompson. January 16, 1849, OA, From the Diary of S. P. Jarvis. MS 787, reel 5, 1849-50.

137. Cotton, *Whisky and Wickedness*, p. 46.

138. ARCAT, *St. Mary's Files*, Caisse to Charbonnel, November 10, 1858.

was closest to Mulcaster Street. It was officially opened on May 30, 1850.

The *Barrie Magnet* reported at the beginning of June 1850 on the blessing. "On Thursday last the 30th instant the ceremony of opening a Roman Catholic Church was performed in Barrie by the Rev'd Amable Charest, of Penetanguishene. The church was blessed to "The Sacred Heart of Mary." The attendance was large considering our population and would have been much larger, we are informed, had there been more notice given. The Reverend Charest was on a visit to a sick member and the Roman Catholic portion of the inhabitants here at once availed themselves of his presence for the ceremony. The building is calculated to accommodate from 300 to 400 persons. It forms a conspicuous feature in the buildings of Barrie. It is situated a little north of the jail and court house and when viewed from the bay occupies a central position between those buildings. We have not had an opportunity of examining the interior, but we are informed that the contractor Mr. William Graham, has given entire satisfaction to those by whom his services were required."[140]

We have the benefit of a description of not only Barrie, but the church in 1852, in a newspaper report on Bishop Charbonnel's visit to Barrie in that year. "He left for the north apparently in excellent health, accompanied by the Rev. Mr. O'Doherty. The following brief outline of his movements will not be uninteresting to our readers:

On the evening of the 17th he reached Barrie, by way of Lake Simcoe, whose quiet water are at length occasionally disturbed by a small steamer.

Barrie is small straggling village, stretching its lank length nearly a mile along the low bank which skirts the head water of Camperfiled Bay.

Directly opposite is the wild coast of Innisfil, presenting the dreary monotony of one continuous chain of stunted pine forest, nearly level with the water, as far as the eye can reach. The village is built in single file, facing the bay; but in the rear, the surface of land, gradually rising to above one hundred feet, furnished some excellent building sites. On one of these stand the jail and court house, and between them, the Catholic church, a plain frame building, 50 feet by 40, unadorned save by a cross above the door, yet less assuming than itself; the interior, though unfinished is clean and sufficiently commodious to admit the large, though very, very poor, congregation sparsely settled over the County of Simcoe. They are nearly without an exception, from the Isle of Saints. On Sunday a considerable congregation assembled. After going through the ususal routine of exhorting, confessions etc. his Lordship administered Confirmation

139. ARCAT, *St. Mary's Files*, Financial statement for 1859.

140. BPL, *Barrie Magnet*, June 6, 1850.

to some sixty person at the last mass, not a few of whom were far advanced in years. On Monday twenty were confirmed; and on Tuesday at five a. m. we left for Orillia."[141]

Slowly the town and the church community were evolving. In 1854, Patrick Smith reported to the diocese that more than twenty-one pounds had been collected to build a house for the priest at Barrie.[142]

A Transient Priesthood.

What can be noted in the study of church records of the settlement era was the fluidity of ministry on the part of the clergy. When the Barrie area was the frontier, a frontier attitude often existed among the priests that were sent to serve. The adherence to boundaries and jurisdiction was it seems loosely defined.

After 1840, the care of the area that was to become the Parish of Barrie with its many missions was not exclusively in the hands of the priests from Newmarket. The records of St. James, Colgan show that priests traveled up into the district of Nottawasaga Township from Adjala Township while the priests from Penetanguishene continued to travel down from the north.

The Nottawasaga Township community coalesced around the fourth line of the township. At this site in 1848 they built a church which was served by Fr. Charest from Pentanguishene.[143] It was also served from Newmarket by Fr. Quinlan who in the fall of 1840 noted that it is almost inaccessible until sledding season.[144]

In Vespra, Medonte and Flos there were areas of strong Catholic presence and by the 1850's a reasonable population of Catholics in the Town of Barrie as well.

Though bishops assiduously recruited priests from Ireland, France and Quebec for Upper Canada, a significant number seem to have been part of the natural flow of immigration as well. There was a surprising lack of stability in ministerial life.

Fr. James Quinlan provides us with evidence of the unsettled nature of priesthood for those leaving Ireland or other countries to come to North Amer-

141. AO, *Toronto Mirror*, August 6, 1852.

142. ARCAT, *St. Mary's Files*, General Correspondence, August 6, 1854.

143. Privately held, Douglas, Agnes, *The History of the Dowling Family*. page 5. There is still a cemetery on the fourth line of Nottawasaga, directly north of the Village of Creemore, that contains the remains of many of these early settlers.

144. AO, *Diocese of Kingston Papers*, BB16-02, Quinlan to Gaulin, October 29, 1840.

ica. He had been born and raised in County Clare, took orders slightly later in life at the age of thirty-four. He came to New Brunswick around 1837 and ministered in St. John for ten months. He made his way to Cincinnati where he worked for twenty-one months and then went to Philadelphia for two months and then on to Canada in the fall of 1840. He was accepted and assigned to Newmarket and its many missions, including Barrie. After five years in Newmarket, he went to Brantford for five years then back to Newmarket. He eventually was assigned again to communities west of Toronto and when the Diocese of Hamilton was formed he found himself in that diocese for the remainder of his life.[145]

Quinlan was a letter writer and so we have the opportunity to know him better than many of the priests who passed through Simcoe County in those pioneer days. Quinlan's letters to bishops and others are rich in observations which help us to identify his personal concerns. Quinlan identifies with the people who are desperately poor and isolated in small disconnected communities. He is burdened by the ineffectiveness of ministry in such a difficult mission field. "The poor people would I believe be well inclined to contribute to my support, but I could not expect from the most of them even the smallest sum, they cannot give what they have not. They are mere paupers, I have no objection, my Lord, to labour and if I had a place where I would get something within reasonable distance of those people would spend a month with them." [146]

At the center of Quinlan's ministry is his concern regarding temperance. His less than hopeful assessment of his flock is reflected in his 1840 observations of those in isolated communities. "As to the peculiar habits of those people composed chiefly of confirmed drunken veterans it would require an Xavier to make good Christians of them. In my feeble effort of preaching I frequently advert to the odious vice of dissipation which is prevalent amongst them. They are indiscriminately poor distressed people."[147]

He did balance his despair with what were perceived to be glimmers of hope when they appeared. "I am also happy to confirm, your Lordship, that the position of the people in that district (Medonte) hither to slaves to the vice of intemperance are thank God, becoming reformed not by the obligation of vows or oaths but a sense of shared duty, but in West Gwillimbury with all the tact that I am capable of I cannot bring the people to any good for the church or themselves.[148]

---

145. Privately held notes, The Quinlan Family.

146. AO, *Diocese of Kingston Papers*, BB16-02, Quinlan to Gaulin, October 23, 1840.

147. Ibid.

148. AO, *Diocese of Kingston Papers*, BB16-01, Quinlan to Gaulin, November 4, 1841.

This fluidity in pastoral ministry was reflected in an interesting problem tackled by the laity of the Barrie and Lake Simcoe area in 1842. It is a clear case of a priest's ambivalence in adherence to boundaries and jurisdiction and the communities willingness to express their concern to the bishop.

They write, "The humble petition of the undersigned inhabitants of Barrie, Lake Simcoe respectfully sheweth our great regret at the confusion excited through our mission by the visitation of the Rev. Mr. Connolly[149] who is now on his second tour amongst us. Petitioners beg leave to assure your Lordship that the people in general feel perfectly satisfied with the gentleman Your Lordship was pleased to appoint in spiritual charge of this mission these fifteen months past, we mean the Rev. Mr. Quinlan[150] whose indefatigable labours and persevering zeal in the advancement of our holy religion together with a strictly exemplary life has been productive of much good. We dread now the contrast, as Mr. Connolly who seems bent on giving him every possible annoyance claims this as part of his mission. We understand the contrary..... We wish to refrain from all recriminations against any of the Lord's anointed as far as religion and conscience would allow, but should your Lordship see fit to grant our prayers, your petitioners humble and earnest prayer would be the continuance of the blessing we hitherto enjoy undisturbed. In addition petitioners beg leave to assure your Lordship that not only we Catholics but those differing from us in religion with which we would wish to cultivate friendship and charity have highly approved of the unaffected humility and meek disposition of Rev. Mr. Quinlan. In his sacerdotal and private capacity such a priest is most likely to do good in this neighbourhood. There is no scandal given as yet as the Rev. Mr. Quinlan avoided the cause in all prudence. Your Lordship's timely prevention of further annoyance to our happiness will confer a peculiar favour for which your humble petitioners shall ever pray." Signed: Mich. Bergin, Francis Lodge, James Lodge, Moyles Kenny, Patrick Doran, Patrick Dunn, Patrick Kenny, Patrick Smith, John Shanahan, Mich. Flanagan, John Hosey, John McEvoy.[151]

This early document of the Catholic community at Barrie is telling on many levels. It makes clear that among the settlers there were those who could ably set pen to paper and though we may find the writing florid, it does reflect

---

149. ord. August 8, 1830.

150. ord. May 24, 1834.

151. ARCAT, *St. Mary's Files*, Petition of Catholics of Barrie, January 12, 1842. We see in this document that the practice of calling parish priests 'Father' had not become the norm at the time the letter was written. In the nineteenth century priests who are members of religious orders were called 'Father', while diocesan or secular priests were called, "Rev. Mr."

an educated mind and an able turn of phrase. It also reflects a lively community where Catholics are in conversation and maybe at least a little bit enticed by gossip. The very fact that they would write suggests a forthrightness that is not generally associated with the image of the passive emigre. One could suspect that Fr. Quinlan is well aware of the letter and is a silent ally.

The other aspect of the letter which is interesting is the desire to create an image as Catholics that will be free from scandal and to make this case to the non-Catholic community.

It reflects a tension that existed in priestly life at the time. Some priests, usually from Ireland, sought to create a ministry which is very much aligned with the the life of the people. The alternate form of priestly life showed itself in being somewhat more distant and restrained in relation to the people. This second approach was seen very much in the men who came from France as missionaries and in the practice of some of the Irish priests too. Fr. Quinlan is clearly of the second discipline committed to sobriety and good orderly direction. This was, of course, the preferred model of the correspondents.

Reverend Mr. Connolly who has recently been stationed at Colgan in south Simcoe was transferred to Mara Point (Uptergrove) and was claiming the Barrie area as part of his parish. It is hardly an accident that this issue would arise when it does, in early January. The salary of priests in early times was essentially the funds that were raised in the Christmas and Easter collections while the funds from the rest of the year were for the management of the church. We find Rev. Connolly hopping on the steamer at the Narrows in Orillia and making his way to Barrie on a winter expedition. In good conscience he will be able to keep for himself the money that he raises in relation to his ministrations around Christmas.

This practice explains the attitude of Fr. Jamot who was to be the first pastor of St. Mary's and had charge of West Gwillimbury near Bradford. The bishop is planning to lighten the load for the overstretched priests of Barrie, by assigning the mission to Newmarket. Fr. Jamot writes back to the bishop to say that he hopes to keep West Gwillimbury until January 15th as it owes him a good deal.[152]

Fr. Quinlan in correspondence with Bishop Gaulin at Kingston frames the issue of tension between him and Connolly in terms that suggest the two men were at odds in their understanding of ministry. Fr. Quinlan refers to Fr. Connolly's 'deplorable propensity'. To put it simply, Quinlan states, "that in public taverns he is at the bar with no more reserve or discretion than a com-

152. ARCAT, *St. Mary's Files*, Jamot to Lynch, November 11, 1862.

mon teamster."[153] Not necessarily the best example of the "unaffected humility and meek disposition" ascribed by the petitioners to Fr. Quinlan.

It is worth noting that Bishop Power gathered all of his priests in the first fall after the formation of the new Diocese of Toronto. In part, it was an opportunity to set some regulations for undertaking priestly ministry. The first of the fourteen regulations was that priests were to stay within the parish assigned them and to not be crossing into other parishes.[154]

Creating a Clergy.

The struggles of the clergy on the frontier were many and profound. Isolation and extreme demands took their toll. This was balanced by periods of inactivity and boredom. Alcohol was a universal problem among the people and priests were not immune.

Many of the men who made their way to Upper Canada may have outstayed their welcome in other ports of call. Whatever training they had for priesthood it had not prepared them well for the frontier.

Early in 1835, John Keegan[155] was assigned to the parish of Penetanguishene. Keegan's short period of service was fraught with conflict and chaos. Fr. Keegan noted that his arrival at Penetanguishene in February was met with "inexpressible marks of joy and esteem." He was pleased with the large and flourishing congregation which was intermixed with large crowds of Indians from Coldwater and other places.[156]

Within a month Keegan had lost the support of the congregation and was responding to an allegation that he had a fist fight with one of his parishioners in the parishioners home. He stated that this was "false and notoriously false." He maintained that they did not come to blows, rather they had only had a shoving match over a disagreement. He believed that those who were spreading these rumors were guilty of greater crimes and in Keegan's mind even worse, the bishop was giving credence to rumors spread by a Protestant.[157]

Within the year he moved on and the last church record regarding him notes that he is teaching school in Monroe, Michigan as a layman.[158]

153. ARCAT, *St. John's, Newmarket Files,* Quinlan to Gaulin, February 5, 1842.
154. McGowan, *Michael Power,* p. 275.
155. served 1834-35.
156. AO, *Diocese of Kingston Papers,* AB26-01, Keegan to McDonell, February 2, 1835.
157. AO, *Diocese of Kingston Papers,* Keegan to Macdonell, March 14, 1835, AB26-2.
158. AO, *Diocese of Kingston Papers,* Macdonell to Gaulin, March 23, 1836, AB 36-3

Persevering Zeal in the Advancement of our Holy Religion

When Michael Power[159] became the first bishop of Toronto in 1842, he made the difficult decision to hold a firm line on those who could minister in the diocese. Though he was leading a diocese absolutely starved for clergy he refused in 1843 and 1844 fifteen men who approached him to work in the diocese because their papers, including proof of education and valid ordination were not in order and it was perceived that they were itinerant.[160]

In the first half of 1847 Bishop Power visited Ireland to recruit priests. Among the places he visited was All Hallows Seminary in Drumcondra, Dublin which was created as a missionary seminary, training men for the colonies.

Power follows up his visit with a letter to Fr. Woodlock, the vice rector of the seminary, to remind him that he is, "to undertake to look for a few qualified young men for this diocese."

As Power continues, we see his clear decision to hold a firm line on those who would be accepted at Toronto, "I have four or five missions and even a greater number if I were to count those places where the Catholics are not quite prepared to support a Priest which stand in need of immediate assistance. I would be willing to do what I could for two or three just now provided you could recommend them in every way.

I hope I shall not lose any of my priests by the fever brought out by the poor Emigrants and which is raging throughout the whole province. We are not so deeply affected as Montreal and Quebec but we have upwards of 500 in our hospital and sheds just now and but two priests to attend all, or I should say, but one for it is arranged that one should attend the town and the other the hospital."

Power concludes his letter by reminding Woodlock, "Young men know little of Canada (Upper Canada) otherwise they would never think of the East or West Indies and prefer tropical temperatures and other numerous inconveniences to the fine healthy bracing climate of Canada West."[161]

Beyond illustrating well, Power's vision for priesthood and his challenges, this letter sent on July 22, 1847 holds a sad irony as well. Power concerned about the well being of his priests in the face of the 'fever' raging in the city was himself to be its victim, dying ten weeks after writing this letter, on October 1, 1847.

Bishop Power's death was to be cataclysmic for the nascent church in Toronto. Power, Canadian born, seemed to mediate the challenges that came his

---

159. born 1804, ordained (priest) 1827, ordained (bishop) 1842, died 1847.

160. McGowan, *Michael Power*, 2005, page 153.

161. AHCA, Correspondence, Toronto 1, Power to Woodlock, July 17, 1847.

way with ease. *The Barrie Magnet* noted his illness, ironically on the day of his death, "Among those suffering from fever of a typhoid character, it is our painful duty to mention the name of the esteemed Roman Catholic bishop, the Right Reverend Dr. Power. It is not only those who have benefitted from his ministration at the altar who will be grieved to be informed of the Right Rev. prelates indisposition, but the many of other persuasions to whom he has become endeared by his charitable bearing and uniform courtesy and kindness."[162]

It would take three years to find a man willing to become bishop of Toronto. The candidate who accepted was Armand Francois Marie de Charbonnel, a French aristocrat.

James Gowan's private correspondence includes an evaluation of Charbonnel. In a letter to Matthew Ryan in the Inspector Generals Office, he comments, "I had the pleasure yesterday of receiving Bishop de Charbonnel here. He is decidedly a superior man and with such fascinating manners. I think, tho I may be mistaken, he is decidedly superior to his predecessor with whom I had a meeting in Toronto.[163]

When Armand Charbonnel became bishop of Toronto in 1850, he continued the relationship begun by Michael Power with All Hallows. He wrote in January 1851 in search of two things; first, priests and second, to seek from All Hallows their services in teaching English to those men who would be inclined to come to Upper Canada from France. He further laid out a six-point plan of requirements for those men who were to be given consideration: they had to serve the diocese, have sound judgement, have solid Ecclesiastical piety, sufficient breadth of knowledge to hear confessions, an amiable temper and firmly resolved to follow in company with another missionary a rule of life like that of your establishment."[164]

Bishop Charbonnel after his initial contact with All Hallows writes three months later asking for twelve priests. A number far beyond a reasonable possibility. Charbonnel pleads that these men in three years will be able to make all Catholics of the immense territory of Toronto true Christians.[165]

A letter three months later perhaps frames the clergy shortage as Charbonnel understands it. "Could you for God's sake send me two or three of your subdeacons, deacons or priests who I would employ immediately or very soon

---

162. BPL, *Barrie Magnet*, October 1, 1847.

163. SCA, *Gowan Letter Books*, Book 8, Gowan to Ryan, 1852. The predecessor would have been Power.

164. All Hallows College Archives, Correspondence, Toronto 2, Charbonnel to Woodlock, January 31, 1951.

165. Ibid, Correspondence, Toronto 3, Charbonnel to All Hallows, April 21, 1851.

in Toronto. I would keep them in my house....you cannot imagine how situated I am, I have few priests and still some are too may; I must discharge several of them; public clamor is against me, for keeping in the ministry drunkards or others of very bad character."[166]

The bishop's campaign of recruitment seems to have been particularly concentrated on his native France. Bishop Charbonnel in seeking Irish priests reminds the rector of All Hallows that he is seeking three priests from Ireland, 'ready made'. He states that in France he could find fifty in three months, but they would not speak English.[167] It is a reflection of Charbonnel's French orientation that when men are identified for him at All Hallows he immediately directs the rector of that college to send them off to St. Sulpice in Paris to complete their education.

The French priests that Charbonnel recruited came with a great sense of zeal for the missionary field. They were the products of a newly revitalized French church which had suffered through the French Revolution a generation before. Perhaps the most successful of all of Charbonnel's recruits was Jean Francois Jamot[168] who came in 1855 by way of Dublin, to Canada West, to form the Parish of St. Mary's in Barrie.

---

166. Ibid, Correspondence, Toronto 4, Charbonnel to All Hallows, August 6, 1851.
167. Ibid, Correspondence, Toronto 7, Charbonnel to All Hallows, November 3, 1851.
169. born 1828, ordained (priest), 1853, ordained (bishop) 1874, died 1886.

Such a Rough and Laborious Mission

IN 1863, the parishioners of St. Mary's Parish petitioned Bishop John Lynch to reconsider the removal of their pastor, Jean Francois Jamot. They wished Jamot to stay among them as there were few, "so well suited to perform the duties of such a rough and laborious mission."[1]

The end of Fr. Jamot's pastorate was in some essential way the end of the foundational years of Catholic life in the Barrie area. It had been eight years since the creation of the parish, in 1855. In this time the structures of parish life had been established at Barrie and at a number of missions. The petition had affixed the names of parishioners not only from Barrie, but also from Collingwood, Sunnidale, Nottawasaga, Angus and Medonte.

On June 1, 1855, Fr. Jean Jamot had arrived in Barrie to take up duties as pastor. He had been born on June 23rd, 1828 at Chatelard, in the Diocese of Limoges, France. After a classical education he was ordained to the priesthood at the age of twenty-six.[2]

It was through his contact with Bishop Charbonnel, the second bishop of Toronto, that he was recruited from the college at Ajain, where he was teaching, to come and be a missionary in Canada. The missionary zeal of French priests of Fr. Jamot's time was not greatly different from that which drew his fellow countryman to Huronia in the 1620's and 30's.

The high idealism of Fr. Jamot found him in 1855 as the twenty-eight-year old pastor of the newly formed parish of St. Mary's in Barrie which included the townships of Vespra, Innisfil, Oro, Essa, West Gwillimbury, Sunnidale, Flos, part of Medonte, Nottawasaga and the Villages of Collingwood and Belle Ewart in Simcoe County as well as Osprey, St. Vincent, Euphrasia, and part of Artemsia Township in Grey County.

To prepare himself for his work among the English speaking people of Canada, Fr. Jamot went to All Hallows Seminary, the missionary seminary in Dublin, Ireland, to learn English.

The seminary published an annual report in which the missionaries related their experiences in the mission field. Letters from Fr. Jamot which were in-

1. ARCAT, *St. Mary's Files*, Parishioners to Lynch, 1863.
2. National Archives on line, *Dictionary of Canadian Biography*, Jamot.

cluded in the All Hallows Annual Report provide us with much information of his journey to Canada and his early work in Barrie and district.

The first letter was written at New York City on May 8, 1855.

The letter relates that Jamot left Liverpool on April 23,1855 and arrived in New York on May 7. He reports regarding the beginning of his journey, "I enjoyed the pleasure of sailing along the shores of dear Ireland. I remained on deck the entire day for that purpose. I loved to gaze on those shores as my heart was still in Ireland . . . When on the evening of this day the sun disappeared amidst the waves of the Atlantic Ocean, Ireland also, this favoured land, blessed by Heaven–this land of faith and suffering, which has lost everything but its unchangeable character of Catholicity–disappeared on the opposite side."[3]

In this first letter, he further relates that he suffered greatly from sea sickness at the outset but settled in as time went on. He turned down an invitation to attend Protestant services, but felt quite comfortable in publicly reading his office and commented on the civility of the Protestants on board.

In October of the same year he writes again. He has been firmly ensconced in Barrie for several months at this point. He reports on his work in the outlying areas, "I am too well received . . . It happens pretty often that they fall down on their knees in the presence of their missionary, kissing his hand and asking his blessing. Sometimes they follow him from house to house saying the day is a good one for them, that it is the first time they have seen a priest in their house, or that they haven't seen one for many years . . . but I have sorrow to add, amidst these consolations, I sometimes feel my heart broken when I see a perversion[4] of someone among these good people. Some have gone astray because of their great distance from a priest, and of the bad example of the Protestants . . .

When visiting our deep forests, I inquire for the Catholics, my guide sometimes answers me: Such a father of a family or such a woman was born of Catholic parents; but now he or she has gone astray. The principle cause of the perversion is the mixed marriages. When they get married to Protestants their salvation is grievously injured, and mixed marriages are too common. In my mission alone I know of more than twenty-five. Another great plague of our people is drunkenness. I establish temperance societies as much as I am able. This vice is awful, especially where such persons are women."[5]

---

3. All Hallows College Archives, Dublin, *Seventh Report of All Hallows*, p. 44.
4. The term 'perversion' at this time referred to someone who converted to another religion.
5. Ibid., p. 48

Fr. Jamot goes on to speak in the same letter of the progress of the people. "The church of Barrie will soon be too small. Every Sunday there is a very good congregation. The next year we shall be obliged to put an addition on to it. I am endeavouring to prepare everything that I may get the Sisters of Mercy next Christmas. His Lordship promised me to get some about that time. We want very much such teachers to bring up in strong Catholic sentiment our young girls, who are very numerous."[6]

In his final letter to All Hallows, Fr. Jamot speaks of the great progress that is being experienced throughout the parish. As he relates, "The greatest part are settled on the land, and their condition is the best, both religiously and temporally speaking. As the soil in general is fertile, after a few years of hard and steady labour, they are in a pretty comfortable way of living; and, besides they stick better to the religious principles and rear their children in the fear and the love of God."[7]

After his time in Barrie, Fr. Jamot was made rector of St. Michael's Cathedral. He then became the bishop of the Vicariate of Northern Canada. His area of ministry was all of Ontario from the Muskoka River north to the Ontario-Manitoba border. He was first stationed at Sault Ste. Marie, but in 1876, he moved the head of his Vicariate to Bracebridge. In 1882, when, Peterborough Diocese was founded, Bishop Jamot was made the first bishop of the diocese a position he held till his death in May of 1886.[8]

The Faith of the People.

The Catholic community of Barrie was for all intent and purposes an Irish community. After the Irish, according to the census of 1861, amongst those who were Catholic the next largest groups were those of Canadian birth who were overwhelmingly of Irish ancestry. There was a sprinkling of English Catholics and Scots Catholics. There was also one household headed by an Italian (Sabastian), one aboriginal (Shilling), one Prussian (Hartmann) and one German (Lorig).[9]

The Catholic Church in the mid 1800's, was an ultramontane institution. The term ultramontane itself is of French origin, it refers to the Alps that divide France and Italy. Loyalty to the Holy Father "over the mountains" was the first

6. Ibid., p. 50, It seems that all active sisters, that worked in society as opposed to remaining in a cloister were called Sisters of Charity.

7. All Hallows College Archives, Dublin, *Ninth Report of All Hallows*, p. 50.

8. Boland, *From Pioneer to the Seventies*, 1976, p. 14.

9. BPL, Census Returns for 1861, Barrie.

mark of living their faith as it assured a refuge from popular thought that had grown out of the Enlightenment and was expressed in secular beliefs.

Ultramontane ideas elevated the place of the papacy in the lives of the faithful, but also centered it on a very strong tradition of piety and a spirit of subjugation to the church's authority. It was easy enough for those on the outside to construe this obedience as political obedience to the Pope, rather than a spiritual expression of the universality of Christian faith.

It also created a context for uniformity in religious practice which was of particular concern on the frontier where the church members could be drawn into other traditions since they were close at hand.

This striving for uniformity in the church was not only to be worked out in culturally sophisticated situations as that found in France, but also among the settling Irish of central Ontario. When Fr. Jamot states that the faithful showed great emotion when he visited their homes and followed him from house to house, he may not have appreciated they were not in the first throes of joy anticipating the creation of structured parishes. They were, in fact, responding as they would have in many parts of Ireland, where for the last many generations the priest came to the people, rather than the people going to the priest in the parish.

It would be easy in the present era to focus on the autocratic and sectarian aspects of this spirituality and miss the more central concern which was a perceived struggle against the world. For the Ultramontanist the struggle against the world included a struggle against Protestantism which was so prevalent in Upper Canada. It was a discussion which was fueled by a strong dose of hyperbole on both sides. Jamot writes in 1856 to Fr. Woodlock, rector of All Hallows in Dublin, "I would have done some things with the grace of God for the happiness and salvation of our dear Irish who are starving for heaven whilst they have plenty for the flesh, the worms and hell. You have no idea of the condition your countrymen immersed in a Protestant ocean of selfishness, of the influence of wealth, with their mixed schools, without having priests or good men. God have mercy on us."[10]

If there is what appears to be a rigorous morality and a certain inflexibility this was not the creation of an ultramontane theology alone but the influence of a strong Jansenistic tendency in Catholic spiritual life and of a Victorian world view, as well.

Jansenism was a spiritual movement that sought to call the believer to a profound sense of responsibility for their own spiritual and moral formation.

---

10. *All Hallows College Archives*, Coresondence, Charbonnel to Woodlock, March 3,1856.

Where it ran into problems was in that it was a short trip to scrupulosity. The moral formation became so rigorous that Jansenists gloried in not receiving communion because they were not worthy. They were on such constant guard against occasions of sin that they, in fact, became what could be called Catholic puritans.

Extreme aspects of Jansenism were rejected by the church, but certainly the rigorous ideals in matters of religion were endorsed and encouraged. The spiritual connection showed itself in deeply emotional expressions of faith which to our view may seem fulsome.

When Fr. Gibra, the curate at St. Mary's with care of the French speaking communities at Bell Ewart and Brentwood extends thanks to the Sisters of St. Joseph for their acknowledging his silver anniversary in the 1880's, he describes it as, "a single drop of honey in an ocean of grief." He promises the sisters that he will, "beg our divine Saviour to drown them all in the sea of His Most Precious Blood."[11]

It is of course important to remember that Victorian sensibilities also played a role in asserting a view of life which was controlled and highly disciplined. A life where boundaries and structures were foremost in the minds of people.

Fr. Jamot writes to his bishop in September of 1858, stating that the ritual for the baptism of adults, in particular, women, causes problems for him since he does not wish to put salt on their tongues or blow in their faces. In his concern we see all of these forces coming together. He is not only an Ultramontane Catholic totally acquiescent to a chain of command, he understands these actions to be highly intimate and a challenge to his Jansenistic theology, but also being a good Victorian he is conscious of boundaries and where they should be set.[12]

The first lay organization established in the parish of St. Mary's was the Sodality of the Blessed Virgin Mary. The Sodality gathered women together to encourage their devotional life and to assist them in creating a community within the parish for their mutual support. As with all parish organizations the secondary realities were not to be underestimated. The Sodality called its members to a particular devotional life but it also offered them a place of fellowship and structure in which they could act on that impulse among like-minded women.

In a time when only a very few women were free to work outside home and of those that did the vast majority were in domestic service, it was a natural way

---

11. Sisters of St. Joseph, Toronto, Archives, *Annals of Barrie*, November 22, 1882.

12. ARCAT, *St. Mary's Files*, Jamot to Charbonnel, September, 28, 1858.

to draw women together who would otherwise not have occasion to gather. This gathering was an effective remedy for isolation from family and from co-religionists as many of the young women found themselves in Protestant homes. It also heightened their identity as Catholic women. Fr. Jamot makes it clear that he depends on the Sisters of St. Joseph for the success of his care of these many young women.[13]

By the 1850's, the structures of community life were being well established in Upper Canada. The jockeying for position for different perspectives politically and religiously were becoming more understood. For those who thought that Upper Canada would be a Protestant stronghold, the presence and activism of the Catholic minority was disconcerting. The structures of the Catholic Church were being established across the province in the mid-1850's causing consternation among some. The fear was that the Catholic community would gain political power and undue influence. The *Northern Advance*, Barrie's paper, noted as a matter of fact, "The Toronto Protestant Alliance is already doing good service. Its lectures in St. Lawrence Hall will no doubt be productive of an essential benefit to the Protestant cause, which needs at present every effort that can be made. We have received a pamphlet entitled "Mary, not immaculate, not the mother of God, nor a perpetual virgin, but only a sinner, saved through the mediation of Jesus Christ. (May be had at the Advance Office)."[14]

The Orange Order had been present in Upper Canada from the late 1820's, but was establishing itself more firmly in the province particularly since the increase of Catholic immigrants in the 1840's. Antagonistic to the Catholic Church, it often strove to position itself as the voice of moderation and good judgement as this report from the *Advance* relates. "Barrie has invariably resounded with the stirring sound of the fife and drum on every anniversary of the Battle of the Boyne and on Friday last was as gay as usual, with a large Orange procession, banners, paraphernalia etc., etc. The marshall for the occasion was Mr. Davis of Essa. The turn out was large and exceedingly orderly. About one o'clock Capt. May's boat, the Emily May, made her first appearance in our bay suffused with maiden blushes and decorated with the colors of an Orange excursion from Sutton and vicinity. The brethren of Barrie assembled to welcome their friends, who were provided with a band, the whole affording a scene of gaiety and animation in which our town folks cordially took part."[15]

---

13. Ibid., August 19, 1858.
14. BPL, *Northern Advance*, May 2, 1855.
15. Ibid., July 17, 1861.

Pastoral care resulted in a rather difficult controversy during Jamot's years of ministry which showed that the Catholics when challenged could be equal in their lack of willingness to rise to civility. While preaching in West Gwillimbury, near Bradford, Jamot emphasized the Catholic understanding of sacred scripture and reminded the faithful that there were many translations of The Bible that Catholics were to avoid.

Rev. John Fletcher, who was the Anglican minister in the same area, maintained that his informant told him that Jamot had told his congregation that the King James' Version should be committed to the flames. Fletcher states that he had tried to reach Jamot by personal letter and since he was not getting a response had sent a letter to the paper.[16]

In a less than pastorally wise response the next week Jamot stated that, "whenever the Romish hierarchy may choose an area of controversy, it will not select for its opponent a vainglorious country parson, who is manifestly ignorant of the first rudiments of English grammar."[17]

The controversy ran from the end of July to the beginning of October.

One wonders why Rev. Fletcher began this public debate, James Gowan, an Anglican like Fletcher, was not overly enamoured with him suspecting he was sympathetic to the Oxford Movement, in other words an advocate of making the Anglican liturgy more "Catholic" with more ritual and decoration in the church.[18] Perhaps, Fletcher was striving to prove his evangelical orientation.

Throughout the summer of 1857 each combatant provided the public, week about, with a letter. Fletcher maintains, and is probably right, that Jamot did not in fact write his letters. Rather, he let his name be attached to letters written by another member of the parish.

The whole rather embarrassing undertaking may have, in fact, had some value in that it did explain the reluctance of Catholics to share scriptures that may have to some extent muted the ideas that emphasized the sacramental life of the church. It also offered the public clear proof that The Bible was not restricted in any way from Catholic homes and listed eleven editions of sacred scripture that had been published in North America in the first half of the eighteen hundreds which were available to Catholics.[19]

Some Anglicans who had felt a certain distinctive place in Upper Canada were not only dismayed by the burgeoning Catholic population and the forma-

16. Ibid., July 30, 1857.
17. Ibid., August 27, 1857.
18. SCA, *Gowan Letters*, Gowan to Bourne, no date (late 1840's.)
19. BPL, *The Northern Advance*, August 1857.

tion of institutions, but also the Methodists were clearly gaining ground and meeting the needs of the population which was often short on opportunities for religious worship.

The Spirit of the Age, the short-lived voice of an Orange Conservative Barrie, mocked the idea of camp meetings.[20]

The press in general maintained a curious but positive attitude to them as this 1855 report in the Northern Advance notes, "The tents encircled an area a little short of an acre and all of them appeared occupied and well supplied with provisions. We found our way tither about six p. m. on Sunday and were not a little surprised to see such a congregation of people, not withstanding the weather. . . . on reaching the grounds we found that afternoon services had commenced, people were seated in front of the minster's stand and listening with marked devotion to plain and wholesome truths delivered with energy and distinction. After service Mrs. Palmer from New York gave an excellent and pointed address to infidels and skeptics and recited a remarkable instance of conversion of one of the latter class during one of her visits to Canada.

While prayer meetings were being carried on in several tents, we accepted the invitation of a kind friend to partake of some refreshment to which everybody seemed welcome and of which numbers partook without a seeming preference to persons or parties."[21]

The Advance noted five years later that a Wesleyan camp meeting that took place on Penetanguishene Road attracted fifteen hundred people, many of them natives.[22]

The vision of a conservative Anglican society was quickly eroding. The increase in the number of Irish Catholics and the willingness of people of all parts of the British Isles to embrace the Methodist faith with its religious enthusiasm and power to be a great leveller was a source of anxiety for the Anglican establishment.

The Initial Efforts in the New Parish.

It is presumed that Fr. Jamot stayed with parishioners when he first arrived, though it is apparent that this was short lived.

During the month he arrived the triangular lot on the west side of Mulcaster and north of McDonald was bought for 145 pounds from William Warnica.

---

20. BPL, *The Spirit of the Age*, July 6, 1859.
21. BPL, *Northern Advance*, June 27, 1855.
22. Ibid., July 18, 1860.

The lot contained a small frame house on the south east corner which served as the first rectory. The money collected the previous year by the trustees under the leadership of Patrick Smith was no doubt put toward this acquisition. The house was enlarged in 1856.[23]

In July 1855, shortly after the founding of the parish, the first curate Fr. James Hobin[24] was appointed to assist at Barrie.

Bishop Charbonnel wrote to All Hallows Seminary in Dublin on the last day of 1855, "Mr. Jamot does wonders; he is with a Rev'd James Hobin of Waterford; they live as two brothers and have in common four churches to attend to alternately. I cannot thank you too much for your special kindness to Mr. Jamot; he will never forget it."[25]

The first years of the new parish were a time of extraordinary industry as a number of material problems which had developed at Barrie's mission church were remedied.

The trustees had stated in 1854 that they were concerned that the roof of the church was in danger of collapsing. We can only presume that the problem was remedied as the church continued to serve the parish for another sixteen years as a church and after that as a school.[26]

In 1856 through further purchase of land the church's property holdings were expanded. Also, during this year the first school was built on the east side of Mulcaster facing the street. During the same year, the church was painted and placed on a stone foundation.

Brief glimpses of rectory life can be found in the correspondence that remains of this early era of parish life. Fr. Jamot defends the employment of a handyman to the bishop in 1858. "Father Hobin and I have again spoken together about what you say concerning the man in our service. We think it would be very hard, not saying impossible, to manage for both houses without a man. Besides he is willing to stop now for $4.00 a month. As he understands things about carpentry, he is also useful to us for many little things about the house, which would cost dear enough were we to employ a regular carpenter. For instance he has put up himself a summer kitchen with a shed for the sisters, he has made also a piquet fence around the sisters. These things have cost us very little, because we got almost all the lumber from him and our people would not have given any money."[27]

---

23. ARCAT, St. Mary's Files, Financial Report.
24. James Hobin, b. in 1833, ord. July 15, 1855, d. August. 7, 1889.
25. Archives of All Hallows College, Dublin, *All Hallows Report* # 10.
26. ARCAT, *St. Mary's Files*, Trustees Correspondence, 1854.
27. ARCAT, *St. Mary's Files*, Jamot to Charbonnel, August 2, 1858.

In May 1859, Fr. Jamot relates to the bishop that their servant has left the house and the sisters will prepare the meals for the priests and look after the house.[28] He further assures the bishop that the priests will be eating their meals in their own house.

In June 1861, to more effectively manage the diocese, Bishop Charbonnel organized deaneries. Barrie was designated as the northern deanery. The dean's responsibility was to be a liaison with the bishop. In return he was the conduit through which information was transferred to the individual parishes.

The dean would also be responsible for clerical discipline. He would be able to keep an eye on the undertakings of his area and also to be able to speak to pastoral issues when they arose.

The year 1861 also saw the expansion of the church property up to the corner of Codrington and Mulcaster. One acre was purchased from George Lount creating a significantly larger parcel of church land. The church now had the full of the triangular lot on the west side of Mulcaster and the full of the frontage from Codrington to McDonald on the east side of Mulcaster.

The house which served as the rectory was not large. We find Fr. Jamot reminding Bishop Charbonnel of this when he agrees to take on John Gribbin[29] who was training for the priesthood. "I think that your Excellency's intention for him is that he stay here and I would willingly give him accommodation for nothing. He is under the impression that he will have to pay something, as it will be hard for me to have a place for him in our small house when we already have three priests, as well as a custodian, a maid and the teachers."[30]

Six years after the formation of the parish the census of 1861 identifies the inhabitants of the house as three priests: Jamot, Rey and Lee, as well Matthew Delaney and Catherine McKoy who were servants and Elizabeth Hussey aged nine who was a servant who was also in school.[31]

In 1862, on the corner of the lot at Mulcaster and Codrington, construction began on a new rectory or as it was more properly called, the deanery. It would be understood as the normal gathering place for the priests of the northern deanery for meetings which may often include overnight stays.

The construction of such a large and expensive house was a source of controversy as the letter of Fr. Jamot to Bishop Lynch in February 1862 attests. "I meet with some kind of resistance from some individuals with regard to our

28. Ibid., May 31, 1859.
29. born 1831, ordained 1863, died 1914.
30. ARCAT, *St. Mary's Files*, Jamot to Charbonnel, August 12, 1860.
31. BPL, 1861 census. Barrie, Microfilm.

house. I would be glad that they would hear you on the matter. For my part I will be perfectly satisfied if your Lordship thinks fit to say a few words on the subject. I submit to any of your own views, faithfully, not caring much about placing some jealous persons who never give anything neither to priest, nor church, and who nevertheless intend to have everything according to their narrow and selfish views."[32]

Beginning with the two lots granted by the government and the purchases to extend the property on the east side of Mulcaster and to acquire the west side of the street, there was created a significant holding of land for the work of the parish. Catholic life coalesced for the next one hundred and thirty years around this area, providing space for the church, rectory, convent and schools.

Barrie and Early Priestly Formation.

When Bishop Charbonnel arrived at Toronto his greatest anxiety was the lack of priests to fulfill the mandate of the church. His predecessor had recruited the Loretto Sisters, and he during his tenure brought the Basilian Fathers and the Sisters of St. Joseph to Toronto. He was constantly on the lookout for potential communities which could bolster the work of the church.

In his constant struggle for priests, Charbonnel's willingness to take men at various stages of preparation resulted in St. Mary's being a centre for formation. Fr. Jamot was given the responsibility of taking on young men who were aspiring to priesthood. This would have been the task of completing a course of study, including a working knowledge of Latin. Correspondence suggests that at the same time he had men nearing ordination in his care as well. This work may have been to observe their skills, train them in liturgy and to be assured of their knowledge of canon law.

This training would have doubtless been in addition to the work students had done at the Grand Seminaire in Quebec or with the recently arrived Basilians who had set up their college in the Bishop's Palace in Toronto.

In December of 1861, Jamot writes to Bishop Lynch regarding potential vocations, "Young O'Mara's father says that he cannot spare the boy, therefore we don't give him any lessons. Mrs. Frawley speaks to me often about her son."[33]

In April 1863, Fr. Jamot writes to Bishop Lynch from Barrie, "Marcel and

32. ARCAT, *St. Mary's Files*, Jamot to Lynch, February 2. 7, 1862.

33. Ibid., December 14, 1861.

Julien are ready to go to Toronto any time you will want them. Father Christy is not ready as of yet for Bradford. They can go at the end of the week. You did not say whether you wanted Ouellette. He can go also if his services are required."[34]

Fr. Philibert Rey[35] was ordained at St. Mary's on January 6, 1860 and remained to serve as curate for four years.

We have the good fortune of having a written record by a parishioner of the ordination of Fr. Rey from a newspaper of the time. "On the following Sunday Bishop Lynch ordained Mr. Rey, a priest before a large concourse of people . . . it was only on Wednesday the 4th instant that we were informed of the intended visit of Bishop Lynch. But the news soon spread in the neighbourhood. A few hours after his arrival in Barrie, his Lordship accompanied by Rev. Mr. Laurent of St. Michael's College visited the pupils of the separate school. A respectable number of people had assembled to give him a hearty welcome. Our pastor, Father Jamot, a member of the congregation and a pupil of the sisters' school successively addressed his Lordship. The right reverend prelate in his reply expressed his great pleasure to be amongst us on this occasion. He said that likely very few had ever before witnessed the ordination of a priest. What they would see on the next day afforded him great pleasure; to be able to give them the satisfaction to be witnesses of the first ordination he was going to perform. He addressed a few words of encouragement to the pupils, recommended they attend regularly the school where they would learn not only reading, writing and the other branches of knowledge, but where above all they would learn how to know and serve God and mark out their own salvation. He congratulated the Catholics of Barrie for the flourishing state of their school which they have the good luck to entrust to the maternal care of the pious Sisters of St. Joseph.

From an early hour on the Sunday, people were seen coming to our church from all directions. His Lordship left the presbytery at ten o'clock headed by the pupils of the school who had formed themselves into a procession. Our church was tastefully decorated for the occasion. The Sisters of St. Joseph spared no trouble. Everything about the altar and sanctuary was clean neat and afforded satisfaction to all. The ceremony lasted about three hours and never had so large a congregation assembled before in the church of Barrie. After the ordination we were again addressed by his Lordship who said that he was happy to leave us the new priest whom he had

34. Ibid., April 23, 1863.

35. bn. October 19, 1834, ord. January 6, 1860, d. October 26, 1867.

ordained . . . he directed the pastors to form a society to promote temperance, showing the immense evil caused by drunkenness . . . in the evening he presided at the meeting of the Sodality of the Immaculate Conception of Mary, lately established in this place . . . we must not forget to mention that our young choir acquitted themselves with credit for their part in the morning and evening services."[36]

John Gribbin had been invited by Bishop Charbonnel to go to Barrie in 1860 and it appears that some significant part of his priestly training was undertaken under the auspices of Fr. Jamot. He was ordained at St. Mary's in December of 1863.[37]

There is found in the archives of the diocese some interesting correspondence between Fr. Jamot and Bishop Charbonnel. It appears that for a brief period in 1858 there was some consideration of the establishing of a religious community in the Barrie area. The targeted lands were on the sixth concession of Vespra at lot 14. It appeared the land was of dubious quality for the proposed use. The alternate site identified was lot 18 in the fifth and sixth concession. It was unclear what the bishop had in mind as far as a religious establishment, though the focus on agricultural land would suggest it was hoped that some form of monastic institution could be established. Jamot's anticipation is heartfelt if not a little sectarian. "I must acknowledge at once that your letter has filled me with joy in every way. And first, I bless God that our Lordship thinks of settling some religious community about Barrie. Everything goes on better since the good sisters are in our midst. And it would yet be better if there were another community in the neighbourhood, this is the way to Christianize this infidel country."[38]

These plans never came to fruition. Whatever the reason, the plan to introduce a religious community in rural Vespra Township probably floundered in Europe where Charbonnel hoped to recruit the foundation for this new religious institution. His correspondence with the rector of All Hallows Seminary in Dublin suggests that it may have been an order of Irish brothers that he hoped would come. "My only chance to succeed with Irish brothers would be to have holy priests who would undertake the good work of an association adapted to our circumstances as . . . others have done in France. I would give to the institute a beautiful land for their central place."[39]

---

36. AO, *Canadian Freeman,* January 20th, 1860.
37. ARCAT, *St. Mary's Files,* Jamot to Lynch, May 29, 1863.
38. ARCAT, *St. Mary's Files,* Jamot to Charbonnel, September 28, 1858.
39. *All Hallows College Archives*, Dublin, All Hallows Report #12.

Worship.

There is little to indicate to us the nature of the life of prayer and worship at St. Mary's in these early years of parish life. The priests who were coming to Canada from other countries truly understood themselves as missionaries. To that end, they would not have expected great refinement in the liturgical life of the communities they served.

When Jamot arrived in Barrie his first project of improvement for the church was to have pews installed.[40] It seems in the first years the people either stood or knelt in the church which was essentially an open room. The installation of pews would lead to a new source of income, since from these earliest times pew rents were a normal part of the church life, though not one without its controversy. Pew rents were a constant source of struggle between pastors seeking income for their church and those coming to church who were happy enough to stand at the back or around the walls. The source of this tension may not have been strictly financial, but also reflected a break with the forms of worship found in Ireland where the faithful, denied churches, would gather before the altar for Eucharist.

In 1859, we find Fr. Jamot asking to hold on to the seminarian, John Gribbin, over another who was being considered for placement in Barrie because Gribbin knows chant well and would be instrumental in forming a choir. The formation of choirs in the past had not succeeded.[41]

In 1860, a new altar was built for the church and two years later a melodion and singing books were purchased.

In 1863, a gallery or choir loft was put in the church.[42]

Establishing the Church in the Countryside.

It is probably not a coincidence that the creation of the Barrie parish coincided with the coming of the railroad. The train came from Toronto and continued on from Allandale to Collingwood.

Fr. Jamot felt the burden of his extensive mission and had surely expressed some serious ambivalence about the extent of the work that needed to done. We find him writing to Bishop Charbonnel on May 16, 1859, "According to your orders I have just passed a week in the mission of West Gwillimbury. I

---

40. ARCAT, *St. Mary's Files*, Jamot's Report on Expenses during his tenure.
41. ARCAT, *St. Mary's Files*, Jamot to Charbonnel, June 27, 1859.
42. ARCAT, *St. Mary's Files*, Jamot's Report on Expenses during his tenure.

visited the Township of Sunnidale and the mission of Nottawasaga. I still have not gone to Collingwood but I have seen nearly everybody in Sunnidale and the mission at Nottawasaga. I've taken it on myself to do my best for the mission that your Excellency has given me."[43]

Travel to Bell Ewart was by boat as was all travel south before 1855. Of course, in the winter sleds were an alternative. The following newspaper account of the visit of Bishop Charbonnel in the winter of 1859 can help us to understand the immensity of the task in the earliest years of St. Mary's Parish.

"On the 23rd inst. His Lordship, Bishop Charbonnel accompanied by Very Rev. J. M. Bruyere, V. G. left Collingwood for Barrie. They reached the latter place at 8 o'clock having traveled 45 miles in about seven hours. Early on the following day, His Lordship, with the Vicar General and Father Jamot, the zealous pastor of Barrie, set out in the direction of Lefroy's Station, distant about 14 miles from this town. There they found the Rev. Father Hobin engaged in the exercise of his holy ministry. Lefroy's Station consists of about thirty families, several of whom were Lower Canadian. The Station is kept in the house of James Cronin, a respectable citizen of the place. There was a large assemblage congregated on this occasion attracted by the desire of receiving the blessing of their beloved Chief Pastor. The holy sacrifice of the mass was offered, a very large number of those present received the Bread of Life. His Lordship then addressed the congregation alternately in English and in French in a tone and spirit well calculated to leave a lasting impression in the minds of the hearers.

Meantime, Very Rev. J. M. Bruyere, V. G. and Fr. Jamot, took their departure for West Gwillimbury, in order to prepare the children and other people for Confirmation, which was to be administered there on the 25th instant, in the church of St. Francis Xavier. On reaching the place, the two reverend gentlemen found a large number of people assembled in the church. They at once commenced their important mission, by examining those who were to be confirmed. The children we found to be intelligent, well instructed and trained. They seemed perfect masters of the letter and of the meaning of their catechism . . . After the Gospel, Charbonnel gave a practical and pathetical exhortation to a large audience delighted to behold and hear their beloved Chief Pastor. He expressed great satisfaction at the gratifying account he received particularly concerning the excellent preparation of the children; and also the progress made by temperance in this locality. The duty of sanctifying the Sunday, of approaching the Sacraments and of bringing up their children in the

43. ARCAT, *St. Mary's Files,* Jamot to Charbonnel, May 16, 1859.

fear of the Lord, was forcibly and eloquently expatiated upon.

Under the spiritual ministrations of these two exemplary clergymen, great revival, if I may be permitted to use an expression familiar to the sons of John Wesley, has been effected in these missions." As a closing comment the paper noted that the church in West Gwillimbury was about four miles from Bradford where it should be relocated as a more central site.[44]

When Fr. Jamot arrived in Barrie, perhaps no other issue preoccupied and stretched his patience like the financial burdens attached to forming missions. His greatest anxiety was that funds had been forwarded by a number of parishioners for the purchase of property and in other cases sureties had been signed by private individuals and the funds were not there to make repayment or cover the loans.

On the northern extreme of the massive parish in 1856, John Gribbin, opened a separate school in the church at Nottawasaga. This, in time, was replaced by a school house of modest standards on the corner of the church lot.

In 1855, St. Patrick's Church was built on the Flos-Vespra Town line at Apto. The land for the Flos church had been donated by Henry and Catherine McAvoy. In 1859 they deeded an additional one hundred acres for the support of the priest at Flos.[45]

In 1856, the church of St. Francis Xavier in West Gwillimbury was added to the Barrie charge. It was renovated shortly afterwards and rededicated in March of 1861.

In 1858, five acres had been granted to the diocese in the settlement of Sudbury, which was located at the mouth of the Batteux Creek, east of Collingwood. Also, efforts were made to establish the church at Wilmot using the school as a gathering place.[46]

In Collingwood the former Anglican Church on Cedar St. was purchased in March 1858. The Church which had been known as Trinity Church was in the same month dedicated to Our Lady of the Annunciation.[47] This would create a more sound footing for the Catholic community in the town which until then had no regular meeting place. The town itself with the coming of the train was growing at an astounding pace. For a pastor located in Barrie,

---

44. AO, *Canadian Freeman*, February 11, 1859.

45. This church site is on the Horseshoe Valley Road, just west of Hwy 400. The cemetery is easily seen at the top of the hill on the north side.

46. ARCAT, *St. Mary's File*, Jamot's Notes. After much research there is still no clarity on the location of Wilmot. It can be safely assumed that this has no connection to Wilmot Township near Kitchener.

47. Ibid.

Collingwood was an obvious destination for a mission. It was accessible by rail from 1855 on. The Northern Railway offered ministers of religion passage on its trains at half fare until 1860 when it was rescinded, because of a belief that the privilege was being abused.[48]

An effort to establish Collingwood and Nottawasaga as a separate parish was proposed in 1858. Fr. Jamot offered advice on how to proceed, "Nottawasaga is fitter place for a rectory . . . which would not be the case in Collingwood, there are not good roads in Collingwood and the train is expensive. There is no fit place in Collingwood for lodging or boarding, but a tavern, and a miserable one. I think the priest would be rather uncomfortable sleeping in the vestry, which is too narrow.

Mr. Dooling would spare a room. If it is not too late, a log home would be built at Nottawasaga containing two rooms for the priest and a large room on the side for the separate school."[49]

The establishment of the parish was moving forward by the end of November, with Jamot actively setting in place all that the new pastor, Fr. Gullion,[50] would need. "We will announce that Mr. Guillon will be in Collingwood for Christmas Day. Mr. Edmund Duggan at Nottawasaga will be happy, he told me, to shelter his new priest till next spring. He will have two pretty good rooms for the priest. They are adjoining his house, though at a sufficient distance that the priest may not be bothered too much by the noise."[51]

In the end the arrangement only lasted five months. Fr. Gullion left the diocese and the missions at Collingwood and Nottawasaga were once again under the care of Barrie.

In the year 1860 a church was built at Bell Ewart. It was blessed on January 1, 1861 and dedicated to the Holy Name of Jesus.[52,53] Bell Ewart had come into its own when a branch line of the Ontario, Simcoe and Huron

---

48. Hunter, *History of Simcoe*, 1948, page 179. For those who take interest in tracing the evolution of language, it is interesting to note that the that time the train came to Simcoe County people did not speak of going "on the train", rather they spoke of going "on the cars".

49. ARCAT, St. Mary's Files, Jamot to Charbonnel, November 9, 1858. Mr. Dooling is in fact probably Matthew Dowling.

50. Michel Guillon, ord December 18, 1858.

51. ARCAT, *St. Mary's Files*, Jamot to Charbonnel, November, 19, 1858.

52. ARCAT, *St. Mary's Files*. Jamot's Notes.

53. Ibid., These notes composed after Jamot was bishop of Peterborough may include an inaccuracy in that the church at Bell Ewart was always called the Assumption.

Union Railroad was built into the community which was to become the hub for lumbering industry around Lake Simcoe.[54]

On June 9, 1861, the new church at Mount St. Louis in Medonte was blessed, replacing the original building.[55]

On the first of January 1862, the new church in Flos was dedicated under the patronage of St. Patrick.[56]

Later the same year land was acquired in the Village of Bradford with the view to building a church there.

By the early 1860's churches were established at Medonte, West Gwillimbury and Nottawasaga in addition to the ones at Collingwood and Flos.

By 1863 the parish received its first relief from the problem of size. The mission at Bradford, West Gwillimbury was attached to the Newmarket parish.

Fr. Jamot writes about the problems of debts and deadlines again and again of which Collingwood proves to be the most problematic. "As for the debt on the church at Collingwood, I beg to remind your Lordship that you told Mr. Coffey, Mr. Boland and another, last July, that you expected to help us to pay it. It is all paid but little over 300 and this 300 is to be paid on the second of next month. We can borrow at the bank but by paying heavy interest (12 percent) and only for three months. I sent to your lordship the names of Mathew Dooling and Edmund Duggan who are kind enough to allow us to borrow in their names. Mr. Feehan knows Mr. Duggan and as for Mr. Dooling he is as safe as Mr. Duggan. Should Mr. Feehan have any doubt about it he can inquire from Dr. Stephens, Mr. Jameson or Mr. Talford the church wardens at the Church of England."

He further communicates to Bishop Charbonnel, "Mr. Feehan of Toronto is owed forty-six louis which will be due the seventh of next month; the ticket is in my name and the names of John O'Neill and David McKernan of Barrie. I will be angry if these gentlemen are bothered by any of this business. They had confidence in me and they gave their signature when I could not find anyone in Collingwood who would do the same for me. I would prefer to see the sale of our house than to see these men responsible for this debt."[57]

We find something of Jamot's personality in this communication as he veers from exasperation to paternal concern in four sentences, "A call was made to the residents of Collingwood for this money, and they replied with silence

---

54. Murdoch et al, *Beautiful Barrie*, 2007, page 89.
55. ARCAT, *St. Mary's Files*, Jamot's Notes.
56. ARCAT, *St. Mary's Files*, Jamot to Lynch, December 14, 1861.
57. ARCAT, *St. Mary's Files*, Jamot to Charbonnel, November 26, 1858.

and joking but taking good care to not give a single dollar. On the other hand, the times are exceedingly hard and at Collingwood even though people of this mission have good will, I believe that they are able to give nothing now; they have been doing their best to pay since last winter.

I believe there will be no difficulty leaving the people of Nottawasaga and certainly those of Collingwood without Sunday Mass because most of them do not do what they are able to. At Collingwood, in particular, they are too proud and this punishment would do well for them."[58]

Jamot wrote Bishop Charbonnel eight months later to update him on the progress in the countryside, "At Nottawasaga they are not too eager to build the room for the priest. Consequently, it is reasonable that they be punished. Furthermore, at Nottawasga, in particular I told them according to your order, that they had to pay the priest and build the house, other than that, you had decided to not leave them their priest. If you want, Monseigneur, in order that your threats make an impression, it is necessary to punish them. So Msgr. it seems to me that it is reasonable to insist that Collingwood pays for the Church in entirety and at Nottawasaga they build the room for the priest first or give them mass alternately every fifteen days. I am ready Msgr. to carry out your orders but it seems to me that to give them mass every fifteen days would be too much certainly since they don't deserve it; once a month could be sufficient until we see their intentions."[59]

The Canadian Freeman provided a very lengthy article on celebrations at Mount St. Louis on Shrove Tuesday 1861 in relation to the construction of the new church. What shines through is the sense of community and commitment that motivated those who invested themselves in this effort.

"With a view of bidding farewell to the old church and of raising funds for the erection and completion of the new one. The people of Mount St. Louis gave a public banquet at which we had the happiness of being present . . . , we drove in sleighs along the Penetanguishene Road a full sixteen miles then turning to the right we entered the Township of Medonte and still had to travel over four miles of heavy splashy roads before arriving . . . Mr. and Mrs. Frawley received us with a real genuine ' cead mille failthe.' Nothing could be more Irish, nothing could be more thoroughly generous than the warm welcome given us by this pious and amiable family. Early on Tuesday morning the silent forests were echoing and sending back in all directions the enlivening sounds

58. Ibid.

59. Ibid., June 27, 1859.

of fife and drum, as a long file of young men were marching in procession from the old church down to the hill to salute Father Proulx the patriarchal missionary who has first preached the gospel in Medonte. After executing some national airs . . . the procession again reformed and marched back to the church preceded by Father Proulx and Father Flannery.

After the banquet a great number of people repaired to the Frawley's home. "Here several neighbours young and old assembled in the course of the evening. Many excellent songs which were inspired by love of fatherland or the good old faith were volunteered . . . and met with great applause. The younger persons present kept up the dance with much spirit until eleven o'clock when they dispersed to their respective homes. We may remark that they did not waste time upon quadrilles, polkas or any of those new fangled specimens of tom foolery, which afford no exercise, and which are, in many instances highly immoral. No the reel and the dear Irish jig were alone patronized. In praise of the latter national dance we cannot do better than insert the following original stanzas, which an esteemed friend present sang with singular effect and pathos.

THE IRISH JIG.

" They tell how this jig came in fashion
and I believe that the story is true
'twas Adam and Eve that first danced it
the reason was partners were few
and altho' they could both dance the polka
even though it was not over chaste
so she preferred the jig to that dancing,
and faith I approve of her taste.

And sure when Herodius' daughter
Was dancing in King Herod's sight
His heart that for years had been frozen
Was melted with joy and delight
And oft and a hundred times over
I heard Fr. Flannigan tell
'Twas this very same jig that she footed

---

60. AO, *Toronto Freeman*, February 21, 1861. The poem is abridged.

that pleasured the old villain so well."[60]

Separate Schools.

With the foundation of St. Mary's Parish, Bishop Armand Charbonnel was not to miss the opportunity of asserting his strongly held opinion regarding separate schools. Charbonnel had assumed his duties as the second bishop of Toronto in September of 1850. He systematically worked to create structures within his diocese to administer the work of the church. Premiere among them was to be separate schools administered by the church and supported by the tax base.

Charbonnel's worthy opponent in his plan was the chief superintendent of schools, Egerton Ryerson. Ryerson was a Methodist minister, who envisioned a system of public education informed by Christian faith. The legislation of 1841 which united the two Canada's supported separate schools in both Upper Canada for Catholics and in Lower Canada for Protestants. Ryerson, however, had a different vision and worked actively against the aims of Charbonnel. By 1855, Ryerson in his annual report stated that if the agitation for separate schools was to continue, aided by the "highest terrors of the ecclesiastical authorities," then there would be no resolve but to create through legislation one public system.[61]

Education in Barrie had kept pace with development of the town. In 1843, a grammar school was opened at Barrie to prepare students for university. Until this time all elementary schools were seen as private initiatives often in the hands of various churches. An elementary school had been opened in 1836, though some believe there may have been a predecessor in 1832.

The Barrie Grammar School included on its staff in 1845, Patrick Smith, a Roman Catholic. After one year he left and taught at a school at the corner of Dunlop and Clapperton. The authors of the centennial history of Barrie Collegiate infer that this was the nascent beginnings of Catholic education in Barrie.[62]

Patrick Smith was a native of Ireland. He was married to Henrietta Wilkie who was a sibling of the Kenny children who died of eating poisonous mushrooms, mentioned at the beginning of the last chapter. It is unclear how long Patrick kept his school or how specifically Catholic it was. It is reasonable that Catholic parents would access a Catholic school master, though this institution

61. Power, Michael, *A Promise Fulfilled*, p. 33.

62. *The History of Barrie Collegiate Institute* 1843 *to* 1943, pages 15 & 16.

had no official church connection. Patrick eventually immigrated to Indiana where he lived the rest of his life and died in 1870.[63] Patrick's brother Eugene lived in the area until he died at 104.

In 1855 the legislature of the united provinces of Upper and Lower Canada passed the Tache Act which provided the necessary permission for Catholics to begin and manage their own schools.

It was in this political climate a Catholic school was opened in Barrie within months of the creation of the parish. The first classes were kept in December of 1855.[64] That first year the school was established in a small house beside the rectory on the west side of Mulcaster at the corner of Codrington Street. This house would in 1858 become the convent. In 1856 a two-room school was built on the east side of Mulcaster, facing the street.

In the first year, the school was taught by a Mrs. Murphy. In May of 1856, she was replaced by Miss Barbara A. Bourk. Miss Bourk[65] served the school until December 1857. The Sisters of St. Jospeh took over in January 1858.[66]

There is little recorded about the life of these schools, but we do find in the public press comment on the value of Catholic schools.

The beginning of the Barrie School was shrouded in controversy because the government grant was so meagre. It appears that there had been some miscalculation. The interested parties put their case before the public in the *Toronto Mirror* which affords us some interesting information on the first built school and the second location of St. Mary's School. "Already this season a school house has been erected in this town at a cost of 150 pounds admirably situated and tastefully laid out in two separate apartments for male and female students. It is a flourishing school with an average attendance of fifty children. The teacher is a young and accomplished lady graduated from the best Catholic teachers college in Ireland. This school has been organized under the Separate School Act and returned on its first report to the Department of Education average attendance of 32½ children and the names on the school list since January last, till June 1 was ninety children of school age. The trustees having received as their share of the school appropriation from

63. Various genealogical sites on the internet. Henrietta Wilkie was the daughter of the James Wilkie and Dorothy Briscoe. When James died Dorothy married Myles Kenny.

64. ARCAT, *St. Mary's Files*, Jamot's Notes.

65. ARCAT, *St. Mary's Files*, Bishop Jamot's notes on Barrie.

66. AO, *Toronto Mirror*, December 19, 1857. Jamot placed the ad recommending the availability and qualities of Miss Burke.

67. Ibid., September 12, 1856.

the hand of the chief superintendent the incredible sum of 9.50."[67]

In May 1857, the *Toronto Mirror* featured an article under the heading, 'The New School House in Barrie." "The Catholic Separate School house in the Town of Barrie, is in a position which is so gratifying as to call for a congratulatory paragraph from us. It is built upon a gentle declivity of Mount Ardagh, which towers to a considerable height above. It is about 48 feet long.....It is apparently divided into two compartments with a door at the front and one window to each; the partition, however, has not been put in. It is considered and with some truth that a large school room has many advantages over two small ones. There is a map of the world, a fine map of Canada and an equally fine map of Ireland suspended on the rollers around the room. This school is supported for the most part by the voluntary contributions of the people of Barrie and the school fees, the amount of the legislative grant being extremely small. To their honor, be it said, the town council never levy a school tax on the Catholics. The number of pupils is about one hundred; they use the Whole Nation Series. The teacher, Miss Burke, who was trained, we believe, in the normal school of Dublin, is an accomplished lady and under her care the children have progressed very well. The school was designed by Father McNulty when missionary on Lake Simcoe and has been brought to this state of perfection under the fostering care of Rev. Mr. Jamot."[68]

High praise for Catholic education was an essential part of the promotion of the same. The *Canadian Freeman* which was the voice of Irish Catholic Ontario noted the work at St. Mary's School in the summer of 1859. "We can scarcely forbear paying a well-earned tribute to the ever devoted and never tired Sisters of St. Joseph, who superintend our Catholic education in Barrie. Let the proficiency of their pupils, both intellectually and morally, proclaim the worth and merit of Sisters Philomena, Camilla and Presentation who devote their whole time and energy to the improvement of those confided to their care."[69]

A year later the *Northern Advance* reports on the work of St. Mary's School. "The yearly examination of the pupils of the Catholic Separate School in Barrie took place on Thursday last, the 28th ult. The children answered with accuracy on the divers branches of the primary education. They were examined in religion, reading, writing, geography, history, English grammar, parsing, elements of arithmetic and etc. and several of the first division read little pieces composed by themselves which would do honour to a more aged person. In

68. Ibid., May 29, 1857.

69. AO, *Canadian Freeman*, August 24, 1859.

the afternoon an interesting lecture was delivered by the Rev. Mr. Hobin, late assistant pastor at Barrie, on "The Action the Church took in the abolition of Domestic Slavery." In a few appropriate remarks the reverend gentleman demonstrated that it had always been the privilege of the Catholic Church to forward individual, but well understood, liberty; that noble faculty imparted by the Creator as a character of man above all other created beings.

Then came various dialogues and dramas by the pupils. During these pleasing performances the audience was kept in good humor and enjoyed themselves heartily. Several of the pupils fulfilled their task with great credit to themselves. The emanation in the morning and the little play in the afternoon were much enlivened by Miss Fraser who kindly volunteered the music. In fact all of the proceedings proved very interesting to those present at the same time we all know that they contribute highly to the mental improvement of youth."[70]

An interesting insight into the early history of the Barrie Catholic School is found in a petition sent to Bishop Charbonnel in the fall of 1862 at the time of the transfer of curate, Fr. Rey to Toronto. The text one would have to presume is not the creation of an elementary school child. It very much reflects an adult hand on the experience of childhood with "all of its innocent mirth and pleasure."

"Very Revd. and Dear Father, We the children of the Barrie School approach you with the sadness and at the same time with respect and hope to ask a favour at your hands. You have been pleased to remove from us a very kind and devoted father whom we all loved with deep affection and respect. One whose kind voice we have listened to with attention and whose cheerful face always brought joy and happiness to our studies and pastimes. His departure, Very Revd. Father, has left a blank in our duties and cast a gloomy shadow over all our innocent mirth and pleasure. We crave thee, very Revd. Father, and we have come all this distance to beg that you will restore him once more to us as one of the greatest favours that our young hearts can demand from you. Grant us then Very Revd. and dear Father this petition and your children of Barrie will always pray. God bless you now and forever."[71]

The list of youthful petitioners offers an interesting insight in to the very earliest years of life at St. Mary's School. Boys outnumbered girls more than two to one on the petition. To be exact there were 55 boys and 23 girls who

70. BPL, *Northern Advance*, July 4, 1860.

71. ARCAT, *St. Mary's Files*, Students of the Barrie School to the Bishop, November 30, 1862.

72. Ibid.

signed their name to the petition.[72]

Part of the challenge of justifying separate schools was played out in the press which reported on the work of St. Mary's School more frequently than one might presume.

It was not only the Catholic press that was called upon to report the efforts of St. Mary's but the local press as well as this report on the school exams in the summer of 1863 attests. "On Friday last, the 17 inst., the annual examination of the school under the charge of the Sisters of St. Joseph of Barrie was held at the school house on Ross Street. At two o'clock the proceedings commenced, the school being tastefully decorated with the maple leaf and in other ways for the occasion. The clergy occupied, with a number of Protestant guests the front seats, the member for North Simcoe Mr. McConkey being among the visitors . . . the pupils displayed a neatness in dress and scrupulousness of demeanour that spoke well for the industry of their teachers . . . The following comprised the various branches the pupils were examined in: Christian Doctrine, Dictionary, Scriptural History, Arithmetic, Grammar, Geography, Philosophy, Astronomy, Reading and Parsing, History modern and ancient . . . the ableness of the girls even in calculation was rather superior to the boys for we noticed one or two of the little fellows look appealingly to the girls especially when the 6x ran up to the 11 x 11 which when answered had to be converted into shillings, pounds and dollars."[73]

If it included a certain sacrifice, this was not seen as negative rather as a source of deepening the students commitment to the privilege of Catholic education. The history that was to follow would clearly communicate that the struggles that presented themselves were met with vigour for Catholic education was something worth fighting for.

In addition to the separate school at Nottawasaga, in 1860, a separate school was established in Vespra Township on the tenth line. The first school was a log construction, which was replaced in 1879 with a frame school house.[74]

Sisters of St. Joseph.

"The sisters are evidently doing good work in the education of the pupils who attend the separate school as a careful training was evident throughout, and we must question whether the pupils of any other school in the county

73. BPL, *Barrie Advance*, July 22, 1863.
74. SMPA, Memorial of the Parish.
75. AO, *Canadian Freeman,* July 24, 1873.

could have better sustained the attention of a public audience for three hours on a warm evening in a sweltering July."[75]

On January 8, 1858, the Sisters of St. Joseph arrived at Barrie. The community which had set down roots in Toronto in 1851 was quickly being dispatched throughout the diocese to help in the newly created separate schools. Their work in Toronto was centered on their first major institution, The House of Providence, which provided shelter and sustenance to the aged and infirmed.

In Barrie, the sisters took up residence in the building which had served as a school for the year 1855. Immediate renovation was required to accommodate the community.[76] The superior of the house that first year was Mother Mary Laurence Treahy. She was accompanied by Sr. Basil Baker, Sr. Mary Rose O'Malley and Sr. Dominic. Of this original four one was to teach music outside the school, one was to be a housekeeper and two were to work in the school. Beyond their specific duties it is apparent that the sisters took on many roles in the parish.

Mother Mary Laurence Treahy was born in 1835 at Askeaton, Co. Limerick, Ireland. She received her education in Ireland and emigrated to Canada with her family as a youth. She entered the Sisters of St. Joseph in 1855 and was quickly given roles of responsibility. She died on April 30, 1859, of tuberculosis, just short of her twenty fourth birthday.[77]

Mention of the first superiors death is found in Jamot's notes written many years later when he was Bishop of Peterborough. He states that she, "carried to the grave a good remembrance from the pastor, congregation and children of Barrie."[78]

Sr. Basil Baker, was a native of Quebec City. She entered the Sisters of St. Joseph at the age of twenty. Though she was part of the foundation in Barrie, most of her long life was spent at The House of Providence where she died in 1915.[79]

Sr. Mary Rose O'Malley was born in Ireland. She entered the Sisters of St. Joseph at fifteen. Because of her young age, her final vows were delayed until 1858, the year she came to Barrie. Her stay in Barrie was brief as she was sent

76. ARCAT, St. Mary's Files, Financial Report.

77. Congregation of the Sisters of St. Joseph, Toronto, Archives, *Dictionary of Biographies of Sisters of St. Joseph.*

78. ARCAT, *St. Mary's Files*, Jamot's Notes.

79. Congregation of the Sisters of St. Joseph, Toronto, Archives, *Dictionary of Biographies of the Sisters of St. Joseph,*

80. Ibid.

on to assist in the foundation at Oshawa. She died in 1929.[80]

On her death Mother Mary Laurence's replacement in Barrie was Mother Mary Philomena Sheridan. A native of Shercock, County Cavan, Ireland, she had been born in 1832 and entered the Sisters of St. Joseph in 1852. She served briefly as Superior General in 1874.

It appears that the sisters taught the girls and the young boys. This may in part explain why the principal of the school in these early years appears to always have been a layman rather than a sister.

It also appears that the sisters all left Barrie in the summer. There may have been a number of reasons for this. Barrie was truly the mission field, with all of the sisters living in a small house and respite was sought for them in the summer at Toronto. The members of the order across the province were all extremely young and a commitment to further formation may have been the reason to gather them in one place. It is not impossible that health considerations were at the heart of sisters leaving. Tuberculosis had taken the first mother superior of Barrie and in the difficult crowded situations they found themselves there could have been a greater potential for disease.

With schools closed it may have been seen as practical to withdraw the sisters from Barrie so they could assist in other places where the needs were great. Part of the summer work of the sisters over the next century was to provide summer schools for children who did not have the opportunity to have religious instruction through attendance at a separate school.[81]

In August of 1860, it is apparent that the sisters have left Barrie for the summer and Fr. Jamot is anxious that some of the ones who had previously been in the parish return. The removal of all of the sisters for Jamot is a perception problem. Will the people believe that there is a local reason that suggested that all the sisters should leave? Further, people may believe they will now need to pay a teacher and will opt to send their children to the public school.

Fr. Jamot is particularly anxious for the return of Sister Philomena for, "she has done much good in her term here. She was very popular not only among the children and parents but even among the young girls who came in great numbers to ask her advice."[82] Sr. Philomena it seems did return for the year as she appears in the 1861 census, but was soon made Mistress of Novices stationed at Toronto.

The census of 1861 reports that the small building used as the original

---

81. ARCAT, St. Mary's Files, Jamot to Charbonnel, August 12, 1860.
82. Ibid.
83. BPL, Census Records, 1861.

convent housed not only Mother Mary Philomena, but Sisters Engele and Ignatius, Mary Keating, a servant and one scholar, Mary Cronyn, aged ten.[83]

As religious communities spread across the diocese, they hoped to attract young women to the order. Their first vocation from Barrie was Susanah McBride, who in the order took the name Sr. Mary Jerome. Her years of service were to be woefully short. Her passing was reported in the *Canadian Freeman*, "The Community of St. Joseph, Clover Hill, Toronto, have to mourn the loss of one of the most valuable members in the person of Sister Mary Jerome McBride who died on the 16th inst. and was interred with due religious solemnity on the 18th.

The deceased had borne the religious habit for nearly seven years. Her zeal, devotedness and aptitude for the training of youth are pleasingly remembered in St. Catherine's and elsewhere.

Having from ill health been obliged to retire for some time prior to her happy demise, she exhibited to the sisterhood an edifying example of patience and resignation to the will of God whose true servant she had been from her tender entrance. Sister M. Jerome had reached her twenty fourth year at the time of her demise.

We offer our sincere condolence to family and friends of the deceased for the bereavement they have sustained and sacrifice they have made in offering a well beloved child at the altar of religion shall be remembered as he told."[84]

The passing of St. Jerome McBride was to be remembered a few months later in the form of a poem that was inserted in the Canadian Freeman.

Month Mind of Sister Jerome.

O pure devotion: spotless zeal
And Faith your virgin truth disclosing
Come chant a prayer in joyful peal
O'er Jerome's soul so calm reposing
And Mother of the incarnate Son
Who came and bled for man's temptation
Oh, grant this soul whom thou has won
A place within thy Father's mansions!

She listened to the song at nigh
And told her beads in your devotion

---

84. AO, *The Canadian Freeman*, March 23, 1871.

Oh give us joy like hers so bright
Inspire our minds with sure emotion
That so may we when Heaven's decree
Shall call us from this anguish wild
Bow down and give our souls to Thee
Just as St. Joseph's humble child.
M."[85]

With eight demanding years behind him, Fr. Jamot left Barrie to take up duties as rector of the cathedral. One cannot help but think that Fr. Jamot must have been profoundly satisfied with the work that had been undertaken and all that had been achieved in the eight years of his pastorate. The parish was firmly established and the beginnings of communities throughout north-west Simcoe County were well on their way to becoming parishes in their own right.

85. Ibid., May 4, 1871. The poem is abridged here.

Hail Happy Barrie, Empress of the North!

THE *Northern Advance*, in 1864, as it announced a fall bazaar to raise funds for a new St. Mary's Church, noted that, "Church architecture in Barrie, up to the present time, has been of the meanest kind but the great exertions are now being made by the different denominations in town to build real structures worthy of the high purpose to which they are to be dedicated.[1]

By the 1860's and 70's the rustic buildings of the pioneer era were disappearing everywhere in Barrie. Log and board structures were being replaced by the grandeur of Victorian brick buildings that communicated economic strength, public duty and permanence.

The new St. Mary's Church which was built on Mulcaster just below Codrington was one of these brick structures that was to stand for a century as a landmark on the horizon.

While Barrie took on a greater permanence, the population in the countryside was diminishing. By the beginning of the First World War the effects of rural depopulation had altered profoundly the Simcoe County which had existed at the time of confederation. The population of the townships around Barrie give clear evidence of this shift. The following numbers give us a comparison of population in 1871 and then in 1913: Essa went from 5,221 to 2,692 residents. Vespra bucked the trend going from 2,071 to 2,375, which may reflect its closeness to Barrie. Oro went from 6,707 to 3,082 and finally Innisfil went from 5,480 to 3,662 citizens.[2] Farms were abandoned by the draw of industrial employment in the large cities, including Toronto and Detroit, as well as smaller towns like Barrie.

Agriculture was becoming less labour intensive as industry provided new equipment to lighten farm work. Improved farm equipment also led to labour surpluses on the farm. The least productive farmers made their way to town and the least productive farmland was quickly abandoned. One of the positive legacies of this period of rural exodus was the eventual creation of large tracts

---

1. BPL, *The Northern Advance*, July 20, 1864.
2. Private Collection, Map of Simcoe County, *The Orillia Times* Printing, 1922.

of reforestation often carrying the name of the original farmer which is still a feature of the county's rural landscape today.

In the decades from the mid-1860's to the First World War, Barrie was transformed from a frontier town, with some small industries into a vital hub of commerce, industry and civic life.

The *Northern Advance* noted in 1867, "Until within the last few years Barrie has been a place of slow growth and the most that could be said of it was that when other towns and villages were retrograding after the land speculation mania had died out, it always held its own.

Since the opening of the switch, however things have, as it were, taken a turn, and it would be difficult today to find any town in the province showing more rapid and at the same time a more healthy advancement.

It is not long since it was considered a matter of some surprise that ten or a dozen stores should be able to find customers enough to pay the proprietors, but now there are nearly fifty such, where merchandise and manufacture are exposed for sale and there is even a demand for more as the fact of a half a dozen new and as yet unfinished stores being already rented will testify. The supply of business premises has perhaps been nearly equal to the demand but we cannot say the same of dwellings as we believe that the accommodation in this respect is at present very much limited and that a score of new ones would readily find as many tenants to pay rent. We hope that some of our monied men will turn their attention toward supplying this want . . .

The evidence of progress is not altogether confined to the rapid increase in the trade of the town, but is perhaps more strikingly displayed in the introduction of manufacturers, and the erection of mills and other establishments requiring the employment of skilled labour.

We are unfortunately without anything worthy of being called a water-power within the limits of the town and it is no doubt owing to the fact that we have been so backward in regard to manufacturers, but it is apparent the businessmen have now found out that the time has arrived when steam power can be made to pay here and the evidences of this option having taken root are already abundant.

The business strides which the town has made of late years appears to be attributed mainly to the building of the switch, and we have no doubt, but that there are some grounds for this opinion. Appearances often produce reality and the dash of the iron horses into our business centre with the consequent stir and excitement it caused added to some very tangible advantages arising from the proximity of a passenger and freight station, has no doubt produced a magical effect in stirring up and arousing business enterprise."[3]

As the editorial rightly stated, the coming of the railroad in 1855 opened the area to distant markets and centered much of Barrie's industrial life at the head of the bay.

Forest industries were central in the years of the development of north and central Simcoe County. The lumber created the opportunity for the manufacture of shingles and staves as well as furniture.

The second economic resource to be found in abundance was agricultural produce. The milling of wheat and grain opened the way for the development of ever larger mills. It also made Barrie a natural venue for breweries and distilleries.

The small boot and shoemakers shops soon gave way to large tanneries which could ship the prepared hides to other larger industrial centres for the manufacture of leather products. The Barrie Tannery eventually evolved into one of the largest industries in Barrie.

The other large industry of the time was the manufacture of carriages and other equipment. These industries evolved out of the development of foundries.

As industry grew so did the population of the city. The population of Barrie in 1861 was 2,070 people and by 1891 the population had increased to 5,511 citizens.[4]

Material Progress.

The most important initiative that was undertaken in the time of Fr. Northgraves, the second pastor of St. Mary's, was the decision to build a new church. The original church, built in 1849, lacked both size and dignity. Apparently, the conversation at the time was energized by speculation in the town. "The church proposed to be built will, we understand occupy the site where now stands the Catholic School House and will we are told be a very handsome structure, costing some twelve or fifteen thousand dollars. There is a rumour current, . . . we do not know whether correct or not . . . that the See of Toronto is to be divided, and a new bishopric erected of these northern missions, and that Barrie will be the cathedral town. In such a case the church would most likely be built larger and with more taste than an ordinary church."[5] *The Advance* was correct when it suggested that it may be a rumour that Barrie was

---

3. BPL, *Northern Advance*, October 3, 1867.
4. BPL, Census Records, 1861 & 1891.
5. BPL, *Northern Advance*, June 30, 1870.

to become a cathedral town.

Mr. Shearman Bird, a local architect, was engaged to draw up plans for the new St. Mary's. It was to be a brick church located north of the corner of Mulcaster and McDonald Streets.

The new church initiated under Fr. Northgraves was to come to fruition under Fr. Richard O'Connor who came to Barrie in October of 1870. Richard Alphonsus O'Connor was the second longest serving pastor of St. Mary's. He was born in Ireland in 1838. His family immigrated to Canada while he was young. O'Connor was one of the first seven students to register in St. Michael's College, in its first semester, in 1852. In 1889 he was raised to the episcopacy, leaving Barrie to become the third bishop of Peterborough, a position he held until his death in 1913.[6]

The pastorate of Fr. O'Connor was followed by the pastorate of Fr. Edward Cassidy in 1890 and in 1893 by Fr. John J. Egan who died at Barrie in August 1909. Dean Egan was known for his activism within the larger community particularly in matters related to education. He, in turn, was replaced by Fr. Moyna in October 1909. Fr. Moyna developed a reputation for his oratory well beyond his pastoral duties.

As a first step in organizing the construction of a new church, Fr. Northgraves purchased fifty acres on the west side of Sunnidale Road at the very western edge of Barrie from the Canada Company. The cost for the land in 1867 was $350.00.[7] The purchase was to provide for a new cemetery to replace the one on the church grounds just east of the corner of Mulcaster and McDonald Streets. The process of moving the graves from the original site to Sunnidale Road began in 1871 and was not completed till 1877 when the church lot was levelled.[8]

The initiative of moving the cemetery was generously endorsed by the local press in an editorial titled '"A Grave Subject": "The action taken by the Roman Catholics of this parish to establish a burial ground near or outside of the town limits was a wise and commendable one, showing a prudential forethought which should be an example to other religious bodies here, and which is likely, we believe, to be followed before long. We understand that at a late meeting of the Episcopal Church vestry a committee was appointed to consider and report upon this question; and whatever suggestion the report to be made may otherwise make on the subject, we cannot doubt but that it will favour the

6. Boland, From Pioneers to the Seventies, page 23.
7. SMPA, Parish Memorial.
8. Ibid.

general principle of having graveyards as far removed from the business centre and populated parts of the town as possible." The editorial notes that there are four burial grounds in the centre of the town and suggests a union cemetery may be the best solution to the problem.[9]

In 1870, five acres of the fifty-acre lot were sold to defray the costs of clearing the cemetery. In 1871, Bernard Hinds, a parishioner, purchased twelve acres of the lot for $350.00, the original cost of the fifty acres, to assist with financing the building of the new church.[10] In 1885, William Lount, purchased seven acres for $300.00. The proceeds from Lount's purchase were used to buy from the Anglican Church, the land on the west side of Berczy between McDonald and Codrington. It was purchased with a view to providing a more adequate playground for the school. Construction of the church began in April 1871 and progressed well under contractor John Palmer of Barrie. Bishop Lynch visited Barrie on June 4, 1871 to bless the cornerstone.

The *Canadian Freeman* provided the following report, "On Sunday last, June 4th, took place the blessing and laying of the cornerstone of the new church which is being erected in Barrie. The ceremony which was very imposing was performed by Bishop Lynch assisted by Fr. Northgraves.

A very instructive and eloquent sermon on the sacredness of the Catholic Church was delivered by Fr. Northgraves who was listened to with marked attention by the large assemblage present more than half of which was composed of Protestants. The church which is of a very beautiful design in the gothic style will be 101 feet by 50 feet with a tower and spire to the height of 170 feet. And will cost about 13,000 dollars."[11]

The following week they noted that the event involved a procession composed of the boys and girls of the sisters' school, neatly dressed and carrying a number of banners, followed by the members of the choir, the building committee and the clergy.

Beneath the stone was placed a casket containing the Barrie papers with the leading journals of the dominion, also the current coins and a beautiful record on parchment of the ecclesiastical and civic officials and the names of the principle donors to the building fund.[12]

When Fr. James O'Donoghue, the curate died the same year, he was buried under the sanctuary of the new church.

---

9. BPL, *Northern Advance*, May 11, 1871.
10. SMPA, Parish Memorial.
11. AO, *Canadian Freeman*, June 8, 1871.
12. Ibid., June 15, 1871.

Bishop Lynch returned on December 15, 1872, to bless the completed church and dedicate it to the Sacred Hearts of Jesus and Mary.

The *Northern Advance* reported four days later, "As the service was expected to be an imposing one, there was a very large gathering of the Protestants in town, as well as those of the Catholic faith, the former attracted chiefly we believe, by a desire to do honour to the zeal of the Catholic body, displayed in the erection of the handsome edifice now open for public worship."[13]

The very lengthy report went on to explain the tenants of the Catholic faith as in a sympathetic way during the liturgy of blessing, and concluded with a general comment on music. "At intervals during the exercises, the choir and band discoursed sweet music, and some solos were also sung with marked good taste, and in a fine voice."[14]

A new organ was installed in the church and noted by the public press, who stated that the Catholics not only had the finest building in town but now had the finest instrumental music as well.[15]

Another improvement which was brought to the church was gas lighting in about 1884. In 1888, Dean O'Connor commissioned a Mr. Dudley of Barrie to paint frescoes on the interior of St. Mary's. Central to the embellishments done at that time were four life size panels of Saints Peter and Paul, Patrick and Andrew.[16]

In 1894 the original stables on the parish grounds were torn down and a new stable for clergy's horses was built at the north side of the property. About the same time, a new shed to shelter parishioners horses was built on the site.[17]

In 1877, the spire was added to the church. The bell which was to serve the parish through the majority of the church's history was in fact purchased in 1892.

As it seems with all religious events in the Town of Barrie, the public press gave generous reportage to the consecration of the new bell. "A large congregation assembled in the Roman Catholic Church, Mulcaster Street, on Sunday morning to witness the ceremony of consecrating the new bell lately purchased for the tower of that church . . . The consecration was a long and elaborate one and performed by the Vicar General McCann and by the Very Reverend Dean Bergin.

The bell had been placed in front of the altar. During the ceremony it was

---

13. BPL, Northern Advance, December 19, 1872.
14. Ibid.
15. Ibid., August 21, 1873.
16. SMPA, Memoriam of the Parish.
17. Ibid.

struck by both priests and by a number of the official members of the church. It has a fine mellow tone and will no doubt sound well from the church tower . . . The musical service was a fine one as is generally the case in the Catholic Church on special occasions."[18]

The cost of heating the church was doubtless the motivation in 1895 for renovating the dining room in the rectory into a chapel under the patronage of St. Francis Xavier.[19]

St. Mary's, over the years, was the benefactor of many gifts offered by the faithful. The earliest of the parish announcement books from 1905, included a 'thank you' to the Beardsley Family for the stained-glass window they had donated in memory of their mother.[20]

The Beardsley Family were part of the parish throughout the 1800's and continued an association with the parish throughout the first half of twentieth century. John and Sarah Beardsley had emigrated from Ireland. John secured the position of constable and caretaker of the jail in 1843.[21] On his death in 1852, Sarah continued in his duties as caretaker, a position she held for fifty years.

The Beardsley Family donated one of the few artifacts that was transferred from the second church to the church on Amelia Street. The large Pieta was given by Alfred and his sister Mary Anne Beardsley in April of 1914.[22]

The parish announcements in May 1907 included the following, "The committee appointed to look into the matter of increased accommodation in the church by way of the addition of a sanctuary and vestry are of the opinion that such an addition is now necessary, and to be recommended and that a plan and specifications be obtained from Mr. Holmes, Architect of Toronto to this effect. The said addition is not to cost more than $2,000 and the Very Rev. Dean Egan is requested to announce to the congregation that as soon as the plans and specifications are received to call a meeting of the congregation in order that the whole matter may be fully gone into. The meeting is to be called on the Sunday after the reception of plans.

If you want the church addition then you will need to subscribe. No other way out of it. Don't leave it to others or wait to find out what others are doing. If adequate subscriptions are not made then we will leave it till the congrega-

---

18. *Northern Advance*, November 3, 1892.

19. SMPA, Parish Memoriam

20. SMPA, Announcement Book.

21. Hunter, page 248. Hunter suggest that John Beardsley died in 1848, it seems his death must have been somewhat later, to have had an eight year old son in 1861.

22. SMPA, *History of Barrie Mission*, page 33.

tion sees the necessity."[23]

The brick and stone from the surrogate court house which was being torn down were purchased for the construction of the addition and the congregation was asked to bring teams and wagons to move the stone to the church site.[24] With the extension of the church and the creation of a sanctuary and vestry, more seating was provided at the front of the church.

In the early years, St. Mary's had the good fortune of having musicians come into the parish who were more than proficient in music and able to direct a choir.

One of these was Herr Heinrich who arrived in Barrie in the spring of 1860. He placed an ad in the *Northern Advance* seeking it seems to make his living through musical training. "Herr Heinrich, begs to state to the ladies and gentlemen of Barrie and neighbourhood that he has taken up permanent residence at Barrie and that he is desirous of organizing a vocal musical society, for this purpose he will devote two evenings in each week to such persons who may patronize him. Terms one dollar per month. All pupils of Herr Heinrich receiving private lessons will be admitted to the musical society free of charge."[25]

It is unclear how long Heinrich stayed in Barrie, but he, it appears, was followed by other choir directors.

St. Mary's found itself as part of a small town drama more appropriate to the wild west than an established and flourishing industrial town in the spring of 1902. We will let the *Northern Advance* pick up the story, "Louis Lawrence and Norman Staely made a mistake by drinking last Wednesday. It made them reckless and as a result their plan of a campaign was upset and they are now contemplating a stay of some years in Kingston Penitentiary. Very Rev. Dean Egan deserves credit for his strategy, which resulted in the capture of these two notorious thieves. He heard them prowling around the church and saw the candle lights moving. This was at 10:30, Wednesday night, and the Dean, suspecting trouble, took a revolver with him, saw the men in the church and covered them. But he changed his mind and decided to have them arrested without bloodshed. Returning to the deanery, he telephoned for assistance. Night watchman Marrin was asked for at the Queen's Hotel and someone found him. Accompanied by a few citizens and followed

23. St. Mary's Parish Archives, Announcement Books, May 19, 1907 (tipped in).

24. SMPA, Announcement Books, April 6, 1908.

25. BPL, *Northern Advance*, April 26, 1860. A picture of Herr Heinrich can be found in the *History of Simcoe County* by Andrew Hunter on page 181, volume 1.

by a dozen or so travellers, Mr. Marrin went up to the church. He went into the church lawn towards the Deanery. The two men heard footsteps and made out of the back door, coming down to the corner where the crowd was and passing them the only person who noticed them was Mr. Wilder Sr. who called for Jim (Marrin). The two men were walking down the hill, Staeley ahead. As soon as they heard the call for the constable they began to run, where upon the crowds realized who they were. Dr. MacLaren who had been in front of the church came out of the yard at the call and passed the crowd running. Reaching Lawrence he threw his foot in front of him bringing him down on his face. The doctor gallantly tackled him and held him for Marrin. The man was a tough looking customer and a little force was needed to hold him when he showed fight." Both men were given five years in Kingston Penitentiary, this in spite of the robbery not garnering anything of significant value.[26]

It is unclear when the church was wired for electric power, but electric lighting was a source of consternation when it became more universally available and, in the case of one concerned Barrie citizen, the reason for a drop off in church attendance. "In considering the causes for the decreased church attendance of which so much is said now days, has it ever occurred to those in charge of the details of church management that the methods of lighting may be a minor but still appreciable factor? An abundance of light during the opening and the closing ceremonies is desirable, but is it necessary to have a full flood of illumination during the whole time of the service? When metered gas was in general use for church lighting it was a common practice to turn the jets down to almost the vanishing point during the sermon, and quite apart from the motive of economy, this action has many advantages which should cause it to be still followed in these days of electric lights. In more than one Barrie church the combined effect of brilliant and upshaded incandescents shining upon brightly tinted walls, light-colored pews, gilded organ pipes and brass electroliers is positively painful to weak and weary eyes, and the result is distinctly trying to the vision and the nerves of many members of the congregation. . . . The rigid posture and concentrated attention which are rightly considered as seemly in church afford no opportunity of escape from the glare of illumination. We have poetic authority for the twin facts that the proper religious light is a dimone and that garishness is not a concomitant of higher aspiration."[27]

---

26. BPL, *Northern Advance*, April 3, 1902.

27. Ibid., November 30, 1911.

Financial Concerns.

St. Mary's had no shortage of initiatives over the years to assist with financially sustaining the parish. The improvements to the church and other buildings, as well as the ongoing care of the parish, made the financial security a constant concern.

Francis Steevens, a Barrie businessman, in his diary mentions in passing on September 1, 1864, that the Catholic Bazaar was at the town hall that day.[28] It included not only the sale of goods and opportunities for eating, but as the Advance noted no expense was spared in prolonging the pleasure of the day as a dance was planned to follow the evening concert. They further noted the trifling cost of tickets at fifty cents which would admit one man and two ladies.[29]

Steevens would know of the bazaar as St. Mary's was extraordinarily effective in promoting its many endeavours and reporting back about the success in the local press and the Catholic press in Toronto.

The bazaar that Steevens believed would be taking place all day was in fact a three-day event.

As was noted in the *Canadian Freeman* late in August, "We earnestly hope the good Catholics of Toronto will liberally support the very Reverend Dean Northgraves in his effort to liquidate the debt on St. Mary's Presbytery in Barrie. Those who desire to cooperate in the good work can enjoy a pleasant day excursion along with performing a meritorious act. Railway tickets can be procured at half fare."[30]

The Freeman later reported on the success of the bazaar which the bishop had also visited. The main prize, a chair, fully embroidered by the Sisters of St. Joseph, was given by the winner to the pastor. On the second and third nights of the bazaar the Barrie Glee Club and the Barrie Brass Band entertained.[31]

The bazaars which were a regular event were a source of inspiration for the bard of South Simcoe, John Colgan. A rather long poem entitled the 'Barrie Bazaar' in 1873 concludes with these lines after the extensive description of the many booths and attractions to be found,

---

28. SCA, *Diary of Francis Steevens*, September 1, 1864.
29. PBL, *Northern Advance*, August 24, 1864.
30. AO, *Canadian Freeman*, August 25, 1864.
31. Ibid., September 8, 1864.

"Escaping from these sirens with a sigh,
To the Refreshment room we next drew nigh;
"Twas here an epicure could please his taste

The tables groaned beneath the tempting feast.
Here Mrs. Moore with brave McDonald stood,
Dispensing blessing in the shape of food.
The Barrie ladies seldom make mistakes,
To please the public with their matchless cakes.

Step forward friends, in case you have the funds,
The one thing needed to redeem the bonds.
Hail happy Barrie, empress of the north!
Where peace and plenty pour their blessings forth!
No bigot breathes within your corporation,
With narrow minds to check civilization.
But men of sterling worth and stainless honor,
Have all assisted Rev. Dean O'Connor."[32]

The efforts at fundraising were varied and reflected a strongly pro-active parish. The *Freeman* reported on a lecture and concert offered by St. Mary's in the winter of 1868. The Basilian, Father Michael Ferguson, offered a lecture on the settlement of Canada which was followed by a concert. Apparently the lecture was a success as the reviewer states, "I have heard many good lecturers, and was many times in the audience moved by eloquence, but I believe such a torrent of eloquence never carried an audience into such a sea of delight."[33]

It is unclear when garden parties began in Barrie. The *Freeman* informed the larger community of St. Mary's garden party of 1871. "On Thursday last a grand picnic was provided in the grounds of W. D. Ardagh's estate the object of which was to realize funds on behalf of the new Catholic church now in course of erection in Barrie. The day proved delightfully fine and entertainment which commenced at nine o'clock in the morning was all that could be desired. Amusements of various kinds were heartily entered into by children of

32. BPL, *Northern Advance*, November 13, 1873.

33. Ibid., February 6, 1868. Father Michael Ferguson was born at Arlington, just west of Alliston. He was the first Canadian ordained in the Basilian order. He has a link to St. Mary's in that his great nephew, Fr. Jim Hayes, was pastor of St. Mary's in the late 1960's.

all growths. Dancing was most patronized. The canvassing for the cake was a great success producing about 1000 votes to the common fund. The attendance was very good, mustering some seven or eight hundred."[34]

This event took place on the grounds of the home of William Davis Ardagh, an Anglican, the son of the long serving incumbent at Trinity, Samuel Ardagh, who spent his early ministry in Ireland trying to convert Catholics. W. D. Ardagh was also the brother-in-law of James Gowan.

A financial report for the years 1871 through 1882 notes that in that time there were four bazaars that raised 5,306 dollars and ten picnics or garden parties which raised 3,339 dollars. Pew rent for that period raised 3,485 dollars.[35]

The getting of money lead to new efforts in the church proper too. The idea of donation envelopes was first tried in 1896, though it appears with little success.[36]

An assessment of each household met with limited success in 1899. Of the two hundred and fifty seven households in the parish one hundred and forty eight paid their assessment.[37]

The memorial of the parish notes that a ways and means committee had been formed in 1902 to assist with paying down the debt. The entry notes that many were resistant, "because the debt was contracted to no useful purpose."[38] Whatever the resistance may have been, the debt, it was noted, was paid off in 1903.

Progress in the Countryside.

When Fr. Northgraves replaced Fr. Jamot the approach to pastoral care changed. In a parish the size of St. Mary's it was a challenge to serve the far-flung missions. One of the ways the problem was remedied was to assign priests to care for specific missions. Fr. J. J. Gribbin was assigned to St. Mary's with particular charge of Mount St. Louis in Medonte and Apto in Flos. This quickly lead to the separation of these missions into a separate parish later in the same year.

The Parish Memoriam gives many details of the missions of St. Mary's. In 1864 land was purchased from John McBride at Brentwood for the establishment of a church at that village. Church construction was delayed until the fall

34. AO, *Canadian Freeman*, September 12, 1871.
35. ARCAT, *St. Mary's Files*, Financial Statement 1871-1882.
36. ARCAT, *St. Mary's Files*, Financial Report 1893-1900.
37. ARCAT, *St. Mary's Files*, Assessment of 1899.
38. SMPA, Parish Memoriam.

of 1871. The new church was opened on June 30, 1872 and dedicated to Our Lady of the Assumption.

In 1865, a lot was purchased in Stayner on which to establish a church. The lot purchased from Gideon Phillips cost $80.00. It was to be a full eight years before a church was built.

On June 19, 1870, a new church was opened at Vigo on the south half of lot 21 in the fourth concession of Flos Township on land donated by Dennis Gallaugher. The church which was 30 by 40 feet cost $1,000 to build. In 1874, a cemetery was opened on the same site.

In September 1871, Fr. Michael O'Reilly who had been curate at Barrie, left to establish a new parish which would include, Collingwood, Stayner, Nottawasaga Township and the northern half of Sunnidale Township.

In these early years both Brentwood and Bell Ewart had large French Canadian populations, which required a French speaking priest. Beginning in 1872, Fr. Gibra for many years served these parishes from Barrie. In 1886, he notes in correspondence with Bishop Lynch that there are only five people in Brentwood who do not speak English and in Bell Ewart there are none.[39]

Progress in Education.

In the summer of 1865 the recent examinations at the Barrie separate school were noted, "Knowing your interest in education, I take the liberty of sending you an account of the examination of the Separate School of this town on last Thursday. The school is taught by the Sisters of St. Joseph and is attended by about 200 pupils during the course of the year, though the daily attendance, is of course, considerably less. The school room is well furnished with maps and tablet lessons. A platform was erected for the pupils and tastefully decorated with fancy work made by the pupils. A large and appreciative audience was present."[40]

The school which had been built in the mid 1850's had a seventeen-year history. It was replaced in 1873 by the renovation of the original church into a school house. The school was removed from the property since it was in front of the new church facing Mulcaster Street.

In 1881, an addition was put on the original church, which at this point had served as a school for eight years, and the older part was significantly renovated. This solution was to last just over a decade.

---

39. Ibid., Gibra to Lynch, January 4, 1886.

40. BPL, *Northern Advance*, July 26, 1864.

In July 1893, A. J. Orr and Sons began construction on a new school which would have four rooms. This school was built behind St. Mary's Church, further east on McDonald Street.[41] The *Catholic Register* noted this initiative, "The contract for the erection of the separate school in Barrie, has been awarded. The building to be well and substantially built of red brick laid in brown mortar. The front and end facades present a very neat appearance. The windows are nicely grouped with elliptical heads. There are two main entrances in a tower which terminates in an artistic belfry. The building contains five rooms, heated and ventilated on the most modern principles, and reflects great credit on the architects, Thomas Kennedy and Co."[42]

It was opened January 1, 1894. The former school which was created out of the renovation of the church was sold for thirty dollars and removed from the property.[43]

In the fall of 1912, the school grounds were levelled so that they could be usable for "scientific games."[44] The Catholic school opened on the tenth line of Vespra in 1870 was still functioning in 1905.[45]

Attendance at school seems to have been an ongoing issue for the church, with announcements in the early part of the last century reminding parents in town and country to send their children to school regularly.

Fr. Northgraves wrote Bishop Lynch regarding a teacher for the Nottawasaga school in February 1864. He assures him that a male or female will do. The school will run for nine months and the successful candidate will receive $80.00. Board, he assures him, can be got for about four dollars a month. He suggests that someone who is just finished school would do as the children are young and backward.[46]

The Sisters of St. Joseph.

The sisters in Barrie were successfully meeting the challenge of ministry. They were the benefactors of the burgeoning response to religious communities by young women.

For the people of St. Mary's their consciousness of the work of the Sisters

---

41. This section of McDonald Street is now the driveway off Mulcaster into the courts and the government building. McDonald at one time ran up to Berczy.

42. AO, *The Catholic Register*, August 10, 1993.

43. ARCAT, *St. Mary's Files*, Financial Statement, 1893 to 1900.

44. SMPA, Memoriam of the Parish.

45. SMPA, Announcement Books, April 20, 1905.

46. ARCAT, *St. Mary's Files*, Northgraves to Lynch, February 1, 1864.

of St. Joseph went well beyond the borders of the town. The *Canadian Freeman* often included notes of thanks from the sisters for those assisting their work at the House of Providence in Toronto. At the end of March 1864 they acknowledged St. Mary's for their donation of 73 bags of wheat, 17 barrels of flour and two barrels of meat.[47]

In 1869, the legacy of land on Penetanguishene Road given to the sisters, by the Bergin and Lodge Families was sold for four thousand dollars.[48]

In 1882, Sr. Antoinette McDonnel, Superior General of the order visited Barrie as the annals report, "Rev Mother returned from Barrie where she has spent a few days with our dear missionary sisters. While there, she discussed the prospects of the erection a new building . . . the present convent being altogether too small for the comfort and accommodation of the sisters."[49] The convent had been in use since 1858, albeit with significant additions, including the addition of a solid board fence to allow for their greater privacy when outside.[50]

In May 1885, excavations began on the site on the west side of Mulcaster Street. The completed building was blessed by Bishop Lynch in January of 1886. The building was built by Robert Fletcher to a design by architect Mr. Kennedy of Barrie for a cost of $8,490.00.[51]

The *Northern Advance* sent a reporter to the new convent in January, "The convent is now nearly ready for occupation . . . , he was enabled to see every part of the building and obtain what information he asked . . . entering the front door into a spacious hall the first room on the right is the parlor finely finished in mahogany. This contains a fireplace though the room is heated by steam from radiators covered by ornamental screens with marble tops. The ceiling has a fine centerpiece. Folding doors open from this room into the chapel, which is also finished with mahogany. On the left of the hall a doorway leads to a corridor that skirts four music rooms. On the second floor there is a large community room for the sisters and to the front a sewing room which looks out on Mulcaster Street. There are some eight rooms on this floor furnished with wardrobes and all conveniences. On this floor there is as very nice bathroom furnished with hot and cold water. The interior of all the rooms on

---

47. AO, *Canadian Freeman*, March 31, 1864.

48. Archives of the Sisters of St. Joseph, Toronto, Annals, July 3, 1869.

49. Ibid., October 25, 1882.

50. ARCAT, *St. Mary's Files,* Northgraves to Lynch, April 26, 1867.

51. Archives of the Sisters of St. Joseph, Toronto. Annals, throughout 1885 & 1886. This building, now law offices still exists, at the time of writing, at the corner of Mulcaster and Codrington.

this floor are finished in stone color tint which gives a pleasant mellow light, very grateful to the eyes."[52]

After Christmas, in 1885, a bazaar was held at the town hall in support of the new convent. "There was a large display of useful fancy and ornamental articles tastefully arranged on the various tables and presenting a most attractive appearance. The prizes for the grand drawing were placed on a separate table and drew remarks of admiration from many on account of their great value. The ladies who had charge of the tables were most obliging and attentive to all visitors, who left the hall, after enjoying their smiles, with lighter hearts and purses. The interest taken in the bazaar by the people of all denominations speaks well for their generosity and good feeling towards the Sisters of St. Joseph who feel very grateful to their benefactors.[53]

The good feeling towards the sisters were undoubtedly genuine though maybe not universal. In June of 1890, an attempt was made to burn down the convent.

The local press took note of the story: "Hearing on Tuesday that an attempt had been made to burn the convent, the young man of the *Advance* went up there to learn the truth of the story. The sister in charge took him to the basement, and there in four places fire had been placed. The worst was in a pantry on the north side of the building where the fire had made considerable headway, burning shelves, drawers and the wood work reaching to the ceiling. In another apartment rags saturated with coal oil had been put into a cupboard and the door shut. In two other places the plaster had been knocked off the wall and the fire started by putting material dipped in coal oil in the holes made. Some ladies passing saw smoke and gave the alarm. Mr. P. Kearns with others were soon on the scene of danger and by prompt measures the fire was extinguished. The sisters were at the church just across the road. They rise at five in the morning and have breakfast before going to church. This deed was evidently done between six and seven o'clock in the morning and must have been done by someone who knows the place and the fact that the sisters were away. The entrance was made through a window in the rear of the basement as all the doors were locked. In one of the rooms where the fire had been put the door had been locked by the incendiary and the key taken but fortunately another key was found that would unlock the door. The sister said they were not suspicious of anyone, not knowing they had an enemy in the world."[54]

---

52. BPL, *Northern Advance*, January 7, 1886.
53. Ibid., January 7, 1886
54. Ibid., June 26, 1890.

The Harsh Realities of Victorian Barrie.

The pervasive problem of alcohol was felt in all aspects of life in Victorian Canada. The concern crossed religious lines. Society in general, through temperance movements, was actively challenging the problem.

The monotony of lives which involved hard work and little social distraction lead easily to drinking which could foster in turn domestic violence and dissolute living. The temperance movement which became very politicized in the twentieth century was at this time not only a critic of the consumption of liquor but functioned as a social alternative to bars and hotels. Temperance groups offered social interaction, excursions and other ways to encourage social intercourse without spirits. Temperance bands became a common feature of many temperance organizations. It is useful to appreciate that temperance was the rejection of imbibing liquor, but it made no comment on the drinking of beer or wine. Total abstinence rejected the use of any form of alcohol.

The commonness of drunken behaviour can be found in an issue that Fr. Northgraves discussed with Bishop Lynch. He relates the situation of a parishioner who had been married before a minister. He assures the bishop, "He was drunk so his consent was doubtful . . . He is looked upon as a good man. Certainly only he was drunk, he would not have done this misdeed."[55]

Judge Gowan in organizing a trial with an official of the court reminds him, "I would also suggest that a proper person be employed to look after the witnesses to keep them from drinking for some of them I am sorry to say are rather given that way and the possibility of their being lured into drinking at the most important moment is by no means remote."[56]

Dean Northgraves wrote to Bishop Lynch shortly after his arrival in Barrie in 1863. "There was a Temperance Society named St. Mary's Temperance Society. It broke down. As I would wish it to be resuscitated and the people also wish it, I would be glad to know whether it should be called St. Mary's as before, or St. John's or any other name you may suggest."[57]

Northgraves came to Barrie with a strong history of temperance work in Toronto.

Temperance was the battle against the bar room. We see in Northgraves concerns the desire to create a place where men could come together other than the bar. A place where men could socialize without the discussion wandering

---

55. Ibid., November 17, 1863.
56. SCA, *Gowan Letter Books*, Gowan to John Norris, October 16, 1843.
57. ARCAT, *St. Mary's Files*, Northgraves to Lynch, October 15, 1863.

into the political debates of the day. A temperance movement that involved only Catholics would provide this goal.

The following letter to the *Canadian Freeman* describes the 1864 St. Patrick's Day celebration organized and hosted by St. Mary's Temperance Society.

"As I know that you are anxious to hear anything in relation to the celebration of St. Patrick's Day in the province, I take the liberty of giving you an account of what was done in this hyper-borean region. Much though we delight in the annual return of our National Feast, we either lacked courage or had not thought of celebrating the day, until this year. However, the St. Mary's Temperance Society . . . lately established in town resolved to atone for past inactivity by celebrating it this time on a grand scale. The town hall was selected for the purpose of holding a social assembly. As soon as the doors were opened it became evident that the expectation of the managing committee would be excelled for it was calculated that there were present at least 600 persons of whom probably half were Protestants . . . Refreshments were served at 8 o'clock of an excellent quality and in great plenty. After tea, the Very Reverend Dean Northgraves delivered an interesting lecture on the Pentateuch. For an hour and quarter the audience composed of the elite of town and country listened with marked attention and great pleasure. The lecture was diversified by sallies, which provoked considerable amusement and served to render agreeable a difficult subject . . . The members of St. Mary's Society are increasing fast. On St. Patrick's Day they appeared for the first time with their new and handsome badges . . . If you deem this account of St. Patrick celebrations in Barrie worthy of a place in your columns, you at your pleasure expunge or alter so as to suit your excellent journal."[58]

The *Northern Advance* further reported with a slight touch of irony on the same event in that they noted that after the reverend gentleman had taken his departure, a dance was improvised at which the younger folk present temperantly enjoyed themselves until they had seen the last of St. Patrick's Day.[59]

The harder side of Victorian Barrie is etched in the following entry in the diary of the Barrie businessman, Francis Steevens, "Mrs. S. awoke this morning at four o'clock by knocking at the front door and raised the bedroom window to ascertain who was there after calling out to whoever was knocking to come to the end of the house without anyone appearing. She went down to the dining room looked out of the window, and saw no one but fancied she heard a

---

58. AO, *Canadian Freeman*, March 24, 1864.
59. BPL, *The Northern Advance*, March 24, 1864.

noise like that of something grunting or like a child breathing heavily. I called for her to come up and not stop there any longer. She then came and communicated to me what she had heard and directly after we heard another knock which of course we did not answer supposing the person who left the child there would take it away again on finding we did not take it in.

When I got up at six thirty a.m. and was washing myself the child was discovered by someone passing who knocked but not being disposed to take in the child I did not open the door but went to fodder the cattle while Mrs. S. answered those who knocked and persistingly demanded we take in the child.

She sent for W. Plaxton being councillor and constable but he did not come until the child was taken to the gaol by Mr. Hudson by order of Mr. Georgan. The child was packed into a basket with some cloth and napkins and covered with a sheepskin and was warm, the weather being mild but snowing fast. It was a female infant about four or five days."[60]

Steevens' obvious reluctance to accept the child, reflected the fact that this was not the first foundling left on the Steevens' doorstep. The same situation had arisen some fifteen months before, when a baby boy was left. In that case the childless couple had accepted the child into their home. They had him baptised at the Anglican Church with the name, Frank Bydoor, a name they settled on eschewing their first choice, Frank Snowdrop. The child unfortunately died the next summer and was buried in the Anglican Cemetery on Berczy St.[61]

In the earliest times of settlement in the region, often there were those who lived in great poverty. The structures to assist with the poor were at best minimal and the needs of the poor were a serious drain on the limited resources that people had.

Fitting In.

Fr. George Northgraves came to Barrie as the second pastor in 1863. If Fr. Jamot was essentially concerned with gathering in the faithful and providing the structures for worship and education. Fr. Northgraves was eager to integrate Catholics into the larger society.

The 1850's had been a time of unprecedented sectarian tension between Catholics and Protestants in Ontario. Northgraves, had been born in 1834 at Lindsay, Ontario. In spite of his effort to integrate Catholics within the larger

60. SCA, *Diary of Francis Steevens*, March 7, 1867.

61. Ibid., Throughout 1866-1867.

community, he found his congregation on more than one occasion under suspicion of disloyalty to crown and country.

By the 1860's, in Canada, the cause of Irish independence with its implied anti-British sentiment had found its voice. Called the Hibernian Movement, it encompassed the ideal of Irish independence from Britain. The more violent aspect of these ideals expressed themselves in the Fenian Brotherhood. The challenge for Irish Catholics was to balance things which were Irish and Catholic and things which were Canadian, which for a majority of English speaking Canadians also meant Protestant. The Hibernians had a political agenda, but they also offered a place for Irish social organization and fellowship other than in the church.

Northgraves reports to the bishop shortly after arriving in Barrie, "The Hibernians are taking steps to start a branch of their society here, as far as we can ascertain. If we remain passive, no doubt, it will be established. Should we take a position of decided hostility, positively discouraging it or should we permit the starting of the branch here? We would start a Temperance Society but though this would be a diversion it would not prevent the establishment of the Hibernians without actual discouragement."[62]

Northgraves encapsulates the church's concern. An organization with strong political overtones within the Catholic community could be a negative while a temperance society would be seen as advocate for community commitment and allow the church to have significant input into the life of the community.

The Irish born Bishop Lynch, who came to Toronto in 1859 had taken an ambivalent attitude toward the Hibernians.

In 1864, Bishop Farrell of Hamilton had gone on record as opposing the Hibernians as a secret society and reiterated his opposition the following year. The leader of the Hibernians, Michael Murphy, spoke at Hamilton and took this time to state that the Hibernians were a temporal group and a Catholic bishop or a renegade or a traitor had no authority to comment on their undertakings.[63]

Northgraves writes shortly after to Fr. Jamot who is now serving as the Vicar General of the diocese, "I see that M. Murphy has grossly insulted Bishop Farrell. I should think the Toronto clergy bound to disclaim sympathy with the outrage. I have taken on myself to discountenance the intended reorganization of the Hibernians, and I believe I will meet with success in preventing it

---

62. ARCAT, *St. Mary's Files*, Northgraves to Lynch, September 1, 1863.

63. Clarke, *Piety and Nationalism*, p. 191.

from being reorganized. Since the Fenian excitement, they fell away and now I believe I will prevent it from being restored unless his Lordship wishes me to remain neutral in the matter. I have spoken very decidedly to many of the Hibernians here against the bad spirit showed by the Hibernian president and newspaper and all agree to have no more to do with the society."

For in spite of his clearly anti-Hibernian, not to mention anti-Fenian sensibilities, there was at the same time deep suspicion which became a celebrated cause in Barrie.[64]

It appears that by the end of 1864 Northgraves had felt required to respond to the excitement in town. It is hard to know how seriously the allegations against the Catholics were taken. The *Canadian Freeman* in editorializing about Fr. Northgraves efforts stated that it was a remedy for the perturbation and alarm in the town of an anticipated Fenian conspiracy and massacre.

Northgraves wrote as follows in the local press, "Dear Gentleman, Certain absurd rumours have caused great alarm here among the Protestants of our community and my own name as well as the names of several of my parishioners have been mentioned as entertaining evil designs on the public. In consequence, I feel it my duty to do all in my power to soothe the alarm which seems to be so general and to deprecate the ill feelings which might be evoked by the circulation of such reports. The rumour is that there is in Barrie a society connected with the Fenians of the United States, the object of which is ultimately to overthrow British rule in Canada or in Ireland and in the meantime desiring to murder the Protestants indiscriminately. Many of the Catholics of Barrie have been accused of being privy to this conspiracy. It has even been asserted and currently believed that a body of men were seen drilling on the verandah of my house, i.e. in the public street and that bodies of Fenians marched through town. These rumours quite unfounded are so absurd that it seems foolish for me to take notice of them; still they are believed by perhaps a majority of the citizens of Barrie; even men who were thither to supposed to be men of sense as they are men of wealth and high standing among us. Of the three Barrie newspapers, two show the good sense of the editors by ridiculing the alarm of the timid men who probably take their cue from the women.

It may be readily inferred that the rumor which makes me a Fenian drill sergeant is without foundation especially as I did not graduate from any military school and scarce know the difference between the two very distinct orders 'to stand at ease and to charge bayonets'."[65]

---

64. ARCAT, *St. Mary's Files*, Northgraves to Jamot, August 11, 1865.
65. AO, *Canadian Freeman*, December 15, 1864.

One would perhaps want to accuse Fr. Northgraves of being alarmist, but the Fenian movement out of the United States did invade Canada, in 1866, and though the incursions were hardly on a concerted basis, still there were deaths and a general anxiety.

Bishop Lynch came out against the Hibernian Society in the summer of 1865.[66] A few days before St. Patrick's Day in 1866 in the height of the Fenian fear, Bishop Lynch stated, "We need not point out to Catholics their duty as loyal subjects is to repel invasion and to celebrate the festival of the Patron Saint of Ireland as pious Catholics, good Irishmen and faithful children of St. Patrick by approaching the Holy Sacrament of the Altar and to pray earnestly to God that through the intercession of His Immaculate and ever virgin Mother and St. Patrick, he would inspire the rulers of Ireland to extend justice and mercy to that poor distracted country."[67]

In Barrie, St. Patrick's Day 1866, the public press noted, "was one of the quietest days we have seen in our usually quiet and orderly town . . . the only honour done to the said saint was in the way of a ball in the town hall which came off the previous night and was well attended and where dancing was kept up by the young folks until the 17th had been well ushered in. Everyone present seemed to enjoy the festivity and to have little thought or care for the Fenians."[68] *The Examiner* added its voice stating, "that it was obvious the commitment of the Irish Roman Catholics of the country as some imagined, was not 'lip loyalty."[69]

This equanimity was not to remain. By the summer, there developed in the town a hysteria once again fueled by the belief that on July 12th, the day of Orange celebration, that the Catholics in aid of the Fenian cause were planning to burn Protestant churches and to bring about a massacre of Protestants in the town. Northgraves told the public through the press that he has been informed by a respectable Protestant gentleman of the rumours and the agitation they were causing. Northgraves learned that guards had been placed on two Protestant churches and that armed bands of men were patrolling the town at night and "prowling around the premises of Catholics while the inmates are unsuspectingly asleep."

Northgraves is not hesitant in identifying the source of the rumours as D'Arcy Boulton. Boulton was the grandson of D'Arcy Boulton who had been

66. BPL, *Northern Advance*, August 23, 1865.
67. BPL, *Barrie Examiner* and *Simcoe Advocate*, March 15, 1866.
68. BPL, *Northern Advance*, March 21, 1866.
69. BPL, *Barrie Examiner*, March 22, 1866.

attorney general in early Upper Canada and nephew of John Beverly Robinson, who had been solicitor general. He came to Barrie to practice law and immerse himself in Conservative and Orange causes. He took part in the creation of "The Spirit of the Age" a short lived newspaper in Barrie that advocated from the Orange and Conservative perspective. He sought election on a number of occasions and sat in provincial legislature for South Simcoe for a period of time.

Boulton's political ambitions ran parallel to his involvement in the Orange movement in which he successfully held many positions at the highest levels in the province. He died at the age of 49. At the time of his "set to" with Fr. Northgraves he was 40 years old.

Boulton, in his own defense, says that he had learned of the news from a woman, it would seem it was his maid, who had been at mass at St. Mary's, where a discussion arose between Northgraves and his parishioners about the plan. Boulton had heard that Northgraves had strongly opposed the plan and put his foot on it, but he had been unsuccessful in his opposition and so it was decided to carry out the massacre on Tuesday night, July 12th.

Northgraves stated at the end of June, the whole story was calumny.[70] The fight was on.

On July 4th, D'Arcy Boulton replied, "I see by last week's *Advance* and *Examiner* that the Rev. Mr. Northgraves of this town has thought fit to have a fling at the Orangemen through me their humble representative . . . and first as to the method of the reverend gentleman's vindication I must say that from my heart I pity the flock whose pastor so far forgets his divine mission (if he has one) as to indulge in the intolerant and malevolent strain that this letter exhibits . . . who can cast aside the garb of peace which his divine master wore and assume so readily the most futile weapon of the flesh known as unmitigated abuse...though it was well known there were Fenians amongst us we did not think that they knew we had spotted them; and now sir, this is the third time within a year that there has been excitement in the town, watches kept and armories guarded; and how come the first time Father Northgraves opens his mouth is after the defeat of the Fenians in the field?"[71]

The next day Northgraves shot the next volley and a week later on the 12th, Boulton responded again. Essentially Northgraves states that the Catholics of Barrie were not Fenians, though Boulton was a convicted slanderer. Boulton in return called Northgraves Jesuitical and daily proof was accumulating that

70. AO, *Canadian Freeman,* June 25, 1866.

71. BPL, *Northern Advance*, July 4, 1866.

would cause Northgraves to draw in his horns."[72]

These flare ups were distressing. At the same time the Catholic community was moving forward making good progress in promotion of the church and the ideals such as temperance which were so pressing at the time. It is obvious that these efforts were being made with the strong support and endorsement of the Catholic community in general.

As the 1860's ended, Canada had become a nation. Confederation was a tonic for easing sectarian tensions. This does not presume that there was not room for disagreement from time to time. The religious issue in the public domain flared again in the early 1880's when Fr. O'Connor was pastor of St. Mary's, though this time on a provincial level. The issue was the use of the novel Marmion in public schools. The book by Walter Scott which carried a rather anti-Catholic bent was to be required reading in the public schools of the province. Among the reasons cited for Catholic opposition was the reference to Catholics as the "vassals and slaves of bloody Rome."[73] The clergy of the northern deanery en masse supported Bishop Lynch in his opposition to the use of the book. As they stated, "The promptitude, with which you called the attention of the Hon. Minister of Education on this subject, is evidence of the zeal and watchfulness with which you guard the interests of your flock and the Catholic people that their religious welfare and that of their children is safe in your keeping."[74] The government conceded the point and withdrew the book near the end of September.[75]

The cry of, "No Popery" was at the heart of the work of the Orange Order. It was to hold influence in varying degrees until the end of the Second World War when its influence began to decline.

From the very beginning of settlement there had been those Protestants ambivalent to the Orange cause. Edward O'Brien of the Shanty Bay O'Brien's summed up this ambivalence to the more vocal opponents of the Catholic community in a letter penned on November 5, 1858. He was commenting on what he called Gunpowder Treason Day or more familiarly known as Guy Fawkes Day. "The consequences being that a variety of Orangemen, the "Bulwark of Protestantism" (who never go to church and have as much Christian liberality as Ferdinand and Isabella) gathered together in the Billiard Room and had a feed this evening followed, I presume, by the usual amount of bad

72. Ibid., July 5 and 12, 1866.
73. Ibid., October 19, 1882.
74. ARCAT, *St. Mary's Files*, O'Connor to Lynch, November 21, 1882.
75. Ibid., September 28, 1882.

speeches and bad wine to say nothing of songs and sentiments."[76]

Beyond its political motivations as O'Brien notes the Orange movement had a social purpose, though he was not sympathetic to their idea of a social evening. The order also created an opportunity for pageantry for folks who belonged to religious traditions that often eschewed ritual and pomp and ironically would have seen it as one of their criticisms of Catholicism.

Through its network of lodges which could be found in the smallest villages of the province as well as the urban centres it created a social network of fellowship for like-minded people. Particularly in the rural outposts the Orange Lodge was a place for creating community. No small part of that community building was the opportunity to parade in the second week of July. The Glorious 12th commemorated the victory of William of Orange at the Battle of Boyne which ended Catholic aspirations for the return of a Catholic to the British throne. The parade was an opportunity to show power in numbers and dominance over the Catholic minority. Parading or processions whatever the group's motivations are very much about marking territory.

For the participants the 12th was also a red letter day of sociability. On July 12, 1866, Francis Steevens notes in his diary that, "The Orangemen walked in procession through Barrie and went to church where Rev. Lett preached a sermon to them. Bauldry and Simpson quit cutting grass at 10 a.m. to see the Orange procession and worked no more today."[77]

The work of the Orange Order was political, and kept politicians vigilant to the interests of the Order. In its desire to be a watchdog, ironically, it strengthened the Catholic community in profound ways, keeping the church leadership ever attentive to its own rights.

The Catholic community could in its own way be provocative. The St. Patrick's Day celebrations in 1865, included a lecture on the Spanish Inquisition by J. G. Moylan the editor of the Toronto Mirror one of the papers serving the Irish community in Ontario. The gist of his case was that the Inquistion was basically a political rather than a religious tool. The audacity of presenting this case resulted in a lengthy correspondence in one of the local papers that stretched over several weeks.[78]

By the end of the nineteenth century the vast majority of the citizens of

---

76. Metropolitan Toronto Reference Library, Baldwin Room, *O'Brien Papers,* Corresepondence, Edward O'Brien to unknown, November 5, 1858. Guy Fawkes and a number of Catholic conspirators were caught trying to blow up the parliament on November 5, 1605. The day has since been celebrated with a strong anti Catholic tone though now in Britain it is more about bonfires than sectarianism.

77. SCA, *Francis Steevens Diary,* July 12, 1866.

Barrie were born in this country. Though strong identities with their nationality still existed there was at the same time a new and deeper awareness of being Canadian. Religious identity took on a greater significance since it was no longer a reflection of the believers native culture but was part of their identity as Canadians.

This did not prevent all controversy and Fr. Egan, in 1898, on returning from Ireland made comments on home rule in the pulpit and was roundly taken to task for it in the public press.

The Editorial for September 29, 1898 noted, "We have always regarded Irish Catholics as loyal citizens and God forbid that our opinion should ever change. We were very much surprised however to hear the speech on Irish Affairs made on Sunday night by Dean Egan. His unsavory remarks touching British law and constitution and even the Queen herself were quite uncalled for from a Canadian pulpit . . . the deans remarks belong to that class of comment which is the greatest hindrance we know of to home rule coming as it does from men who are teachers of their people and should be the last to give vent to such objectionable and unwarranted criticism. That kind of speech in this country is apt to perpetuate an unfriendliness among the different classes and creeds and stimulate such societies as the P. P. A.[79]

The Dean's reply appeared in the paper two weeks later and it is apparent that he does not feel in an apologetic mood, "The editor of the Advance has been grievously scandalized, the tender skin of his loyalty has been sorely lacerated, and his religious flesh bleeds." Egan concludes by reminding the editorialist of the "loyal poetry and music which graces these Orange celebrations such as "Arise ye sons of King William arise, we will kick the pope before us."[80]

This changing society encouraged cooperation and though there were many reasons for disagreement between Catholics and their fellow citizens from the Protestant traditions, it is clear that there was proactive service as well.

When Queen Victoria died in 1901, the local press noted the undertakings of the various churches. It was acknowledged that no special service would be sanctioned in the Catholic Church so no memorial sermon was preached. It was noted that Dean Egan did pay eloquent tribute to the memory of her maj-

78. BPL, *Northern Advance*, March 22, 1865 and following.

79. Ibid., September 29, 1898. The P. P. A. was the Protestant Protective Association, as the name implies an organization seeking political influence on behalf of it constituents. It was a secret oath bound organization. It had connection to Dalton McCarthy of Barrie who was a significant force in its foundation.

80. Ibid., October 13, 1898.

esty and many prayers from devout Catholics went up on her behalf.[81]

One of the areas where there is clear evidence of this religious cooperation is in the support for the local hospital. On October 27, 1907, the pulpit announcements included the following, "It has been suggested that the ladies of the congregation, as well as the others in town, send during their canning week a donation of one or two jars of preserved fruit to the Royal Victoria Hospital where such a donation would be most gratefully received. Each contributor will kindly attach their name as the gifts will be acknowledged in the public press. "

The graduation exercises of nurses in 1910 from Royal Victoria Hospital included the minister of St. Andrew's Presbyterian Church presiding at the convocation and the scholarly address being given by Dean Moyna the pastor of St. Mary's.[82]

The Laity in Action.

The majority of the lay organizations were focused on the spiritual well being of the community and the members of the organizations.

The Canadian Mutual Benefit Association (CMBA) had been formed in 1886 at Barrie, the fifty first branch of this organization. It provided its members with insurance and medical aid.[83]

The CMBA also was a social organization which provided excursions and other diversions for its members. It was clearly focused on those in the Catholic community who had the ability to pay the fees. The members would have been drawn from the commercial and business class rather than the poorer members of the parish. As the reports in the local paper made clear it held views that were strongly nationalistic and were committed to the effective integration of Catholics in the larger society.

When Fr. O'Connor left Barrie in 1889, to become Bishop of Peterborough, the parting address of the CMBA and his response was noted in the paper. The members acknowledged his interest during the three years of their existence. O'Connor in turn thanked the members of the lodge for their kindly sentiments and for the valuable benefits in financial, social, intellectual and even spiritual points of view. He further thanked them emphasizing the importance of liberality and kindness to all denominations and preserving har-

81. Ibid., January 31, 1901.

82. SMPA, News clippings, *Barrie Examiner*, "Down Memory Lane" July 3, 1965.

83. SMPA, Parish Guide for 1902.

mony among all classes of people.[84]

The CMBA Banquet at Bothwell's Hall in Allandale in January 1896 reflects that desire. "The chair was ably filled by the retiring president, Mr. M. Shanacy and the vice chair by Very Rev. Dean Egan. The menu was choice and table finery was tastefully arranged to the satiation of the most fastidious epicure. About ninety sat down to the tempting tables.

Upon the removal of the cloth, toasts, sentiments, songs and speeches filled up the passing hour. The toast of the Queen and the Royal Family was responded to by the national anthem sung with special heartiness by the company."[85]

The CMBA offered opportunities that were probably not accessible to all in the parish but show clearly that parish undertakings were not restricted to the town hall or the church. One case in point was the annual excursion of the CMBA, one of which was described in the summer of 1898. "The annual excursion of the CMBA on Tuesday to Jackson's Point per the steamer Enterprise, was the best, financially and otherwise, the society has ever had. At 9:30 the boat left with a large crowd, and after calling at Big Bay Point arrived at Jackson's Point about noon. The afternoon races were provided for children from five years old upwards and first, second and third prizes were given for every event. After the program was finished all children who had not obtained any of the three positions were lined up and each given a prize. . . The boat left for Barrie at five o'clock and on the way back 10 lbs. of candy and half a bushel of peanuts were distributed among the children. In the evening a large number took advantage of a delightful three hour sail down the lake. Keenan's orchestra furnished music for dancing."[86]

The organization sought to connect themselves within the city and the wider community. Their event at the very beginning of January 1900 reflects this desire. "During the evening the Honorable F. R. Latchford, Minister of Public Works for Ontario, gave a short address. He dwelt on the extent of Ontario's natural resources, which he claimed are greater than those of any other country and will stop the emigration of young men to the United States, particularly from the eastern part of the province. The duty of Canadians is first last and all the time to Canada our home and having in view the cementing into one Canadianism the various elements of population in Canada, it is the duty of all citizens to refrain from doing anything that might divide the people along racial or religious lines.[87]

---

84. BPL, *Northern Advance*, April 25, 1889.

85. BPL, *Northern Advance*, January 9, 1896.

86. Ibid., August 4, 1898.

A St. Mary's Literary Society was formed in the late 1890's. It seems to have been of short duration, but in its time gathered parishioners for a program of debates and other intellectual pursuits.[88]

In May of 1893, it was announced in the public press that a conference of the St. Vincent de Paul Society was formed in Barrie. The news item stated that the society would look after the poor of the congregation.[89]

This misconception about the society serving only Catholics was clarified by the fall when a report was made on a fundraiser in the form of a musical vespers and lecture by Fr. Teefy, the president of St. Michael's College. It was noted, "The principle object of the society was to visit the poor in their dwellings and bring them such consolation and assistance as they may need, and to which the resources of the society may be adequate.

Though the society is composed of Catholic laymen, it is non sectarian in the distribution of its charities. They are the dispensers of the gifts of God, who is the common Father of mankind, and makes his sun to shine upon all. The title of poor, to their commiseration is simply their poverty regardless of their religious creed . . . hence the society having this understanding and concern for the needy and the poor, there will be the best possible guarantee that whatever may be placed in their hands by those urged to do so by true charity and tender compassion for the misery of our less favoured fellow creatures, will find its way to serving their objects."[90]

The St. Vincent de Paul Society was first instituted at Toronto in 1850, the oldest lay organization in the diocese.

As we trace the history of the St. Vincent de Paul in Barrie, we find that it was an organization which had a cyclical existence with periods of great success and then periods of disarray. There is something uniquely practical about its work that brings it back into service again and again.

The Altar Society was formed to centre the efforts of the laity in maintaining a standard of decoration and beauty in the church. They also concerned themselves with the purchase of vestments and other accouterments of the sanctuary.

Limited minutes from the Altar Society's meetings exist beginning in 1907. They solicited Catholic homes door to door to raise funds for their work. They oversaw the maintenance of linens and other church effects. During that year

---

87. Ibid., January 4, 1900.
88. Ibid., November 11, 1897.
89. Ibid., May 11, 1893
90. Ibid., November 9, 1893.

they hosted a garden party, and an "at home" to raise funds for stained glass windows in the church. The 'at home' was to take place at the town hall and would include euchre and dancing.[91]

The beginning of 1908 saw the Altar Society relieved of one of its important duties; sweeping the church, as a caretaker had been hired. By the end of 1908, the Altar Society had rescinded their goal of purchasing windows and had committed themselves to carpeting the sanctuary of the church, during this time of significant renovations. They also contracted to have the altar and the adoring angels painted.[92]

Among its other responsibilities in 1909 the Altar Society was asked to cover the hydro bill which was about forty-five dollars for the year. Funds for the expense were procured from the garden party in the summer with excess proceeds of the garden party turned over to the building fund.[93]

In 1911, when the sisters who did a significant amount of work in the care of the sanctuary and maintenance of decoration asked for felt for a table, the Altar Society agreed that "Miss Cassin would accompany the sisters to procure the same."[94] The Altar Society cautioned the sisters that they would only be given one dollar a month "and not more" for the purchase of fresh flowers.[95]

The Altar Society also took some oversight of music in the parish, ordering hymnals for the choir, including Dumont's Missa de Angeles, Carr's Chant Mass and Fischer's Mass in F opus 193.[96]

The Holy Name Society was established on February 21, 1907 at the end of a parish mission preached by the Redemptorist Fathers with one hundred and forty-seven members joining. The organization was exclusively a male society to encourage devotion and piety. As was noted in the press that the object and aim of the initial group was to curtail profane and indecent language.[97]

The Holy Name society offered men an opportunity to gather, though not of the privileged station in life like members of the CMBA and not drawn by the highly structured organization the Knights of Columbus would be.

Information on the Holy Name Society appeared in the press from time to time, as when they had a talk on temperance by Dean Moyna. As the newspaper noted, "the Holy Name Society make a specialty of clean speech and the

---

91. SMPA, Minutes of the Altar Society, October 8, 1907.
92. Ibid., January 6, 1908.
93. Ibid., June & July, 1909.
94. Ibid., February 26, 1911.
95. Ibid., April 1, 1910.
96. Ibid., loose sheet.
97. BPL, *Northern Advance*, April 11, 1907.

avoidance of blasphemy."[98]

The memorial of the parish notes that in 1910, in addition to the Holy Name Society which now had 194 members, there was a Sacred Heart League with 859 members, a Sodality of the Blessed Virgin Mary which had 78 members and a John Berchman's Society which had 23 members.

The John Berchman's Society had been formed in 1910. This was an attempt to elevate the role of the altar server.[99]

In June of 1912, the Knights of Columbus of Barrie received their charter, being the 28th council in Ontario and 1626th in the world. The first home for the Knights was rented space above the A & P store on Dunlop Street.

The first meeting established some norms for the organization. Smoking was only to be allowed in the anteroom of the Knight's space. The Deputy Grand Knight, Shanancy, played the violin and the chaplain, Fr. Flanagan the curate of St. Mary's, recited, "Priest Hunting in Ireland."[100]

In January of 1914, the Confraternity of Christian Mothers was established with 121 members.

The Devotional Revolution and Discipline.

On the parish level the creation of devotional movements reflected in a particularly effective way the preoccupations of the faithful and the clergy. The impulse to create devotional organizations has been a significant part of the history of St. Mary's Parish since its foundation.

The emphasis on pious devotions that the faithful could share is called by historians the devotional revolution. The devotional revolution not only deepened their connectedness as a Catholic community but encouraged a deeper connection with the sacramental life of the church. It called people to a more conventional practice of their religious duties by attending mass regularly and following the disciplines of the church, in particular, the habit of regular confession and frequent reception of communion.

The strengthening of religious identity was to a large extent encouraged through the devotional revolution which swept through Catholicism in the mid eighteenth century. This change in religious sensibility was reflected in a deeper commitment to public and private devotions. The role that pious activities took on was a profound influence on the way church came to be understood over the next one hundred years.

---

98. Ibid. April 9, 1914.
99. SMPA, Parish Memoriam.
100. Beaudoin, *Glancing Over our Shoulders at Eighty Five Years*, 1997.

There are many roots to this change in religious life. It was a natural outgrowth of ultramontanism, but was also a response to the modern age and the unsettled nature of society. The turmoil that swept Europe in the middle of the nineteenth century and the rapid industrialization caused people to cast their eyes and minds back to a time when religious life was more intimately entwined with emotion and personal responsibility. There was a romance that was found in the religious practice of the middle ages. In a world where personal identity was more and more lost in the great industrial complex of the city, devotions provided an autonomy, which was totally tied to personal relationship with God. This idea of the personal relationship through particular devotions also answered an observation that was made that Catholics were essentially tied to the directives of their priests.

In fact, for many the rich experience of faith practiced each day was of their own design and choosing.

This autonomy reflected increased literacy as well. Devotional activities presumed that the faithful could take down a missal or book of devotions and independent of the priest enter into a discipline of prayer and personal quest for the sacred.

The devotional revolution was also about community. These devotions which often had a parish event attached created community and allowed people to focus on what was unique about their religious practice. Devotions to Our Lady of Perpetual Help, The Sacred Heart or the Rosary all could allow for a coming together of people for weekly devotions in the parish church.

The devotional revolution also gave autonomy to families to deepen within the family the devotional life of their children in a particular way. Devotional images in the home and family prayer became firmly rooted in the life of the good Catholic home. It became a remedy for the anxieties of life and a bulwark against bad habit, particularly the temptation to drink. It could also be carried away from the family home. The presumption of sacramental commitment was to stand beside the commitment to carry your beads and to use them once you had gone to the city.

One of the most significant devotional moments for the church in Simcoe County was the opening of the Martyrs' Shrine. The first shrine was, in fact, at Waubashene, which was close to where it was presumed the martyrs died. For this first shrine which was opened in August of 1907, only the sanctuary was enclosed. The worshipers were in fact in the open air.[101]

The spiritual life of the church centered as it has throughout history on the Eucharist. Since it was only at mid twentieth century that mass could

---

101. BPL, *Northern Advance*, August 22, 1907.

be celebrated after noon hour, for evening gatherings other forms of worship were used. For evening gatherings, vespers, benediction and the rosary were common undertakings. Vespers seem to have been particularly significant on Sunday evenings, which was also a frequent time for parish meetings. We find that vespers, which is the recitation of the psalms, were often used to highlight a particular moment in the year. In mid March 1906 a panegyric in honour of St. Patrick was to be preached after vespers. Later the same year the pastor would speak Sunday evening on the use and the abuse of the Bible.[102]

Religious instruction for children was undertaken in the school and for those that were a distance from school there was summer school. Christian doctrine classes were offered for parents as well. The oft heard complaint through the ages was noted 'that some take an interest and others do not.'[103]

The precision of how sacraments were to be celebrated was of the utmost significance and disciplined Catholicism demanded that the faithful be well informed of these expectations. It would not have been seen as peculiar that the St. Mary's 1902 parish guide would include a section called Service and Rules of St. Mary's Church. This little publication includes many indications of the rigour that was aspired to and at the same time the directives which veered toward the pedantic.

The directives on Lenten observance remind all that the days of Lent except Sundays are fast days. Beyond the one full meal which is to be eaten at mid day, the faithful may in the morning have a cup of tea or coffee and a small piece of bread–nothing else–and in the evening about eight ounces of food. Flesh meat is permitted on Mondays, Tuesday, Thursday and Saturday at the main meal of the day. Flesh meat and fish are never to be served at the same meal. Further the faithful are to take no role in public amusements. The use of lard dripping is permitted for cooking. Alcohol is to be avoided in remembrance of the sacred thirst of the Lord on the cross. Exceptions are made for those under 21 and over 60, as well as expectant and nursing mothers, the sick and infirm and all engaged in servile work.[104]

In the same booklet the faithful are offered the following advice for those occasions when the priest may be called to the bed of a sick parishioner. "When the Blessed Sacrament is coming to the house, prepare by putting the sick room in order. If there are other people, beside the sick person, sleeping in it, see that they get up and that the beds are decently adjusted. Sponge the sick person's

---

102. SMPA, *Announcement books*, various place, 1906-7.

103. SMPA, *Announcement books*, September 2, 1906.

104. SMPA, *Parish Guide of St. Mary's*, 1902, Announcements, February 20, 1908.

face and hands, to refresh him and if Extreme Unction is to be administered, see also that the feet are clean and stockings removed."[105]

As has been reviewed above, the parish, as the First World War appeared on the horizon, was a vital and active community seeking to connect people with their faith and each other. One might be surprised to find that this burgeoning of activity followed a period of unprecedented reaction against church activism by the bishop of the diocese, Denis O'Connor.

Bishop O'Connor had come to Toronto as bishop in 1899, a native of Pickering, he was Toronto's first Canadian born bishop since the time of Bishop Power. The preoccupation with modernism in the church, the introduction of progressive ideas, particularly in academic fields created the anxiety that all things would become relative. The Catholic Church found itself trying to stem the tide of change by imposing a number of regulations which were to discourage what were seen as some of the more problematic tendencies.

In 1902, the local press noted with fulsome praise the music that marked Easter at St. Mary's Church. "At 8:30 a.m. mass the sisters' choir, composed of 50 boys and girls sang very sweetly several anthems assisted by a boy violin soloist. At 10:30 St. Mary's choir sang Millard's Mass in C and in this they showed excellent training by their leader Mr. O'Meara. The solo parts were taken by Misses Byrnes, Graham, Logue, Mahoney, Power and Soules and Messrs. Power and Warde. Mr. O'Meara sang a fine offertory bass solo, Ecce Sacerdos. Misses Logue, Mahoney and Graham and Mr. Warde gave an excellent quartet Benedictus."[106]

St. Mary's would have been one of those places that felt strongly about the directives a year later in which the Vatican had directed that all music must be Gregorian Chant at mass and all instruments other than the organ were banned. Part singing was abolished and women were no longer to sing in choirs, only in the congregation with an exception being made for convents and girls schools.[107] The prohibition on women was rescinded in 1909 as long as women were separate from the men and well away from the altar.[108] The Vatican was not quite prepared to concede and tried to reinforce the same directive in 1912.

The music was not the only area of concern. A stringent stand was taken on interfaith marriages and the use of parish space for other than spiritual un-

105. Ibid.

106. BPL, *Northern Advance*, April 3, 1902.

107. Ibid., March 7, 1912.

108. *McGowan*, page 79.

dertakings was discouraged. All things that suggested socializing in the parish were likewise discouraged.

Bishop O'Connor was frustrated by the less than warm reception to his strict enforcement of the regulations. He by his own admission did not have the support of a large number of the priests of his diocese and he eventually chose to resign in 1908.

Many of the priests, also Canadian, had grown up in Toronto and in the towns and villages of Ontario as a minority attending more often than not public high schools and learning the discipline of accommodation and mutual interchange with their non-Catholic neighbours.

The restrictions around social gatherings were likewise a reflection of a positive motivation in that O'Connor wished to centre the church in the truths of the faith. This, however, met with even greater resistance in that churches depended on the financial support of the social gatherings and picnics. These offered an opportunity for lay integration, especially the integration of women which was seen as essential. We see the way that organizations in Barrie circumvented the strict prohibition of social gatherings for fundraising was to integrate fundraising into liturgical events, such as sung Vespers.

O'Connor's strictness to the contemporary mind may seem confusing. O'Connor would not even permit Holy Name parades and emphatically denied the Knights of Columbus the right to establish itself in his diocese.

It is not as if the struggle was simply Bishop's O'Connor's, but it was something that the church would wrestle with over many years. This anxiety bridged over the whole of the decades as we find, Archbishop McGuigan in 1946, reminding the editor of the *Catholic Register* to not be advertising dances as they are strictly speaking forbidden by O'Connor's directive on church property. McGuigan is not, it is clear, going to interfere at the parish level, but suggests that such events be identified as social gatherings.[109]

With the departure of Bishop O'Connor the primary form of social undertaking was the 'at home' a coming together for a time of hospitality in parish space. Admissions to these parish events which were hosted by all groups were a source of fundraising and introducing the work of the group to the larger parish.

It was not only Catholics who were wrestling with questions that had a broad implication for their community. It was noted in Barrie in 1914 that the pastor of Collier Methodist Church denounced ultra fashionable attire. The Reverend Turk noted that the fashions come from hell by way of Paris

109. Ibid., page 37.

and New York. "Many women are so hobbled that they cannot walk and their appearance made them appear as deformities. Public dances were condemned, but skipping around to music in the house was permissible."[110]

Very soon not only in Barrie but throughout the western world the concerns of the public and ministers of religion in their own particular way would be called on to face the cataclysm of war.

---

[110] BPL, *Northern Advance*, February 26, 1914.

Jean Baptiste Assiginack
(Blackbird)
from a drawing by the Jesuit Fr. LePointe.

Courtesy of the Jesuit Archives of Canada

Barrie's first vocation,
Fr. Richard Baxter, S.J.

Courtesy of the Jesuit Archives of Canada

Fr. James Quinlan,
early missionary to Barrie.

Courtesy of the Quinlan Family

Susanah McBride, in religious life, Sister Mary Jerome, the first woman religious from Barrie.
Pencil sketch by an unknown artist.

Courtesy of the Archives of the Sisters of St. Joseph.

Fr. Jean Francois Jamot, first pastor of St. Mary's, later in life, when Bishop of Peterborough

The first two St. Mary's Churches.
The frame church in the background
and the newly built brick church.
The street in front is McDonald Street
below Mulcaster Street.

Courtesy of Simcoe County Archives

Interior of the second church.

The boys of St. Mary's School in about 1880. The school building is the original church with the cross still above the door. Nothing makes a man like a good hat.

Courtesy of Simcoe County Archives

An outing of the CMBA (Catholic Mutual Benefit Association)
Courtesy of Simcoe County Archives

The fourth St. Mary's School.

A typical classroom in the fourth school

Courtesy of St. Mary's School

Funeral for the Australian airmen at St. Mary's Church, 1942.

Two pictures from the enclosure of the Redemptoristine Sisters in 1952.
Monsignor Clair locks the gate and hands through the key to the Mother Superior.

Courtesy of the Redemptorist Archives of Canada

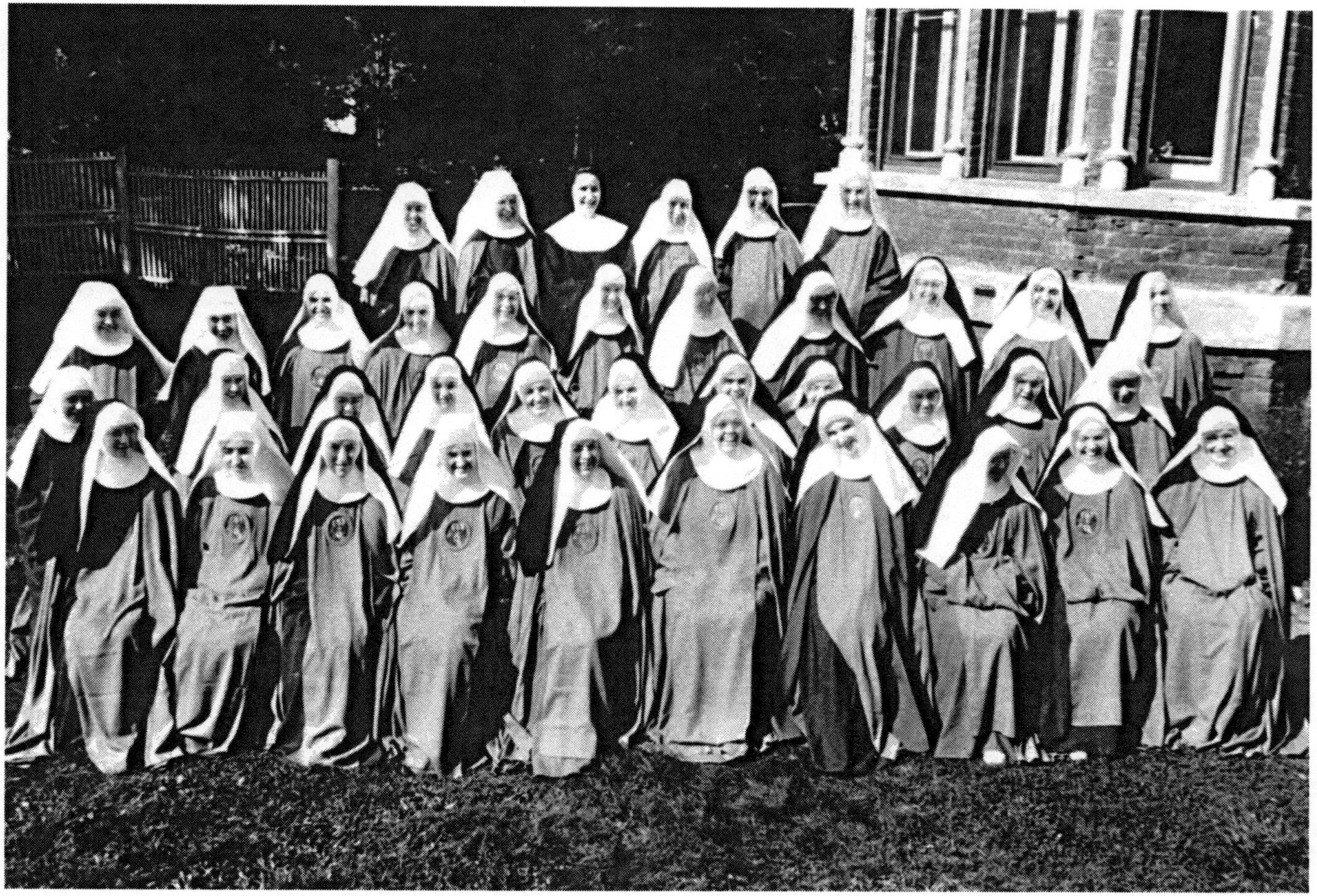

The Redemptoristine Community at Barrie in the late 1950's.
Courtesy of the Redemptorist Archives of Canada

The original St. Joseph's High School formerly the second convent of The Sisters of St. Joseph. In the foreground, the parish hall.

Interior of the new St. Mary's Church 1969.

So That Our Parish Can Make a Good Showing

FROM the beginning of the First World War to the end of the Second World War, Canada was faced with problems that consumed the daily life of citizens on an enormous scale. The effects of prosperity and then the great depression sandwiched between the two wars defined the era. These events were very much an imposition on the life of the town as they were on every town. Churches were an active part of the response to those challenges. Canada was already on the move to becoming an urban nation. Barrie was no longer a small town. The growth of urban centres, as families were established away from the farm, in households financed by employment in industry led to more disposable time and greater mobility.

Structuring Parish Life.

At St. Mary's the Sodality of the Blessed Virgin which had existed from the beginning of the parish was still active. We find by 1921 there were also the Knights of Columbus, The Christian Mothers, The Altar Society, Confraternity of the Holy Souls, The Catholic Women's League, The Catholic Church Extension, The League of the Sacred Heart, The juvenile and senior Holy Name Societies and The St. Vincent de Paul Society. All of these groups were vying for the same parishioners to assist them in their particular mission.

Pope Pius X had at the beginning of the century encouraged reception of communion at the age of six or seven, rather than thirteen or fourteen. He also encouraged more regular reception of communion, not just once or twice a year as would have been the practice of many. The fast from food beginning at midnight, the night before communion was received, and the strong connection between confession and communion, caused the shift to more frequent reception of communion to be only gradual.

One of the strategies to encourage reception of communion was Communion Sundays. On a particular Sunday, all members of a group or sodality would receive communion and after have a communion breakfast, an event which often included a guest speaker.

Sacramental life was much more structured in ways which later generations would find problematic. Children were expected to attend "nursery" masses which were the earlier masses on a Sunday. In 1915, St. Mary's mass on Sunday at 7:30 a. m. was exclusively for children and parents.[1] By implication later masses were not to include small children.

For a number of years Ascension Thursday, was the normal day for First Communion at St. Mary's. This was a holy day of obligation, and as such was treated like a Sunday. All who could were to avoid work. Needless to say, those involved in industry would not have been free to attend a first communion even if their child was receiving.[2] By 1937, we find that first communion is on the Feast of the Sacred Heart at the beginning of June on which day all first communicants would receive at the 7:30 a.m. mass.[3]

It was common to have a mass at which communion was not received by the congregation. In 1922, the pastor reminded the parish that communion would be given out at all the Christmas masses.[4] On the other hand, communion was offered without mass at 7:30 a.m. sharp on the Feast of St. Joseph in 1923 since there would only be one mass later on that day.[5]

It was noted that on average in the first half of 1924, there were 2,400 receptions of communion each month at St. Mary's. This would indicate about six hundred a week spread over several masses on Sunday and during the week.[6] It is apparent that an Easter season was included in this number and the participation of the school children in parish weekday mass would have been more frequent, especially during Lent. Going to mass each day before school started was a regular discipline for part of the student body.

On the other hand, the preoccupation with the faithful arriving at mass before the end of the Liturgy of the Word so that they fulfilled their Sunday obligation, resulted in the following announcement in 1925, "During the summer vacation we will have low masses and short sermons (if any), so all should be on time for both masses as it will be easy to be late."[7] By 1935 the announcement about the briefness of mass in the summer was to be explained as necessary, "as many are anxious to go motor driving on Sunday."[8]

The preoccupation with disciplined church attendance is highlighted in this

1. SMPA, Announcement Books, November 14, 1915.
2. Ibid., May 10, 1931.
3. Ibid., May 30, 1937.
4. Ibid., December 24, 1922.
5. Ibid., March 18, 1923.
6. Ibid., June 29, 1924.
7. Ibid., June 25, 1925.
8. Ibid., June 24, 1934.

poem, 'The Rear Guard', included with the announcements in May 1931,

"He strolls to mass at the "Sanctus"
Or maybe a moment before,
And, lest he should bother his neighbours
He drops on one knee at the door.

Good seats near the altar are vacant
In fact there is room and to spare,
But why should he push himself forward
He'd be so conspicuous there.

He doesn't look up at the altar,
But keeps his gaze bent on the floor:
We notice him yawning a little
As though it was rather a bore.

He squats for the last benediction,
And then, ere the service is through,
We look for him there in the background,
And find he has melted from view."[9]

We see this structuring of parish life around confessions as well. Sunday evening confessions were restricted to men only, who by implication would have been working on Saturday and unable to attend.[10]

The priest of the parish in 1922 included in his Lenten announcements a number of challenges for a keener commitment to Lent. He stated in mid-March, "Lent is passing quickly. What have you really done by way of penance? We had a large gathering at morning mass for a few mornings, but the flesh will win if you let it."[11]

This was followed two weeks later, "We have only two weeks of Lent. What have you done? Have you spent the days of Lent the way you would like to spend your last Lent on earth?"[12]

The call to discipline was a matter of personal practice and of public wit-

9. Ibid., May 3, 1931.
10. Ibid., September 30, 1917.
11. Ibid., March 19, 1922.
12. Ibid., April 2, 1922.

ness as attested that the pastor was pleased with the attendance at Lenten devotions, "but if reports be true some are not as careful about places of amusement as they should be."[13]

The discipline of parish life included a bare minimum for those wishing to consider themselves as a Catholic in good standing. This centred on the Easter duty. The faithful were to go to confession and communion between Ash Wednesday and the end of the Easter season at least once. We have the pastor reminding the faithful of this in April of 1923, "We hope, pray and trust that there will be no one in St. Mary's Parish who will not make their Easter duty. If there be any old or sick or infirm who cannot come to church please send in names soon and we will attend to them. All who are slow making their duty may expect to be called upon."[14]

Other practices strongly opposed by the church were coming to the priest's attention as this 1924 announcement attests, "Should anyone receive a copy of a chain prayer through the mail or any other way put it in the stove at once and have nothing to do with either reciting it or circulating it.[15]

Change was constant, sometimes it was subtle and at other times significant enough to be noted in the public press. After the stringent years of serious limitations on liturgy and church life in the decade earlier, we find that when Dean O'Malley celebrated his silver jubilee, in 1918, the Barrie newspaper reported that the 'The young ladies' of the Sodality presented their pastor with a gift and an address 'inside the communion rail.'[16]

For those who maintain the church has a history of being ambivalent about the sacred scriptures, it is worth noting that there was a regular class on scripture held biweekly on Sunday afternoons in 1921.[17]

The original site of the Martyrs' Shrine at Waubaushene was replaced when the new church was built in 1925 near the site of Ste. Marie Among the Hurons at Midland.[18] It was a significant focus for the faithful of the diocese and in a particular way for those of Simcoe County who claimed a particular connection to this historic and devotional site. This was only increased when the

13. Ibid., March 23, 1924.

14. Ibid., April 1, 1923.

15. Ibid., March 23, 1924. The *Northern Advance* noted a chain letter craze was sweeping Barrie again ten years later in June of 1935. Ibid., June 13, 1935.

16. SMPA, News clipping, "*Dean O'Malley 25 years a Priest.*" The communion rail in Catholic church offered the faithful a place to kneel to receive communion. It also clearly separated the sanctuary from the body of the church.

17. SMPA, Announcement Books, November 6, 1921.

18. BPL, *Northern Advance*, October 1, 1925.

martyrs were canonized in the spring of 1930.

The growth in the ownership of cars was to be a great boon for the shrine. Cars were not the only way to get there; beginning in 1931 trains were leaving Barrie on a regular basis with stops at the Martyrs' Shrine.[19]

The remoteness of those in the rural areas was the constant source of adaptation. The parish was to go to the country people since it was a challenge for them to get to the church. An announcement in February 1922 fairly summed up the situation for country people in the dead of winter. "Mrs. McBride's funeral is tomorrow morning. The mass will be about 9:30 or as soon as they can get here from the country."[20]

Creating opportunities for the faithful to practice the disciplines of their faith was an ongoing mission of the church. In the summer of 1933 copies of the Catholic Manual of Prayer were placed in every home in the parish.[21]

Christmas practices too, were considered and comment offered as was done in 1938. "During the past few years a certain organization having great influence in the lithography business has attempted to paganize Christmas. One of the powerful means used has been the gradual obliteration from Christmas cards of any mention or hint of Christmas as the birthday of Christ. No Catholic should ever even think of buying such cards."[22]

Not only the laity but the clergy were a concern in matters relating to discipline. In 1937, Archbishop McGuigan made it clear that priests under no circumstances were to drive a car if they had imbibed even the slightest amount of alcohol in the last eight hours, an exception for sacramental wine, of course, was made.

Further to this, no priest was to be at any time in a motor vehicle with a woman, the only exception being made for their mother.[23]

Financial Support.

The first half of the twentieth century was a time of new sophistication coming to the financial support of the church. Before this time the collection basket was passed and each gave what they could. This income was bolstered

---

19. Ibid., August 4, 1929 and July 13, 1930.

20. SMPA, Announcement Books, February 26, 1922. At the time what is commonly called visitation or the wake took place in the home. It is not only a concern that the family get in from the country, but the casket as well.

21. Ibid., July 30, 1933.

22. Ibid., November 13, 1938.

23. Moir, p. 69.

by special collections for any number of efforts as well as pew rents and collections which were undertaken door to door. There were also fundraisers often under the auspices of one of the many organizations of the parish, or in the case of the parish bazaar in December of 1921, it was a shared event of all groups of the parish which lasted three days.[24]

The publication of donations in print on an annual basis was the norm. Parishioners were reminded again and again of the need to get their donations in as the list would soon be published. By 1916, the pastor reminds them that they will still publish a list of donors, but the list will no longer be read at the Sunday masses.[25]

In 1915 an envelope committee was formed. Those that were not supporting the parish through the new innovative idea of envelopes had a monthly collection in which they were to give their support. In February 1917, those not using envelopes were reminded that the monthly collection would be taken up by the priests of the parish after the sermon.[26]

The inception of the use of envelopes also marked the beginning of constant reminders for people to put their name on their envelopes.[27] Curiously, annual packs of envelopes only became the norm in 1939.[28]

Early in 1921, the announcements reminded parishioners that the usual collection was twenty-five cents per adult in the household.[29]

From the earliest history of the church in the Diocese of Toronto, pew rents were a source of income and equally a cause of debate and contention.

This practice which began with Fr. Jamot at St. Mary's persisted until the mid-twentieth century. Those who paid their pew rent secured the pew for their family and of course this inferred that interlopers were not to make their way into a rented pew. It was a system fraught with problems. Each pew had a card holder on the end in which the tenants name was placed. If rents were in arrears, it may lead to the removal of the name card and the pew being identified as vacant. By November 1923, Dean Sweeney's ongoing frustration with pew rent is seen in that he reminds the congregation that there is still $150.00 of pew rent unpaid. He reminds them, "that it is not pleasant to talk about money. But expenses are going on and need to be met.

24. SMPA, Announcement Books, October 16, 1921.
25. Ibid., January 9, 1916.
26. Ibid., February 5, 1917.
27. Ibid., October 22, 1916 and ff.
28. Ibid., August 13, 1939.
29. Ibid., February 13, 1921.

Surely it cannot be necessary to talk about money. Money talks in church have gone out of fashion."[30]

The frustration with the system was still palatable in this 1937 announcement. "Pew rent for the first quarter of 1937 was due last Sunday. There are many pews to rent. So if you desire one just speak to the collectors. Persons who have not a pew should not enter a pew with a white ticket on the side. Children have been removing the white tickets from pews. This must be stopped. The gallery is reserved for members of the choir and no one else is supposed to be up there."[31]

Improvements to the Church.

Under the auspices of the Holy Name Society a pipe organ was purchased for the church in 1914 and blessed in January of 1915. The Carnegie foundation gave a grant of $1250.00 that covered almost half of the $2,785.00 expense. The organ was built by Kam Morris of Woodstock Ontario.[32] The organ that was installed in the church in 1873 was given to the Bell Ewart church.[33]

In January of 1915, the *Northern Advance* announced for the general public that, "The formal opening of the new pipe organ in St. Mary's Roman Catholic Church will be the occasion of special services on Sunday evening January 24th at 7 p.m. Archbishop McNeill of Toronto will conduct the services and the Very Rev. Dean Harris L.L.D., a brilliant speaker, will deliver a lecture on that occasion. During the service, Professor Cummer of Aurora and Mr. Jules Brazil of Toronto, two well-known musicians, will give special selections to test the capabilities of the new organ, which is said to be an excellent instrument with the new tubular pneumatic action. Every person is welcome to attend this service on January 24th.[34]

The prosperity that followed The First World War saw a new round of renovations to the church property.

In 1918 the rectory was renovated and wired for hydro.[35]

In March 1921, it was announced that the farmers in the parish were asked to meet after mass to talk about the sheds. These sheds located behind the

30. Ibid., November 11, 1923.
31. Ibid., January 10, 1937.
32. SMPA, Parish Memorium.
33. Ibid.
34. BPL, *Northern Advance*, January 14, 1915.
35. SMPA, Parish Memorium.

church provided shelter for horses while rural families were attending mass. It is unclear if this is a routine meeting to consider practical matters such as a spring cleaning or was it to consider the discontinuance of the sheds with the coming of cars?[36]

The Church's Response to Those in Need in the Nation and the Town.

The Catholic Church Extension was formed in Canada to secure the progress of the church in new and isolated regions of the country in September 1908. The work of the Extension was taken up quickly in St. Mary's. A combination of fundraising and works of charity combined to raise consciousness of how Catholics in established parts of the country could assist areas of new settlement. The Catholic Church Extension in 1920 was inviting all in the parish who were interested to make altar linens for the western missions.[37]

The financial commitments for causes outside the parish were ongoing and consistent. We find collections regularly being taken up for the needs of immigrants.[38] Also religious communities that served the immigrants of the west were often invited to solicit the support of the congregation. In December 1929, the "Ruthenian Sisters"were pleased with the support of the parish during their campaign in Ontario for their work in the west.[39]

The Sisters of Service, co-founded by Simcoe County native, Sr. Catherine Donnelly, were particularly focused on ministry among immigrant people. As was reported to the people, their 1932 campaign found them making their way to Barrie; "Tomorrow evening at eight o'clock there will be an illustrated lecture in the parish hall. This lecture will be given by the Sisters of Service. There will be pictures of their great work shown. They feel that some of our young ladies may desire to enter their community. All of our young ladies and others more than 16 years are invited to be present. Let us hope for a large crowd."[40]

In the nineteen thirties, the west was impacted greatly by the depression and several years of drought. In October of 1936, the pastor announced,

---

36. SMPA, Announcement Books, March 19, 1921.

37. Ibid., January 25, 1920.

38. Ibid., January 1, 1922.

39. Ibid., December 15, 1929 Ruthenian is an antiquated term for Ukranians. In this case Ukranian Catholic nuns.

40. Ibid., April 17, 1932.

"People having clothing to send to the west may send them to the school and Christian Mothers will try to repair them and send them west."[41] The same project was undertaken two years later by the Catholic Women's League.[42]

By the fall of 1937, the deepening crisis on the prairies found the people of the parish assisting the aid trains going west with relief. With the Ontario harvest completed and the gardens prepared for winter it was announced to the parish, "The vegetables and canned goods promised for relief in the drought areas of the west are to be brought to the parish hall on Monday or Tuesday of this week as the car is being loaded in Phelpston on Wednesday. Those who said they could not deliver these things themselves will be called on either Monday or Tuesday. If there are any others who have not promised to give anything and who are in a position to give something may either bring what they have to the hall on those days or leave word at the deanery and they will be called for."[43]

The First World War had brought great change in the life of Canadians. The technological advances moved Canadians toward the consumer boom of the 1920's. The support for those needing assistance was still heavily stressed and the structures were poorly formed at the local level to assist the disadvantaged. The following announcement from January 1920 is a concrete witness to that reality. "Children at the shelter are to be given out if taken."[44]

Four years later there was perhaps a more benign sensibility expressed by the pastor in confronting the same serious problem, "There is a nice healthy boy for adoption, who is Catholic. He is seven years of age and seems a bright little fellow. Any person who feels that they would like to give him a home, let me know soon."[45]

The concern for Catholic children was expressed in far more emphatic detail fifteen years later, "There are several Catholic children of various ages at the shelter. Some of these are infants. It would be a great work of charity for Catholic families to adopt one or two of them or even take them temporarily. If Catholics do not take them there is a great danger of their being adopted into non-Catholic homes."[46]

The ongoing concern for the poor has for a century and a half been identified with the work of the St. Vincent de Paul Society. References are made

41. Ibid., October 18, 1936.
42. Ibid., February 6, 1938.
43. Ibid., October 24, 1939.
44. Ibid., January 11, 1920.
45. Ibid., January 18,1925.
46. Ibid., November 19, 1939.

to the group in the summer of 1916 and in 1919 when they were organizing picnics for the children of the parish.[47] By the fall of 1921, the Society was in need of reorganization and early in December it was announced that collection of boxes were by the door for the work of the Society.[48]

Beginning in the fall of 1929, the depression brought ever greater demands on the Saint Vincent de Paul Society which was constantly seeking more men to assist with the work.[49]

The common awareness of the economic struggle was reflected in the call for prayers in 1932, for relief of the depression.[50]

The relief efforts were not only an undertaking of people of faith, but was a community-based endeavour as well. In 1932, the Town of Barrie had initiated a Relief Fund and support for the drive to raise $4,000 was announced at the masses.[51]

We find throughout this time many announcements of an essentially secular nature. Help needed at the canning factory was announced in 1916 and in 1927 an announcement at the masses stated, "Men out of work may be glad to know that they are sure of employment with the C. N. R. at Allendale handling coal. The pay is 35 cents an hour and work will last for over a month or six weeks. This is a good opportunity for idle men. They may go to work in the morning."[52]

The local labour force and those even harder to employ were a concern of the parish in this 1930 announcement, "Farmers requiring help on their farms and who would be willing to give immigrants a trial, please send their request to the deanery, stating how much they would be willing to pay per month, also how many months they would require help."[53]

The cooperative movement which was in part a response to the depression was actively pursued by the church. Particular success was realized in eastern Canada, but the movement also took hold in different parts of the diocese, particularly in relation to the creation of affordable housing. Information on the movement was provided at a meeting of men and boys at the Knights of Columbus Hall. They were reminded that, "Father Peter Lockwood will give a short talk on the cooperative work he is promoting in St. Patrick's Parish in

47. Ibid., July 16, 1916 & July 20, 1919.
48. Ibid., December 4, 1921.
49. Ibid., March 13, 1932.
50. Ibid., June 5, 1932.
51. Ibid., November 27, 1932.
52. Ibid., August 5, 1916 & February 13, 1927.
53. Ibid., January 26, 1930.

Toronto. He will be prepared to answer any questions you may wish to ask on the subject. Lunch will be served. Bring your smokes. Those who can should bring sandwiches or cake."[54]

Perhaps the most concrete result of the cooperative movement in Barrie was the creation of the parish credit union. A month after Fr. Lockwood's visit a study club on credit unions was formed in the parish. A month later a credit union had been formed with a provisional executive.[55]

A Canadian Church.

At the time of the First World War, St. Mary's Parish, like all other churches in the Barrie area, was called on to respond to challenges close to home and on the battlefields of Europe.

Patriotic Societies and National Service were spoken of from the pulpit. In February 1917, a letter from the Canadian Minister of Finance was read at all masses on saving money and on November 11 of the same year, a letter from Bishop McNeil was read on bonds and patriotism.[56]

The parish was actively involved in war aid, also, through the work of the Red Cross. Even children were called to do their part. The parish announced a Red Cross entertainment to be given by the children in February 1916. The admission for parents was to be ten cents each.[57]

The *Northern Advance* noted in 1918 that a Sister of St. Joseph of Barrie had composed a military march entitled, "The Canadian Heroes." The composition which pictured scenes of military life, it was noted, was filled with brilliant harmonies. Copies of the piece were available at the convent or at the music store in town.[58]

The Great War was a national cataclysm. The parish could list eight parishioners who had lost their life in the war; Walter Nugent, December 1915, Willard Touchette, September 1916, John McDonell, September 1916, Ernest Delaney, May 1917, Joseph Desourdie, August 1917, Francis McAvoy, February 1918 and Ernest Hanmer, October 1918.[59]

There were events within this time which stood out as particularly horrific. One of these was the Halifax explosion which killed sixteen hundred citizens of

---

54. Ibid., February 6, 1940.
55. Ibid., March 3, 1940 & March 17, 1940.
56. Ibid., October 15 & November 24, 1916, February 5 & November 11, 1917.
57. Ibid., February 13, 1916.
58. BPL, *Northern Advance,* May 23, 1918.
59. As recorded in the vestibule of the church. Veterans Affairs Canada Website.

the city and injured several thousand. At the request of Archbishop McNeil all parishes, including Barrie, took up a collection on the last Sunday of 1917.[60]

The end of the First World War was overshadowed in a crisis at home that called for action on an unparalleled scale. It was significantly urgent that it robbed St. Mary's Parish of the right to say that mass has been celebrated every Sunday since it was established in June 1855. On Sunday, October 27, 1918, there was no mass at St. Mary's by order of the health department. This was a universal order to all places of assembly in response to the Spanish Flu Epidemic. The week before the parish school was closed, Sunday school classes had been cancelled, and the church services directed to be shorter before the outright ban on October 27.[61]

One of the effects of war was that there was on the part of the Catholic community a greater preparedness to work within the social structures and movements of the larger society. The work of the Red Cross Society and the Victory Loan campaigns drew the community together beyond sectarian lines.

This reflected a dissipation of the influence of organizations such as the Orange Lodge which were in some ways hostile to Catholicism. Dean O'Malley addressed the Women's Institute in 1918. The chair of the meeting was a Protestant minister, Rev. Mr. Raymond, and the Dean, as guest speaker, spoke on, "Jealousy in Shakespeare's Plays."[62]

For many years to come Catholic attendance at Protestant services, even weddings and funerals was discouraged. Likewise, interfaith marriages were celebrated in the sacristy or the rectory of the church. On the other hand, Catholics in Barrie were encouraged to attend meetings to elect directors for the Victorian Order of Community Service Nurses and to attend the annual meeting of the Children's Aid Society.[63] The hospital was assisted by the various organizations of the parish raising funds to furnish a ward.[64]

The parishioners were reminded from the pulpit in June 1930, of the introduction of daylight-saving time for two months that summer. The announcement was bolstered with an announcement from the town council soliciting the hearty cooperation of all citizens.[65]

---

60. SMPA, Announcement Books, December 23, 1917.

61. Ibid., October 20 & 27, 1918. Twenty years later in 1937, the same anxiety caused the cancellation of the parish picnic due to the increased number of cases of infantile paralysis in the town. In 1937, the school year began a month late.

62. BPL, *Northern Advance*, February 14, 1918.

63. SMPA, Announcement Books, November 18, 1923.

64. *Beaudoin*, p. 9.

65. SMPA ,Announcement Books, June 29, 1930. Daylight Saving time had also been tried immediately after the war in 1918. (See *Northern Advance*, April 11, 1918).

This sense of shared community was acknowledged when those who were not members of St. Mary's supported the parish endeavours as well. The generosity of businessmen in their support of the children's picnic was acknowledged from the pulpit in 1931.[66]

Even the tag day of the Ladies Auxiliary of the Lions Club for the benefit of the blind was announced in the parish in 1938.[67]

Over the years, the commitment to remembering the dead of the First World War was noted, with small gestures. This was more emphatically taken up by the church in 1937 when all Catholic veterans and those in active military service were invited to assemble at Queen's Park in Toronto to march to the cathedral for a special memorial and peace service on Sunday, November 7.[68]

Perhaps no aspect of this shared life within the larger community could be seen more clearly than in the simple announcement from May 9, 1937, "Prayers will be offered at devotions this evening, as requested, marking the coronation of the king which takes place on May 12."[69]

The royal tour of 1939 indicates the attitude of the Catholic Church in Canada toward the monarchy. It was announced that special efforts would be made because King George VI and Queen Elizabeth, were among their Canadian subjects, "The 10:30 mass today will be offered for their majesties the King and Queen and for the peace and prosperity of the Empire. The liturgical prayer "Pro Rege" (For the King) is added to the mass each day during the royal visit."[70]

During both world wars a national registration of all citizens 16 and over was undertaken and the pulpit of the church was used to remind all citizens that their full cooperation was anticipated.[71]

Civic duty was also strongly encouraged at the time of elections. Announcements in anticipation of elections not only reminded the congregation of their franchise, but in a particular way reminded women that they too had the franchise. In January of 1924, the announcement suggested that every man and every woman should have enough interest in their town to go out and vote.[72]

Later the same year, the people were reminded, "voting is on Thursday the

66. Ibid., August 2, 1931.
67. Ibid., May 29, 1938.
68. Ibid., October 24, 1937.
69. Ibid., May 9, 1937.
70. Ibid., May 28, 1939.
71. Ibid., June 16, 1918 & August 18, 1940.
72. Ibid., January 6, 1924.

23rd; vote as you like, but all vote. Many years ago there was a great struggle for the franchise. So now be sure to use it."[73] The pastor reinforced the theme of duty to vote in November 1927, reminding the parishioners to vote for whoever they would like to vote for, but vote. He further reminds the women of the parish that Monday is not a wash day.[74] The importance of voting was reinforced in 1934 by a campaign sponsored by the Catholic Women's League, called, "Votes Count."[75]

Nationalistic themes were integrated into the life of the parish as the prayer offered in anticipation of Dominion Day to mark the sixtieth anniversary of confederation attests, "O God, Eternal Father, We return thanks to Thee for the many graces thou hast bestowed upon us, and for the temporal blessing we have received from Thy bounty. We thank Thee especially this day for the privilege and the blessing of being Canadians, and having given us a country of great promise. We thank Thee for having preserved the union of our Canadian provinces, during the sixty years since they began to unite. We beseech Thee to bless our country through Jesus Christ, Our Lord, Amen.

O God of unity and peace, grant, we beseech Thee, in the holy name of Jesus, that we who are many races and tongues, may be united in heart and mind, in all that pertains to the advancement of religion and the best interests of our country: Through the same Christ our Lord. Amen."[76]

The Church Bombing.

On the evening of June 10, 1926, three sticks of dynamite were detonated in the basement of St. Mary's Church. The explosion blew a hole in the floor of the church and broke windows. Whether it should be or not, the story over the years has been understood more as a novelty than as an act of raw violence. It was the work of the Ku Klux Klan.

In the 1920's, Barrie was a place where religious sensibilities strove to validate the efforts of all Christians. It is true that the Orange Lodge was still quite active and marches were undertaken annually on the twelfth of July. These were balanced by Holy Name processions through town. In July of 1925, 1,800 members of the Holy Name Society of the northern region of the Diocese of Toronto marched from armories along Dunlop Street to St. Mary's

73. Ibid., October 19, 1924.
74. Ibid., January 1, 1928.
75. Ibid., February 18, 1934.
76. Ibid., June 26, 1927.
77. BPL, *Barrie Examiner*, July 16, 1925.

Church.[77]

In many cases, there was still a less than enlightened understanding of racial equality. In Oro Township there had been an Afro Canadian community from the eighteen hundreds. By the 1920's this community had, for the most part, moved on and some had taken up residence in Barrie.

Barrie's small black community had been a source of controversy in the years leading up to 1926, for religious reasons. As the *Advance* noted in its May 15, 1924 edition, "Tomorrow morning John Thompson, coloured, charged with disturbing the peace will know what fate has in store for him. The case, which alleges an offence of disturbing the peace on or about April 29, was heard by Magistrate Jeffes last Friday and judgement reserved for one week. All of this arose out of holding religious services in Thompson's house, 86 John Street. The neighbours objected to the religious fervour of the Pentecostal Brethren's meetings, claiming that it was impossible to put their children to sleep or go to bed themselves until after 11 o'clock on the nights these services are observed. Thomson admitted that they made a great deal of noise but declared that it was not of their own volition, but by the direction of the Lord."[78]

In fact, the charges were thrown out and Thompson and the other Pentecostals were free to worship.[79]

Casual prejudice was very much a part of life in Barrie. In 1923 the *Northern Advance* noted that a musical comedy was presented by the youth of St. Mary's in Barrie. The second half opened with a minstrel show in which the featured solo was, "My Coal Black Mammy." Minstrel shows which were standard fare for musical evenings involved the performers dressing up in black face and performing in exaggerated ways their ideas of black mannerisms.[80] They were not the exclusive domain of Catholics, but the Catholics had little reticence in participating in and patronizing such performances. The attitude of prejudice was pervasive. In April of 1926, the youth of St. Mary's put on a play in which one of the characters was identified as a "melancholy coon."[81]

The ambivalent attitudes towards blacks was certainly exacerbated by showing movies such as "The Birth of a Nation," which was featured in a Barrie theatre in May of 1926.[82] The Birth of a Nation was highly sympathetic to the

78. BPL, *Northern Advance*, May 15, 1924.

79. Ibid., May 22, 1924.

80. BPL, *Northern Advance*, April 12, 1923. In 1938 the CYO of the diocese undertook a three-day minstrel review at Columbus Hall in Toronto. (Parish Announcements, January 30, 1938)

81. BPL, *Barrie Examiner*, April 26, 1926.

82. Ibid., May 6, 1926. The ad notes that Uncle Tom's Cabin will be coming later. Though more sympathetic to black people it still was rich in stereotypes.

Klan. That same May the Ku Klux Klan undertook a large rally in Barrie.

The Ku Klux Klan had come into existence in the southern states during the period of reconstruction after the American Civil War. The first focus of their endeavours was to discourage the advancement of black people. As they extended their influence into the northern states they included on their roster those that were not welcome in a Klan world view; Jews, Catholics and immigrants. In Canada they added French speaking people to their list of groups who needed to be kept in their place. The gist of the organization was to seek the power to suppress those groups mentioned and to enhance the power of their own who were essentially white Protestants of British Isles and Western European origin.

The Klan made its way into Ontario in the early 1920's and sought a charter from the province in 1925.[83] Their first planned rally for Barrie was in July of 1925.[84] Nothing seems to have come of this initial effort.

A second rally was planned for May 26, 1926. The *Northern Advance* discussed the upcoming event the week before the event under the byline, "A Konklave Koming of the Ku Klux Klan." The article notes that about 2,000 people were anticipated. A representative of the organization fashioning himself as the representative of a religious organization had approached Mayor Craig for the use of a town park for camping and parking cars. The mayor had sent the man onto the secretary of the Parks Commission who gave permission with certain conditions. Neither the mayor nor the secretary was aware of the nature of the meetings and when they learned that it was in fact the Klan wanting the use of facilities, access to the agricultural park was denied on grounds that the Klan shrouds their activities in secrecy. The Klan quickly regrouped and gained access to land at the top of Toronto Street. It was understood the event was to be comprised of afternoon and evening sessions.[85]

The day after the rally the *Barrie Examiner* reported at length on the events of the previous day. A Dr. Fowler seems to have been the main speaker in the afternoon and evening, though a Mrs. Smith invited white, Protestant, Gentile women to join the ranks of the Klan as well.

The *Barrie Examiner* noted that three of the most important aims of the Klan were dealt with by Dr. Fowler. " They were the preservation of Anglo Saxon and Celtic blood; preservation of the country for the use and benefit of the Anglo Saxons and preservation of the Protestant faith and the English

---

83. BPL, *Northern Advance*, February 18, 1925.

84. Ibid., May 21, 1925.

85. Ibid., May 20, 1926.

language. In his opening remarks Dr. Fowler stated that the Klan is the greatest movement on the earth today and that it is the most exclusive organization for it admits only people of Anglo Saxon and Celtic blood. While possessing no antipathy towards Negroes or those of the Mongolian or Semitic races the speaker was eloquent in his condemnation of intermarriage of white people with those of other races. Intermarriage with coloured or Mongolian blood was the greatest crime Anglo Saxons could commit. He declared that it was greater even than murder or arson.

The laundry business and the café and restaurant business should be taken away from the foreigners and put in the hands of Canadian men and women, he stated. If this were done hundreds of Canadians who have been forced to seek a living in other countries could return to their native land, find employment and opportunity. The motion picture business, also the jewelry, wool, leather, shoe and clothing trades are in the hands of the non Anglo Saxon people."

The *Examiner* had further reported on the evening event that, "Ceremonies started at eight. While the fifty-foot cross was being raised one of the wires snapped and it was with difficulty that the cross was prevented from crashing to the ground and perhaps injuring some of the Klansmen. One hooded member climbed the great cross as it was supported by poles in mid air and adjusted the wire and the raising proceeded."[86]

The raising of the cross was described as a symbol of liberty and the coming together of the Protestant people of this country. It was a symbol of one school system and only one.

There were clear voices of opposition to the Klan and its presence in the community. The editorial comment in the *Northern Advance* for the same week was that the Klan was contrary to British ideals and The Bible.[87]

Among those who responded to the call of the Klan was a rather hapless Irish immigrant named William Skelly. Skelly was a shoemaker, by trade, who had come to Canada in 1925. He was slowly moving west taking odd jobs in various towns, arriving in Barrie sometime in late April or early May 1926.

On the evening of June 10 he bombed St. Mary's Church.

Press reports stated that Skelly, was a native of Belfast, who had been injured in the First World War. He then enlisted with the Black and Tans, a security wing of the British army, dedicated to the quelling unrest in Ireland. Skelly maintained at his arrest that he was widowed in Ireland when his wife

---

86. BPL, *Barrie Examiner*, May 27, 1926.

87. BPL, *Northern Barrie Advance*, May 27, 1926.

was shot by Sein Fein, the Irish provisional army. There is no reason to believe that this was true. Like so much in Skelly's life, truth seems to have been a movable feature.[88]

Regrettably, most of the archival material on this trial has been lost and that which is held by the Ontario Archives is mostly correspondence on the administration of the trial.

There is, however, a report by a psychiatrist which covers Skelly's history and helps us to give this elusive character more context. Skelly was in fact born in 1900 into a Presbyterian family in Belfast. He was an average student. He began school at eight and withdrew to become an apprentice at thirteen. At the age of fourteen, in 1914, he joined the Royal Irish Fusiliers. He was injured three times at the first battle of the Somme. He was wounded in the mouth, the head and the leg.

He also lost the middle finger of his right hand. He was discharged from the army for being too young. On discharge he joined the navy and worked as a stoker at the Chatham Depot. After demobilization he worked in the shipyards in Belfast.

In 1920, he married a widow with three children and over the next couple of years they had two more children. He experienced extended periods of unemployment.

He left for Canada in 1925. He did farm labour, then opened a shoe repair shop in Prescott and later Campbellford. He eventually ended up in Lefroy as a farm labourer and then drifted onto Barrie where he found work.

While in Ireland, he spent eleven months in jail; nine for attacking a policeman and two for hitting his wife.

In the same record Skelly states that on his arrival in Barrie, a barber named Lee encouraged him to join the KKK as they would see that he got work. He borrowed the ten dollars to join, five for membership and five for the uniform.

He received his little brown dog card, which read, "Ancient, Honorable, Transcendental and Effervescent order of the little brown dog. This is to certify that William Skelly has been raised from the common mongrel pup to the effervescent degree of dogdom, and is entitled to gnaw in peace and harmony."[89]

---

88. The two Barrie newspapers covered the events around the bombing extensively in the weeks following the incident. The first stories included some information that reflected the hysteria of the moment, including the report that a twelve year old boy was shot at near the top of the Dundonald Street hill on his way home from a band concert in St. Vincent Street Park. (June 24).

89. BPL, *Norther Advance,* October 21, 1926.

So That Our Parish Can Make a Good Showing

On June 9, in Barrie, a meeting of the Klan discussed an act of terrorism. Among others present at the meeting were William Butler and Clare Lee who were both implicated in the crime. The first choice of action was to blow up a "Roman Catholic Monument" in Orillia. They, in fact, were probably talking about the Champlain monument which had been unveiled on Dominion Day the year before. Skelly stated that at a meeting at the Klavern that they drew lots and he drew the "Fiery Cross" and was the candidate to undertake the act of violence.

Skelly went to the hardware and bought three sticks of dynamite and caps and hid them in Lee's barbershop. He states that the next night he and William Butler, after an evening of drinking dandelion wine, went to St. Mary's where the dynamite was placed in the basement and detonated.

On Thursday night they decided on a target closer to home because Butler's car was not working. According to Skelly, Butler suggested blowing up St. Mary's," to let the Catholics know the Klan was in town."

After the explosion they ran down the street throwing KKK handbills. They also fired two shots from a revolver in the air. He states that on his way home by the post office he met two Jews and a Frenchman and gave them Klan material.[90]

When talk had turned to action the Klan became a little unnerved. After the explosion Skelly consulted with the officers of the Klan in Barrie and they arranged for him to meet Col. Proctor the head of the Klan in Toronto. When he met with Proctor, there was also a lawyer present who induced him to sign a statement absolving the Ku Klux Klan of any responsibility in the bombing. He said that he signed since he was afraid they would kill him.[91]

This was Skelly's original story which evolved over time. The dandelion wine part of the story was probably true, but it seems that Skelly entered the building on his own. Butler and Lee had only supporting roles.

Skelly was the prime object of police concern, but when he was arrested he implicated Clare Lee, aged 24 and William Butler, aged 27, both Barrie residents, who worked together at the shoe factory. Both Butler and Lee at first denied any involvement. Lee stated that he met Skelly that night and walked up Mulcaster as far as Worsley to show him where the Catholic church was. Butler stated that he had been at the Klavern, but his little girl had been with him. Skelly also implicated three others in the bombing, including one

---

90. BPL, *Barrie Examiner,* July 1, 1926.

91. AO, Department of the Attorney General, File 4-32 1926, No. 1526. *Synopsis of History of William Skelly*, C. Crawford, M.D., October 6, 1926, taken at Barrie Jail.

resident who assisted in the effort by getting him drunk on dandelion wine and driving him to the church, showing him how to break in and waiting for him.

These are the sketchy details. There probably can never be a clear understanding of what happened. There are those in Barrie who would state that involvement extended beyond these three young men and in fact some who participated had positions of respect in the community and were able to distance themselves from the fiasco.

The damage was not discovered until the next morning when the caretaker opened the church in anticipation of the 6:30 a.m. mass. The mass was said in the chapel of the convent across the street and quick repairs were made so that the church could be used for mass on the weekend.[92]

The trial of all three took place in mid October and all three were found guilty after the jury deliberated for less than two hours. Skelly was found guilty of causing the explosion. Lee was found guilty of complicity in pointing out the church and assisting Skelly evade arrest, and Butler with aiding his escape.[93]

Though the *Advance* had cautioned in its editorial at the time of the arrests, that those arrested were innocent till proven guilty, it had little sympathy for the Ku Klux Klan that spent all its time distancing itself from the crime. The *Advance* clearly stated that after the explosion all the members of the Klan should identify themselves.[94] It seems the *Advance* at the time also suspected greater involvement than just these three hapless youth.

Both Barrie papers consistently reminded the public that this incident would not have occurred at all except the Klan had made a move into Barrie. They challenged the contention of the Klan that they were a peaceful organization, especially when they went so far as to say they did not believe in any public demonstrations at all.[95]

Dean Sweeney who was the pastor at the time had been proactive in dampening any possible sectarian tension that could arise out of the crime. He acknowledged frequently that the feelings between the Catholics and Protestants

---

90. BPL, *Barrie Examiner,* July 1, 1926.

91. AO, Department of the Attorney General, File 4-32 1926, No. 1526. Synopsis of History of William Skelly, C. Crawford, M.D., October 6, 1926, taken at Barrie Jail.

92. BPL, *Barrie Examiner*, June 24, 1926.

93. BPL, *Barrie Examiner,* October 21, 1926.

94. BPL, *Northern Advance,* June 24, 1926.

95. BPL, *Barrie Examiner,* July 1, 1926.

of Barrie were excellent and that, in fact, on the Sundays leading up to the crime no comment had been made about the Klan or its activities in the pulpit at St. Mary's.

Judge Logie in his comments at the end of the trial stated, "You have justified my faith in Ontario jurors. In this county, well known for its prosperity and patriotism as witnessed by the great number of young men who went to the war, it is expected that their fathers and brothers would uphold their ideals of liberty which their sons and brothers fought for. In this county, I am told, for many years Catholics and Protestants have lived in amity, side by side, never troubling each other. That is as it should be. We do not want in this country conditions which formerly prevailed in that distressful isle, Ireland, nor do we want those conditions, if the press is to be believed, which prevail at the present moment in the republic to the south. One may safely say that man may leave his rights in the hands of his peer without fear that they will be moved by prejudice or favour. I am told that some of you are Orangemen. If that is so, it is all the more credit to you, in view of the fact that you have laid aside any feelings that you might have toward the Roman Catholic Church. You have dealt a blow for liberty which will show that the hearts of the people of this county and of Canada are sound."[96]

The aftermath in the parish is hard to gauge.

On the first Sunday in July 1926, Dean Sweeney told the parish that they must consider repairing the church at once. He did not however focus on the bombing but suggested a much more extensive program of physical renewal inside and outside. He noted the outside of the church needs repointing. He also suggested replacing the wooden sidewalks and putting in a fence to discourage short cuts through the property. He is hoping to gather a good wise committee to oversee the task.[97]

By May of the following year, Dean Sweeney was full of praise for the people of the parish. The Altar Society replaced the hardwood floors, the Christian Mothers purchased a new baptism font, the League of the Sacred Heart covered the cost of painting the altars and the sanctuary, and the Catholic Women's League gave funds to renew the exterior of the church."[98]

The other concrete impact the incident had was to double the cost for insurance on the church.[99]

96. BPL, *Northern Advance* October 21, 1926.
97. SMPA, Announcement Books, July 3, 1926.
98. Ibid., May 15, 1927.
99. Ibid., March 6, 1927.

Children and Youth in the Parish.

The parish's work with children extended well beyond the classroom. If Catholic education was foundational in the fostering of identity, it by no means, ended there. For children in rural areas who did not attend Catholic schools, religious instruction was required. Secondly, the church recognized that it must strive to give the young an enriched experience of church life.

The Christian Mothers, had been founded as an organization to give support to women and family life. Among their works they provided social occasions for children. In November 1915, it was announced that during the week following Christmas a festival was planned.[100] The primary focus of this special event would be a Christmas tree. Members of the parish were invited to send presents to the hall to be distributed to the children.[101]

For younger boys there was the opportunity to serve on the altar as sanctuary boys. They were offered social opportunities as this note from the Barrie Examiner in 1915 attests; "Tuesday afternoon the altar boys of St. Mary's Church enjoyed a sleigh ride and afterwards a banquet at Boldger's Restaurant."[102]

A more elaborate event was described in the announcements over subsequent weeks in 1926. "On Wednesday evening, the sanctuary boys are intent on having a sleigh ride and supper. They will assemble in front of the church at 4:30. Now we must all go together and make this a success. For my part I intend to provide the sleighs. Unless someone with sleighs should volunteer. We expect the good ladies of the parish to provide the banquet which should consist of sandwiches and good fresh cakes, the kind mother used to make.

There are about 30 boys and I would say each boy will eat about twice as much as he would at home. Some nice fruit would be very acceptable such as apples and oranges. These boys deserve decent refreshment. Persons who wish to send good things may do so on Wednesday afternoon to the parish hall."[103]

The following week the success of the event was reported, "I wish to thank the ladies and gentlemen of the parish who helped in any way in connection with the sanctuary boy's banquet. It was a great success so far as the eating was concerned."[104]

At various times in the history of the parish there have been initiatives

---

100. Ibid., November 21, 1915.
101. Ibid., December 26, 1915.
102. BPL, *Barrie Examiner*, January 7, 1915
103. SMPA, Announcement Books., February 19, 1922.
104. Ibid., February 26, 1922.

which focused on recreational needs of the parish youth.

A Glee Club existed early in 1915. Club meetings cost those under 15, a nickel a meeting and those over 15, a dime. Each meeting would be followed by an "at home."[105]

In the spring of 1934, there was an announcement regarding a meeting for all of those interested in the tennis courts.[106]

In October 1922, the pastor announced the upcoming retreat for the members of the Sodality. "The Sodality will meet at three o'clock as usual. All members should make an effort to be present today as there are some preparations to be made for the approaching retreat. The retreat opens next Sunday evening right after the usual Sunday devotions. This retreat is for all unmarried women more than 16 years of age. If younger girls wish to attend, they must make special arrangements with the sister in charge. The preacher, Fr. Roehr, is said to be one of the very best available in this kind of work.....He has given retreats to young ladies all over the province. So you will understand that a very special privilege awaits you. This is a time of special grace. This retreat may be the turning point in the lives of many. But you must correspond with God's grace. The way to correspond with grace in the first place is to attend.

Parents should make every effort to see that their daughters attend. It may be the means of averting a great many misfortunes and sorrows."[107]

Though organizations for boys were not as quickly formed, the Holy Name Society included a juvenile branch.

Ministry to youth in part sought to bring young people from further afield. The young people's clubs of Midland and Barrie had a moonlight excursion in June 1936.[108] The next spring the young people's clubs of Mimico came to Barrie to present two plays. After the plays, dancing was planned.[109]

The Catholic Youth Organization, the CYO, was active in the diocese though it did not seem to have been present in a structured way in Barrie before the Second World War. In 1939, it undertook a "National Crusade of Good Reading." The goal of the campaign was to promote the reading of good, clean and wholesome literature and to rid Canada of all immoral and suggestive publications. They sought a commitment of all through the signing of pledge cards.[110]

---

105. Ibid., November 14, 1915.
106. Ibid., May 13, 1934.
107. Ibid., October 15, 1922.
108. Ibid., June 21, 1936.
109. Ibid., May 30, 1937.
110. Ibid., March 12, 1939.

Holy Name Society.

The value of the many fraternal organizations was to enhance the life of the participants and to organize the parish effectively. A little competition amongst different organizations was not beyond the realm of the work. In 1922, the Sodality is reminded that the meeting at the usual hour should be well attended as there is to be a singing practice in anticipation of the event for the reception of new members. They are reminded, "The Holy Name men have raised the standard of singing on their communion Sunday."[111]

The Holy Name Society found an expression of its presence in the broader Catholic community through rallies. The first in the region was in June of 1924 at Orillia when 200 from Barrie attended.[112] The nature of the rally was to show strength. So the pastor was often found reminding the men of the parish of the importance of their participation in the rallies. The 1926 rally at Midland included some directions for the participants. "Processionists will march four abreast and wear their badges. As much as possible military discipline will prevail, and order will be maintained by the Marshal of each Branch Society.

Ladies and children are not admitted onto the School Grounds until after all the processionists have entered.

The use of tobacco is strictly forbidden during the parade."[113]

The rallies of the Holy Name Society moved throughout the region on an annual basis.

Knights of Columbus.

The Knights rented the hall from M. J. Frawley that was to be the locus of their activities for many years. When Frawley died the hall came into the possession of his sisters who continued the arrangement. The parish having few venues in which to gather was often dependant on the Knights for their hospitality.

Like any organization, the Knights experienced a waxing and waning of membership. This was often related to the availability of men to bolster the ranks. After the First World War the quorum was lowered to five members for meetings.[114]

---

111. IIbid., May 21, 1922.
112. BPL, *Northern Advance*, June 26, 1924.
113. SMPA, Announcement Books, June 13, 1926.
114. Beaudoin, p. 6.

During the First and Second World Wars the local Knights were active in their support of the Army Huts which were an integral part of the organization's response to the war and showing support for military personnel. Catholic huts provided opportunities for socialization and comradery away from the seedier side of life. The men who were going off to new places were young, often from sheltered backgrounds and it is important to remember that not all were prepared to cut loose and seek out the extremes of life. Much of this work was done in Europe, but closer to home, military personnel were also a particular concern.[115]

The Catholic Huts as a worthy cause was strongly endorsed by Archbishop McNeil who saw it as a natural opportunity to emphasize that the time of war was bearing fruit through cooperation across denominational lines. "No matter how hard the Catholics of the city work or give, the Protestants of Toronto will do more in their campaign for Catholic Huts. They ranged their best organizations on our side this time, and we shall certainly do no less."[116]

The First World War provided its own challenges for the City of Barrie. Camp Borden was opened in July 1916 as part of the Canadian effort to train soldiers. In Barrie, the Knights during the First World War provided social occasions for soldiers. It is unclear what form these events took, but they would needless to say be a haven for young men who were anxious for a break from the routine, in a safe and hospitable environment.[117]

By the 1920's, the Knights were encouraging a council in Phelpston, sending money to the suffering of Ireland and to those left homeless by the Haileybury fire, seeking to encourage Catholic scouting and adding their voice to Catholic education rights. All of these endeavours were reflected in a response to a 1923 address from Dean Sweeney encouraging men to take a more active part in public affairs.[118]

Over the years the Knights of Columbus distinguished themselves by their many programs. In the fall of 1935, they organized classes of public speaking, took the children of the shelter for automobile rides and gathered in the cemetery to pray for deceased members.

Like the Holy Name Society, the Knights, were seen as a bulwark against elements hostile to Catholic causes. We find the Knights hosting Fr. Lamphier, in 1938, in the waning days of the depression. Fr. Lamphier was the director

---

115. SMPA, *A Century of Service*, Knights of Columbus of Barrie.
116. Moir, p. 197.
117. SMPA, Announcement Books, November 21, 1915.
118. Beaudoin, p. 7.

of the Radio League of St. Michael, a ministry focused on keeping Catholics vigilant to the dangers of communism.[119]

The Knights, in the same season, celebrated their twenty fifth anniversary with a meal prepared and served by the Catholic Women's League, at their Dunlop Street hall.[120]

The ongoing demands on the Knights for causes that grew out of the depression were to be balanced with an ongoing drop off in membership. By 1946 the membership dropped to an all time low of twenty nine. It raised the question of persevering at all, though it was decided that if costs could be covered the council should continue.[121]

The Catholic Women's League.

The Northern Advance informed the general public in April of 1921 that, "A branch of the Catholic Women's League has been formed in Barrie . . . the first public meeting was held on Thursday evening in the parish hall on Collier Street and was well attended. A highly instructive literary program was interspersed with piano, violin and vocal selections. Making it a very pleasant evening. Rev. Dean O'Malley and Rev. Father Kirby were present and each expressed gratification at the ability shown in the papers read. Much latent talent, it is hoped will be brought out in future meetings and the women of the parish will be given opportunities to discuss the important questions of the day."[122]

The Catholic Women's League was formed in western Canada and it moved quickly across the country, creating a vast network of groups from coast to coast, advocating for women and the concerns which were prevalent in the lives of women. The League also asserted the place of women in a way which may have been a particular challenge to the status quo in many homes as the following announcement suggests, "The Catholic Women's League is holding a Garden Party at the home of Mrs. W. L. Patterson, on Dominion Day, July 1, 1923 from 2:30 to 7:00. Every member of the League is invited to be present, also every old lady of the congregation, whether a member of the League or not is especially invited. No admission fee will be charged. Leave your purse at home as you will not need it. The very old will be sent for. It is hoped the

119. Ibid., June 6, 1937.
120. BPL, *Northern Advance*, October 25, 1933.
121. Beaudoin, p. 13, 14.
122. BPL, *Northern Advance*, April 21, 1921.

husbands and fathers will assume the responsibilities of the home for that afternoon and allow the ladies to attend the Garden Party."[123]

The Catholic Women's League was first introduced in the Barrie area in 1920, when Fr. O'Malley invited Miss Gertrude Lawlor to come to Barrie to speak of the work of the League.[124] By the spring of 1921 they were having regular meetings and had organized an executive for their work.[125]

By 1926, the League was solely responsible for the parish bazaar.[126]

The League's commitment to social action on a national scale has been a cornerstone of its work since its inception. We find the League in Barrie in 1923, arranging a toy shower for the western missions. Admission to the event was a piece of material which could be converted into an article for a sale of work, to aid the Sisters of Service in Western Canada.[127] The next year we find them in March selling shamrocks to aid St. Joseph's Orphanage in Toronto.[128] In March of 1930, they committed themselves to furnishing a room at the Royal Victoria Hospital.[129]

The confidence that was exhibited by the C. W. L. could result in tension on occasion as well. In February of 1932, the pastor announced, "That the Ladies of the C. W. L. intend carrying on their good work in the Knights of Columbus Hall during the rest of the duration. I am inviting myself to make a very friendly visit with them on next Friday at 3:00 P.M. I would like to meet all the ladies of the congregation on this occasion."[130]

Whatever the tension between the pastor and the League, the fence was adequately mended for the Barrie League to host the C. W. L. Convention for the diocese in the fall of 1933. Among the reports that were presented were reports from the convenors of education, immigration, traveler's aid, the magazine, Sisters of Service, social welfare, membership and junior and senior study groups.[131]

Like the Knights of Columbus, the Catholic Women's League invested in

---

123. SMPA, Announcement Books, June 24, 1923.

124. ARCAT, *St. Mary's Files,* O'Malley to McNeil, November 11, 1920. Anyone seeking some models of proactive Catholic women in earlier eras of the church would do well to spend some time exploring the life of Gertrude Lawlor.

125. SMPA, Announcement Books, April 3, 1921.

126. Ibid., November 21, 1926.

127. Ibid., October 28, 1923.

128. Ibid., March 9, 1924.

129. BPL, *Barrie Examiner,* March 13, 1930.

130. SMPA, Announcement Books, February 7, 1932.

131. BPL, *Northern Advance,* October 5, 1933.

the war effort. In 1941 the promotion of war stamps and certificates were utmost in the minds of the League. In February, the diocesan executive clearly saw itself as responsible for leading the cause of encouraging savings. The month of February 1941 was set aside to encourage two million Canadians to become war savers. As the Archdiocesan convenor emphasized, "As Canadian civilians we are not called upon to see our homes laid in ruins . . . so far we are not asked to risk our lives . . . but Canada is asking us to lend our dollars to keep our homes and lives secure. As a national organization we shall be depended upon to lend active assistance in the purchase of stamps during the month of February.[132]

The C. W. L. was also promoting the moral well being of the men in uniform. The letter regarding war savings noted further that the diocesan convenor would be pleased to hear whether Catholic and other good literature is being sent to the Roman Catholic chaplain at Camp Borden for distribution among the troops. In return mail, the convenor was assured that this was so and in fact Fr. Wilhelm, the chaplain, had been guest speaker at a League meeting.[133]

Though the League was concerned about the moral as well as the physical well being of the troops. Msgr. Clair felt in June 1942, the C. W. L. was being stampeded into support of the Christian Women's Temperance Union. The W. C. T. U. was in the light of the war effort anxious to promote some more stringent regulations around the sale and distribution of alcohol. At this juncture, the Temperance Union was seeking the support of the C. W. L. to petition for a number of things dear to their heart: the curtailment of the manufacture of beer, wine and liquor, the closing of all women's beverage rooms, strict ban on drinking by minors, drastic shortening of the hours of sale of alcohol and finally the removal of all chairs and tables from beverage rooms.

Msgr. Clair sought the advice of Fr. E. J. McGrath, diocesan chaplain for the League, to see if, in fact, the League at a higher level had made a decision about the petition. It is presumed by the tone of the correspondence that the support of the C. W. L. would not be forthcoming.[134] Msgr. Clair, who was not known as a spontaneous wit, does conclude his letter with a comment that Fr. McGrath's answer would determine whether he was in need of a retreat or not.

---

132. SMPA, Correspondence, Walker to Madam President, 1941.
133. SMPA, Correspondence, Clair to McGrath, June 1942.
134. SMPA, Correspondence, Clair to McGrath, June 1942.

Catholic Education.

The effort for financial parity for separate schools was a long ongoing struggle. Throughout the thirties the Catholic schools worked to gain a more equitable share of the tax base.

In 1932, the concern centered on assessment of homes supporting Catholic education and was bolstered by a collection to defray expenses in pursuing the "Separate School Taxation Question" by the diocese.[135] Dean Clair was at the end of the decade complementing the parish on the strong interest shown in the meeting of the Catholic Taxpayers Association.[136]

During Dean Clair's time he was a proactive advocate for any dollar that the separate schools were entitled to. In 1939, early in his pastorate, he reminds the parishioners, "Newcomers to the parish are requested to please phone the Deanery or call and leave their address within the next two or three days. It is important that this be done at once in order that our parochial school may receive a due share of taxes. Not only owners but tenants have the right to direct taxes. It makes no difference if the owner is a non-Catholic, the tenant governs the taxes. Thousands of dollars have been lost to our schools during the past year on account of the carelessness of people in the matter. This applies to all who are within three miles of the school."[137]

The spiritual care of children from the countryside was likewise a concern.

The parish had organized centers for religious instruction. We find the pastor, in May 1919, reminding parishioners that the reports for each month are needed from the country catechism centres. Further in the same announcement, it was noted that a new centre had opened at the home of Michael Shanahan in Oro.[138]

In addition to the centres of instruction, summer school was provided for the children who attended public schools. The logistical challenges of summer schools were obvious. "Vacation School begins on July 6. All children in the parish who have been attending public schools should come to vacation school for special training in religion. All parents who have not means of transportation or any place for children to stay in town should let us know, at once. The Archbishop demands that all children who have not been in Separate Schools

---

135. SMPA, Announcement Book, March 20, 1932 & April 10, 1932.
136. Ibid., February 12, 1939.
137. Ibid., October 8, 1939.
138. Ibid., May 4, 1919.

during the past year shall attend vacation school. This is not a burden to the children and is a serious loss of a means of grace to neglect."[139]

The funding of separate schools was still a great source of resentment and activists during the years when Mitchell Hepburn was premier gathered momentum once again in asserting their opposition. A 'monster' rally, in Barrie, at the IOOF Temple in May of 1936, featured a Reverend Dr. Shields who spoke on the question, 'Will the Church of Rome Rule Ontario?'

A synopsis of the talk appeared in the Advance, "Dr. Shields said he believed in the fullest religious liberty and Roman Catholics should be free to exercise their religious freedom if they believe in it. Roman Catholicism is not Christianity, said Dr. Shields, because it sells salvation for a price. The Roman Catholic Church is the world's biggest racket. It is a political institution as well as a religious institution. The speaker said he abhorred communism and there was not room for it in Canada but the Roman Catholic Church was a thousand times more dangerous than all the communists put together.[140]

Priests.

The period of the late eighteen hundreds and early nineteen hundreds was marked after the eighteen year pastorate of Dean O'Connor, by a number of short terms of service.

Fr. Moyna left Barrie in 1915 and Dean Andrew O'Malley[141] became pastor of St. Mary's from 1915 until his death in 1921. Dean O'Malley was a poet and essayist. His essays on literary topics were edited by Dean Harris a rather well known cleric and man of letters of the time. O'Malley had published the Wreck of the Titanic in 1912, Shakespearean Lectures, American Statesman and Joan of Arc. Other than those designated as lectures all works were poetry. His most ambitious endeavour was a collection of poems called Sonnets of a Recluse. This work was contained in three volumes though the intention was to have it run to ten volumes.[142] Dean Harris, wrote the preface which begins, "It is a daring adventure in these days of heroic iliads, ephemeral verses and fugitive compositions in rhyme, for a writer to publish his poems in book form, especially if these poems are cast in a sonnetal mould. But genius cannot be fettered, and an original and gifted mind, dowered with rich exuberance, will, when the spirit of poetry visits it, burst out in spontaneous gushing,

---

139. Ibid., June 21, 1942.
140. BPL, *Northern Advance*, May 21, 1936.
141. bn 1863, ordained 1893, died 1921.
142. See catalogues of National Library and Amicus.

or open for itself new channels through which the treasure of its thoughts will flow in rich and joyous currents. Again, genius, indifferent to criticism, is ever prepared to break all fetters of rules and suggestion, and, like the eagle, dare to soar aloft in its own independent flight."

It is probably useful to give voice to O'Malley's muse in one of his sonnets from this volume on a perennial Barrie topic, "The Snow",

"Think you these flakes are Manna flung from heaven,
that fall in benediction on thy head,
And 'neath thy feet; make carpet where you tread,
As white as hawthorn buds, by zephyrs driven?

Are they the floss that float across the walls
Of paradise, wherein they keep sweet flowers,
To perfume their own happy homes and bowers,
And garland with bouquets their banquet halls?

Not so! They're messengers all robed in white,
Their faces blanched, for they have in their keeping
Such words, as make men meditate on death.
They typify, but speak not of the blight
Of years; for winter comes awake or sleeping,
On our heads, and chokes us with frosty breath."[143]

When Hugh Sweeney[144] became pastor and Dean, he was a radical change from the academic O'Malley. Raised on a farm in Caledon he was noted for advocacy of children and down to earth approach to ministry. He was to be pastor for seventeen years dying in 1938.[145]

He in turn was followed by Monsignor James Clair[146] who served the parish of Barrie for thirty-one years. After his retirement as pastor he continued to minister in the parish till infirmity required care closer to his family. Born in 1894 at Cayuga, Ontario he was educated at the local schools and entered St. Augustine's Seminary near the end of the First World War. He was ordained in 1921 and served the diocese in a number of roles. In 1928 he was appointed

143. MetroToronto Reference Library, CIHM 75341, O'Malley, Andrew, *Sonnets of a Recluse*,.

144. bn 1864, ordained 1896, died 1937.

145. It is a source of contemplation to note that St. Mary's had two pastors between 1921 and 1968.

146. bn 1894, ordained 1921, died 1988.

chancellor, the official who oversees the effective running of the diocese, during the episcopacy of Archbishop Neil McNeil. In 1938 he was appointed pastor of Barrie and dean of the northern region of the diocese.

Social Life.

Parish picnics were standard summer events. The earliest host of a parish picnic seems to have been the St. Vincent de Paul Society who passed the responsibility off to the school board. Throughout the 1920's, the parish picnic which took place at St. Vincent Park, at the foot of St. Vincent Street, was concluded with parishioners taking the children for car rides.

The pastor makes us aware of a small, town-country tension in an announcement which was essentially to congratulate the work of the school board in organizing the parish picnic in July 1923. "The school picnic was a great success. The school board deserves great credit. All should be proud of the children who so nicely conducted themselves. Parents provided an excellent and bountiful feed, as the boys say, "the eats were good." The success of the day was crowned with the evening auto drive. We wish to thank one and all as I feel that anything done for children is done for me. Next year I hope to see all the Catholic children of the parish included . . . country children as well."[149]

We have the schedule for the picnic for 1930:

1) All children belonging to the parish and their parents, also others belonging to the parish are very welcome.
2) The Christian Mothers will, as usual, look after the good things to eat.
3) The boys' and girls' soft ball games begin at 1:15 o'clock.
4) Horseshoe contests for men of the parish at 2:30.
5) Races for boys and girls of different ages at 2:30.
6) Races for high school boys and girls who are members of the parish will take place about 2:30.
7) There will be a fat ladies race and ladies balloon races.

In a word, everything will be carried out along the same line as on other occasions of this kind other years. Everybody may feel sure of a pleasant time. So we trust that as many of our people, as possible, will try to be present to encourage our children."[150]

---

149. SMPA, Announcement Books, July 23, 1923.
150. Ibid., July 23, 1930.

With the arrival of Fr. Clair the announcements often included recommendations of movies, such as "Boys Town" in 1938. Fundraisers by way of hosting movies at the Roxy Theatre were undertaken by the Sodality in 1939, with the presentation of "Angels with Dirty Faces."

The opportunity that movies provided even led to a relaxing of the stringent norms of Lent. "One of the greatest musicians of our time is Ignace Jan Paderewski. He is approaching four score years of age and the evening of his career. His first and perhaps his last appearance in moving pictures is in "Moonlight Sonata" to be shown at the Roxy Theatre Monday, Tuesday and Wednesday of the week. We think it would be too bad, for those who love good music, to miss the opportunity of hearing this great master. It is an opportunity that may not come again. We think that will be sufficient excuse for going to a show this once during Lent."

The report in the bulletin regarding a recently released Bing Crosby vehicle was somewhat more fulsome. It is apparently written by one of the curates as it does not sound like Msgr. Clair. "Believe it or not it's better than 'Going My Way'. The portrayal of the sisters in 'Keys of the Kingdom' and 'Song of Bernadette' were rather unfavourable, but they really get a break in this last picture. The girls will all want to be sisters after they see Sister Mary Benedict, who is none other than Ingrid Bergman."

The Cemetery.

St. Mary's Cemetery on Sunnidale Road had come into existence when the brick church was built in the 1870's.[152]

Regular bees were organized for the maintenance of the burial ground. These events were usually in the spring. We find a call for workers on the Wednesday afternoon of the coming week on May 13, 1934.[153] Wednesdays at the time were half holidays. Stores and businesses were closed regularly on Wednesdays at noon.

In the spring and summer of 1939, the parish invested itself in an ongoing improvement of the cemetery. The bees over the years had been a stop gap measure. Dean Clair himself states that the cemetery is to be a particular concern of that year. Cemeteries before the age of gas powered lawn mowers and higher expectations on the part of the public, tended to be rather rustic places.

151. Ibid., March 12, 1939.

152. SMPA, Bulletin, January 1946.

153. SMPA, Announcement Books, May 13, 1934

Dean Clair states by mid summer that great headway has been made in making the cemetery a credit to the parish.[154]

The perennial challenges for people to engage in the work of the parish are probably as old as parishes themselves. On the Sunday before a bee in 1939, Dean Clair reminded the people that the cemetery clean up should come first and plans made later. A mower or a rake can do a great deal and is better than golf.[155] The following week it was announced that, "We wish to thank all those parishioners who helped at the cemetery during the past week. Wednesday and Thursday of this week, extra help will be needed from the people in town. Dean Clair will communicate with the people in the country to arrange for a day most suitable. This is to avoid having too many on one day and also interfering with farm work."[156]

Later in the month the announcements at mass reported, "Work at the cemetery is progressing favourably. You are invited to visit it today or any day and give us your opinions and advice. The appearance of the cemetery would be very much improved by the addition of a new fence along the front. We propose to ask for donations to promote this work in the near future. A strong permanent fence with iron posts should be our first objective. Our intention is to concentrate on this project for the summer of 1939."[157]

Clearly the endeavour was a long term success. The parishioners were reminded in 1940, "As you may have noticed all plots in the cemetery are mowed regularly. Anyone wishing to give donations for upkeep of plots may do so. All money received will be placed in the cemetery fund.[158]

Parish Hall.

At some point the parish acquired a hall. There are announcements from 1915 on which invite parishioners to activities which will occur in the parish hall which was located on Collier Street between Collier Street United and Mulcaster Street It seems that the hall was not in regular use and an announcement was made by the pastor on March 19, 1916, that, "owing to the fact that the parish hall is not paying expenses, I will promptly close it up."[159] It is not

154. Ibid., July 23, 1939.
155. Ibid., May 28, 1939.
156. Ibid., June 4, 1939.
157. Ibid., June 18, 1939.
158. Ibid., June 9, 1940.
159. Ibid., March 19, 1916. This lot now holds the law offices of Stewart and Esten.

clear how long the hall was closed. In fact, it may have been only a winter initiative related to keeping the building heated.

Fr. O'Malley reopened the hall in 1920 after a period of it being closed, though it would seem he was not totally supportive of the undertaking as he relates to Archbishop McNeil, "I opened the parish hall here a month ago. but had to raise $1,000 . . . The people are quite proud of it, and some of my forty old maids and 40 gentlemen will have a chance for their levies now."[160]

The *Barrie Examiner* noted that the debt on the hall was wiped out by the parish bazaar in 1921.[161]

The hall had two levels, kitchen facilities and was used not only by adults of the parish but was used as well by the school for concerts and various other activities.

Early in 1923 the hall was still causing anxiety as this announcement related, "The parish hall is not patronized as it should be. Perhaps the entertainments are not to people's liking . . . well then why not complain to the committee."[162]

By 1943, Msgr. Clair is writing to the chancery to ask for an accounting of the parish funds on deposit. His goal is to interest the people in building a parish hall after the war. "It is very much needed here. We haven't a place for meetings of parish societies and for religious instruction."[163] It seems that the monsignor's early enthusiasm was tempered as consideration turned to the development of education. In good time a new hall was built in tandem with responding to education needs.

World War Two.

The Second World War found St. Mary's fully immersed in the national cause, spiritually and materially

At the beginning of October 1939, all are called to pray the rosary with peace foremost in their mind.[164] In May 1940, it was announced that the four

---

160. ARCAT, *St. Mary's Files*, O'Malley to McNeil, November 11, 1920. There is a woeful lack of information on the hall. There are some references in the Simcoe County Archives that suggest that the hall may have been housed in what had been the Sevigny Family home. They had a carriage works beside it.

161. BPL, *Barrie Examiner*, December 15, 1921.

162. SMPA, Anounncement Books, January 21, 1923.

163. Ibid., December 11, 1943. This would seem to suggest that the hall on Collier Street no longer existed.

164. Ibid., October 1, 1939.

societies; The Catholic Women's League, The Christian Mothers, The Holy Name Society and the Knights of Columbus had agreed to have a mass said each month for the success of the allies and for peace.[165] This was, in part, a response to a call by Pope Pius XII that May is set aside as a month to pray for peace. By June of the same year, the Archbishop was requesting that parishes mark the crisis in France by holy hours in every parish.[166]

In October 1945, when the Rosary Sunday Rally at Maple Leaf Gardens is recommended as a time for prayers for final victory and the safe homecoming of our loved ones."[167]

The ecumenical theme which was to become such a strong force thirty years later showed itself during the time of war as this 1941 announcement attests, "Wednesday is the Feast of St. George, Patron of England. All denominations will celebrate the feast of this Catholic saint with a day of prayer and patriotism. A special service will be held in St. Michael's Cathedral on Wednesday at noon. His honor the Lieutenant-Governor and other civic dignitaries will be present. In Barrie we will celebrate the occasion by a mass at 8:30 o'clock. Everyone who can, should attend, especially the school children. There will also be a short address suitable to the occasion. We hope to have one of the army chaplains speak." [168]

The same cooperation continued throughout the war. "Sunday, September 6, 1942 has been set aside by his Majesty, the King and our Canadian Government as a day of prayer and renewal of our efforts for God and country. There will be a holy hour from 7 till 8 p.m.."[169]

On the secular side, the Red Cross was central to the work in relation to the war. By January 1940, work on the home front was well underway, as the announcement to all the women of the parish attests, "The sewing meeting of the Catholic Women's League in aid of the Red Cross War Work will be held in the Red Cross Rooms . . . It is hoped that a good number of ladies for both sewing and knitting will attend, so that our parish will make a good showing."[170]

The Red Cross work had an effective way of personalizing the work of those on the home front as is seen in the announcement that there is an urgent need for "Seaman's Long Stockings, 18" and 14" socks. Your knitting convenor has been supplied with wool and is most anxious to contact all who can help com-

165. Ibid., May 19, 1940.
166. Ibid., June 16, 1940.
167. Ibid., October 7, 1945.
168. Ibid., April 20, 1941.
169. Ibid., September 6, 1942.
170. Ibid., January 14, 1940.

plete this quota at an early date.[171] Quotas were set for particular groups and St. Mary's is reminded that their quota is 10 turtle neck sweaters, 10 pairs of socks, 15 pairs of gloves. This quota is to be finished before December 15."[172]

The sewing work was in part focused on the troops overseas, but also on the civilian victims of war in Europe as well. In March of 1940 the sewers are asked to up their effort for the relief of Poland.[173] The same month the C. W. L. hosted a guest talk at Central Collegiate by Rev. P. J. Klite entitled, "I Saw Poland Crucified." The proceeds from the talk were to go to the Red Cross Polish Relief.[174]

The parishioners were reminded that any endeavours to raise funds for the civilian victims of war were firmly endorsed by the Archbishop. This included British War Relief in September of 1941.[175] The collection realized at St. Mary's $142.47 and in Bell Ewart $20.03.[176]

The 25th anniversary of Pope Pius XII's ordination as a bishop was to be marked with collections in all the parishes of Canada. Money collected in Canada was to be used exclusively within the British Empire.[77]

The parish was a natural conduit for information on war endeavours of all types. The Women's War Service Unit planned to collect waste paper.[178]

In April 1942, the National plebiscite on the draft was undertaken with all parishioners reminded to go out and vote.[179] The plebiscite was publicly endorsed by Archbishop McGuigan in terms which have rarely been seen in Canada. "No sensible and patriotic Canadian can contemplate without horror the civic paralysis that would afflict this country in war time, if the Government was refused the power to govern effectively. It is now abundantly clear that the efficacy of our war effort and the security of our homes and sacred altars require that our government and Parliament should have the fullest liberty to study and adopt whatever measure they deem necessary for our national safety and the victory of the United Nations."[180]

The plebiscite gave the government the authority to introduce conscription

---

171. Ibid., October 24, 1943.
172. Ibid., October 29, 1944.
173. Ibid., March 3, 1940.
174. Ibid., March 17, 1940.
175. Ibid., September 21, 1941.
176. Ibid., September 21, 1941.
177. Ibid., May 3, 1942.
178. Ibid., July 14, 1940. To save paper there was no box with the envelopes in 1942.
179. Ibid., April 19 1942.
180. Moir, p. 199.

under the slogan, "conscription if necessary, not necessarily conscription."

In 1940, the call for the Dominion registration was drawn to the parishioners' attention from the pulpit on several Sundays with the expectation that, "everyone 16 years of age and over should register as soon as possible."[181]

Of equal concern was that the church aid the government in the financial demands of undertaking a war. It was announced in November of 1941, "The War Savings Campaign begins this week. Canvassers will call at your home. People who give their time to increase Canada's war effort should be received courteously. Besides, we should do all we can to increase our efforts by buying war savings certificates."[182]

The home front was not touched only by volunteer work and the financial challenges but in far more practical ways. The ideas of self sufficiency at home were emphasized. A course in home nursing was offered in the winter of 1941 by the Red Cross.[183] The following announcement strove to resolve the shortages that were being experienced as a special dinner in the parish was on the horizon. "There will be a meeting of the ladies of the parish in the vestry on Monday night at 8 o'clock. We ask the ladies to please look up recipes for food for the supper, so that it will then be possible to announce what kind of eatables should be prepared. Let us have suggestions as to how you are able to overcome the effects of the sugar shortage in your own home."[184]

Catholics were in some ways conscious of validating their loyalty and protecting against the perception that they were less loyal. Catholic Quebec had adamantly opposed conscription and so in the English speaking part of the country, Catholic loyalty was an ongoing concern. "All members of the C. W. L. and also non-members who are willing to do so, may report purchases of War Saving Stamps and Certificates to the War Service Convenor of Barrie Subdivision. The purpose of this is that Catholics may receive credit for doing their share in the "Help Win the War Effort."[185]

The same disposition was found when discussing the Children's Aid Society's efforts on behalf of refugee children from the British Isles. The parishioners were reminded, "that Catholics should lead the way in charity."[186]

On occasion the tragedy of war touched very close to home. Two Aus-

---

181. SMPA, Announcement Books, July 14, 1940, June 30, 1940, August 18, 1940.
182. Ibid., November 2, 1941.
183. Ibid., January 19, 1941.
184. Ibid., June 21, 1942.
185. Ibid., February 9, 1941.
186. Ibid., June 30, 1940.

tralian airmen, William Hogan and Neville Loginoff, had their funerals at St. Mary's Church on February 27, 1942 and were buried at St. Mary's Cemetery. They had died as the result of a plane crash at Camp Borden.[187]

The Catholic Women's League lead an appeal in the fall of 1941 for rosaries and pocket size crucifixes. "Members of the C. W. L. will be present at the back of the church before and after masses next Sunday. They will be glad to receive any Rosaries or Crucifixes that you can spare. The manufacture of these articles is stopped and there is a great need for them in the parts of England where there are many refugees from the rest of Europe. Even parts of rosaries or broken ones will be accepted and The C. W. L. will have them repaired."[188]

As the war progressed there is some shift in emphasis from concerns about the war as a general crisis, to concern for the individual soldiers and their families. Part of this concern was for the families of those located at Base Borden. Among the efforts of the larger community that was endorsed by the parish was the creation of daycare at the armories, two afternoons a week for the wives of the soldiers at Camp Borden.[189] The families attached to Base Borden created a tremendous demand on the city as wives and children of soldiers required housing as in September of 1939, women and children were evacuated from the camp.[190]

The first extant parish bulletin, from June 1942, featured the Canadian Bishops pastoral regarding the war effort. They commend the generous response of the country and then go on to say, "Let us pray for our fighting men that inspired with such thoughts and with a pure intention, they may persevere to the end, determined, intrepid, heroic." They then go further, "We feel obliged to sound a warning against certain lamentable abuses in the matter of strong drink . . . with all our heart we deplore the practice of blaspheming and profaning the Name of God . . . we call attention to the proper authorities to the respect due the Lord's Day . . . the true welfare of the nation demands that all working people be guaranteed an opportunity on Sunday of getting some bodily rest, and fulfill their religious duties and receiving moral instruction . . . Finally, once more we wish to warn those who have the authority to unmask the propaganda of atheistic communism.[191]

---

187. SMPA, Parochial Records
188. SMPA, Announcement Books, September 21, 1941,
189. Ibid., August 17, 1941.
190. Murdoch et al, p. 258.
191. SMPA, Bulletin, June 13, 1942.

Msgr. Clair and the Soldiers.

The Christian Mothers organized boxes to be sent to all men from the parish serving in Europe and in Canada.

Among the sparse collection of material left from Msgr. Clair's thirty years of ministry in Barrie is a file of letters from soldiers on active duty during the Second World War. The letters for the most part are thank you notes to the parish for its efforts on their behalf.

Because of security restrictions the letters often do not carry a great deal of factual information, rather, they include experiences with travel and much on the common complaint of boredom, while waiting to go to the front.

"Dear Dean Clair: I have visited many places in London and one of the most impressive sights I have yet seen is St. Paul's Cathedral in London. Although surrounded with destruction and debris it still stands . . . I often wish I was home on a Sunday just to walk up to Mass in the morn, meet the boys after and have a jolly time. Is there many boys left?......You know Father, I think I will be having a little job for you to do when I return. That is to marry my girl friend and I. No she isn't anyone you know. She is a girl from Toronto. Mary Proudfoot is her name and really a swell girl. So if I may have it, I would like your promise to perform the rituals."[192] P.E. Fred Arsenault

"Dear Father: The O. C. of our squadron is a Catholic so I had no trouble whatever to get off for the ordination and first mass. The time for that has come really fast. They do not give us very much leave here, but for such occasions they are very good to us."[193] Wilfrid (Bill) Firth

"Dear Dean Clair:. You cannot possibly know how much it means to us to know the people in Barrie still keep us in their thoughts and try to help our morale by little kindnesses.

I sincerely hope that next Easter will find my son and myself back in St. Mary's, Barrie."[194] Major Jack Wallace

"Reverend Dean Clair: It is with deep gratitude that I write this short letter of thanks to you and through you to the kind ladies of the best little parish in the world . . . I write this thanksgiving for the feeling that I have friends wait-

---

192. SMPA, Correspondence, Arseneault to Clair.
193. Ibid., Firth to Clair, November 22, 1943.
194. Ibid., April 5, 1942, Wallace to Clair.

ing to welcome me home when I once more return to my hometown."[195] John Murphy

"Dear Rev. Father . . . Receiving parcels and letters from home make up our brightest moments; you'd realize that if you could see the boys crowd around the post office when the word goes around, 'There's some Canadian mail in today." I can tell you though that I enjoy my work and seeing all there is to see of the world. It isn't fair to make an opinion of a country while it's at war but as you've probably already guessed Canada was never more appreciated in all its life than it is now with the boys over here."[196] Mike Murphy

"Rev Dean Clair: I am fine except that I miss my wife and children very much, but hope it will not be long before this is all over. We are kept pretty busy tunneling every day, and as we work Sunday I do not get to mass often."[197] Sapper A. Miller

Dear Dean Clair: I have just come back from a film shown by the K of C. They usually bring one a week to the unit and they are always good. Once or twice a month there is a special night, when lights out is extended for the occasion. First a film is shown, then we play bingo until ten o'clock for the Canadian chocolate bars and cigarettes. Afterward, comes a very popular treat, coffee and biscuits. Yes, the K of C certainly does a lot for the soldiers and more than the other services. You might envoy my thanks and everyone else's over here to the Knights for their wonderful work."[198] Lloyd Rolston.

"Dear Reverend Dean Clair: I'm just waiting for the time to get back to good old Canada although it's not too bad over here in the summer time. Coming in on the train to London it is a really picturesque scene with all its stately old fashioned buildings. I shall close for now as there is a couple of girls calling to me from across the road. Much love to all." Brian Rolston.[199]

"Dear Dean Clair: I hope that everything is running smoothly over there at Saint Mary's Parish. I want to thank you and the rest of the kind people who sent me that nice parcel . . . I guess you will be getting snow pretty soon over

195. Ibid., May 13, 1942, Murphy to Clair.
196. Ibid., June 21, 1942, Murphy to Clair.
197. Ibid., April 21, 1942, Miller to Clair.
198. Ibid., April 29, 1942, Rolston to Clair.
199. Ibid., June 21, 1942, Rolston to Clair.

there . . . this is a pretty fair country over here, but you cannot compare it in the least with good old Canada . . . Well I have to go on guard tonight so I guess I had better go and get cleaned up for the inspection. Give my love to the gang. Yours affectionately, Brian Rolston."[200]

Fred Arsenault did not get married at St. Mary's. Jack Wallace did return to Canada having lost one of his legs. In time two of his sons were at the front. One returned, the other did not. Both Murphy boys returned, married and raised families. Mike died in 2006. John, at the time of writing was still an usher at the noon mass on Sundays. Bill Firth, after the war followed his brother into the priesthood and became a highly respected pastor in the Toronto Diocese. He was buried at St. Mary's Cemetery in the winter of 2009.

Brian Rolston who wrote with such easy affection to his pastor never saw dear old Canada again, he was killed in Italy in 1944.

The war had, in many ways, allowed the parish to establish itself clearly within the mainstream of Barrie life. The assiduous detail to duty on behalf of the nation allowed St. Mary's to see itself clearly within the heart of civic life at the time. The success of the war and the defeat of nazism as well as the hostile forces in the Pacific theatre allowed the sense of success to be palatable. This was balanced however by the cost of the war to the parish as the following announcement attests powerfully,

"There will be a Requiem High Mass on Monday at 8:10 for the following who were killed overseas: Fl. Sgt. Leonard Hogan, Fl. Sgt. Gerard McDougall, Sgt. Air Gunner George Jones, Pl. of. Dalton McDougall, Gnr. Brian Rolston, Tpr. Ted. Wallace, Cprl. Dominic D'Ambrosio. This mass is requested by their parents."[201]

The toll in lives seems to have been concentrated in the later part of the war. In April of 1944 Sunday mass included prayers for the sick and Gerald Shaughnessy who was missing in action.[202] By July, the Confraternity of Christian Mothers had requested a mass for the repose of his soul.[203]

In 1943 and 1944 the deaths from the parish were unremitting: Dalton McDougall (January 1943) and his cousin Gerard McDougall who in June of 1943 was recommended to the parish as missing in action, was presumed

---

200. SMPA, Ibid., Rolston to Clair, October 25, 1942.
201. SMPA, Announcement Books, December 16, 1945.
202. SMPA, Announcement Books, April 23, 1944.
203. SMPA, Announcement Books, July 9, 1944.

dead in January of 1944, Leonard Hogan, (January 1944), George Jones, (July 1944), Dominic D'Ambrosio, (July 1944), Brian Rolston, (August 1944), Ernest Montferrand, (September 1944), Ted Wallace (April 1945) and finally merchant navy mariner, Joseph McVeigh in January of 1945.[204]

The war came to an end and the men came home. If those observers of public life felt that they were safe in saying that society had been changed because of the war, then surely it is no surprise that coming decades would be a time of extraordinary change in the life of the church.

204. Lovell, various pages. also Verteran's Affairs, Canada website.

The New Order Will Have to be Different

THE end of the Second World War found the parishioners of St. Mary's with two significant tasks. The first was the continuing call to charity in the wake of the war. In 1946 the parish was busy collecting clothing for the destitute of Europe.[1]

Secondly, in June 1946, it was announced that, "A bronze plaque listing the names of the men of the parish killed during the war has been presented by the youth of the parish."[2]

With the end of the war, Canada found itself in a world focused on change. War production had enhanced the power of technology and industry. Manufacturing became an essential part of the economy, providing employment to many of those no longer involved in the war effort. New products and a population of active consumers made the 1950's a time of prosperity.

Where once the Saturday movie and the frequent recommendations of Msgr. Clair to attend a particular movie of proven moral value was at the core of entertainment, over the next decade the family began to center its recreational time around the television.

In 1950, a television station was opened by Ralph Snelgrove. CKVR was a new link with the world, but also provided a forum for activities and talents which were close to home.

The use of the public media for the promotion of the Catholic faith was new. The local radio station CKBB offered the "Ave Maria" program beginning in 1949.[3] A few years later, CKVR began to broadcast Bishop Fulton Sheen's, "A Life Worth Living." The parishioners were encouraged to show their appreciation by extending their thanks to the local stations.[4]

The idea of community which had not been considered as central to the core of parish life before the war was taking on a new significance. This in part reflects the diminishment of movements and sodalities.

In the post war era, Catholicism took on a new confidence, for on the

1. SMPA, Announcement Books, May and June 1946.
2. Ibid., June 23, 1946.
3. Ibid., October 16, 1949.
4. Ibid., October 23, 1955.

battlefields and behind the lines there was no questioning the patriotism of Catholics. In 1952, a series was initiated in the parish to inform non-Catholics what Catholics believed. Leaflets were distributed to the public. A particular invitation was directed to those who were keeping company with a Catholic to find out what they believe. It was also made clear that attendance would not be presumed as a desire to convert, one was more than welcome to attend if all they wish to do is criticize.[5]

In the same year the Christian Mothers put 20 Christmas scenes in the front windows of the stores in the business district of Barrie.[6]

In the spring of 1953, it was announced that a parish bulletin would be published weekly.[7] This was hardly the beginning of this endeavour. Attempts were made throughout the 1940's to provide bulletins.[8] The bulletin, for a period in the later forties, was the responsibility of the CYO.[9]

In 1953, a Social Club was formed that offered evenings with the view to allowing parishioners to be better acquainted. A particular interest was outreach to the air force personnel at the radar station at Edgar. The invitation in March 1953 promised an evening of "Catholic entertainment," of which its main feature would be dancing."[10]

The war had called all citizens to act and one of the fruits of the war was a greater sense of inclusivity in the period after the war. The following report of the recital by the St. Mary's School Choir, perhaps more than most, reflects that desire to not only exhibit loyalty, but to express shared values. "Several two part songs were beautifully rendered by the St. Mary's School Choir. During the singing of God Bless our Queen the girls stepped aside in a "V" formation, revealing a picture of Her Majesty occupying a position of honor at center stage."[11]

This event of course followed the death King George the VI in February 1952. On the day of his funeral, school was cancelled and the parish cel-

5. SMPA, "*The Catholic Church, What she Teaches*," a leaflet, 1952.

6. SMPA, Year Book, 1953, p. 49.

7. SMPA, Announcement Books, March 29, 1953.

8. The earliest one in the parish archives is June 13, 1942.

9. SMPA, Bulletin Nov 25 1945, Human nature and behaviour changes little as this bulletin attests. The Question box inquired: "Is it all right to move over when someone tries to get into the pew that you are occupying or must you have them climb over you? Answer: It's O. K. to move over so try it sometime." The same bulletin reminded Christian Doctrine students that they must bring pencils to class.

10. SMPA, Announcement Books, March 1, 1953.

11. SMPA, Year Book 1953, p. 37.

ebrated mass for the welfare of the Royal Family. In the annals of the Sisters of St. Joseph it is noted that at the end of mass, "God Save the Queen" was sung. They further noted that the church was full and most received communion.[12]

It is notable that not only was the day of the king's funeral a day off in 1952, it was also the last year that St. Patrick's Day was a holiday for the separate schools.[13]

The parish strove to integrate itself into public efforts as is reflected in a letter from Robert Saunders, the chairman of the hydro commission, in 1948, to remind parishioners to turn off lights when they were not needed.[14] Across the diocese the faithful were reminded to patronize the Poppy Fund Tag Day in 1948.[15] Parishioners were also encouraged to enrol in the Blue Cross hospitalization plan from the pulpit in 1948.[16]

Social programs became an important part of government policy. In 1946, the struggle to eradicate tuberculosis lead to the creation of community clinics. Churches were enlisted to reinforce the shared responsibility for this cause. "Every citizen is earnestly asked to co-operate in the great effort to stamp out tuberculosis by making an appointment and coming to the clinic. The x-ray takes only a moment to complete and the results will be treated as confidential."[17]

St. Mary's Parish into the 1950's was addressing needs which were particular to the families at Camp Borden. This included the Catholic Women's League seeking out rooms in town for families from the camp.[18]

The Credit Union was in full swing by 1954, providing an alternative source of credit and for investment by parishioners.[19] Credit Union loans were by their nature not large sums. Rather, they tended to be amounts that allowed households to improve on their furniture or appliances or to tide them over with car repairs. By 1957 the credit union had established offices in the parish hall.[20]

---

12. Sisters of St Joseph of Toronto Archives, *Annals of Barrie*, February 15, 1952.
13. Ibid., March 17, 1953.
14. SMPA, Announcement Books, September 26, 1948.
15. Ibid., October 31, 1948.
16. Ibid., November 7, 1948.
17. Ibid., September 16, 1946.
18. Ibid., January 14, 1951.
19. Ibid., May 23, 1954.
20. Ibid., October 15, 1957.

New Canadians.

The Annals of the Sisters of St. Joseph in Barrie, note that, Camp Borden and emigration from Europe have given Sr. Mary Richard a good sprinkling of non-English speaking pupils.[21]

The first great wave of European immigration to impact on Barrie in the twentieth century was from Italy. The Italians who settled in Barrie were strongly connected to the railroad, though others made their way into produce marketing. To a large extent families with a railroad connection settled in Allandale. This immigration occurred before and after the First World War.

In spite of the fact that a great Italian immigration to the region had occurred at the beginning of the twentieth century, there was sufficient new immigration for the bulletin to include the following urgent message in June 1959, "Avviso! Attenzione! Confessioni in Italiano. Avvertiamo gli Italiani che possono fare la confessioni e lingua Italiana, presso il Padre Michele Perna, l'orario delle confessioni e 'Mercoledi' prossimo dalle ore 7:30 p.m. alle 8:30 di sera."[22]

With the end of the war, European immigration became a huge force for change socially, particularly in the urban centers but in the rural heartland a large immigration of Dutch farmers changed the population makeup of the townships around Barrie. Immigration from many European countries touched the lives of Catholic parishes recognizing the need to include and to accommodate this new population of parishiners with particular needs.

An area of particular concern in ministry was to provide opportunities for confession. Fr. Lannoye, a Dutch imnmigre himself, was enlisted to minister to the Dutch community and to teach them the rudiments of going to confession in English.[23] This effort for ministry to the Dutch also showed itself in the creation of pilgrimages to the Martyrs' Shrine for the Dutch community.[24]

This early work among the Dutch immigrants is curious in light of the fact that of all national groups who took up residence in Canada, the Dutch, more than any other sought to integrate into the life of their host country. Since the Dutch, either Catholic or Reformed, maintained strong ties to religion, the creation of national clubs was less significant and the preparedness to learn English if it had not already been acquired before became universal.

The other moments of ethnic ministry reflected international realities.

---

22. SMPA, Parish Bulletin, June 7, 1959.
23. Ibid., October 4, 1953, March 27, 1955.
24. Ibid., September 9, 1956.

In December 1956, ministry to Hungarian immigrants was highlighted. The Catholic Women's League had taken on responsibility for finding accommodation for refugees in the town for which they hoped the government would provide a subsidy.[25]

In December 1968, in the months following the "Prague Spring" the parish had accessed Fr. Kadlec to celebrate mass and hear confessions of the Czech and Slovak people. The Knights of Columbus provided a reception following the liturgy at their hall.[26]

Fighting Materialism and Communism.

In 1950, John Woods of St. Joseph High School won the Archdiocesan Rosary Essay Contest with his short story on the power of the rosary over communism. The story was about a man incarcerated by communists who silently says his rosary. As the story unfolds a guard enters the cell. "All at once he spied my rosary, falling to his knees he asked in short sobs if I were a Catholic. I said, yes Comrade. He choked, I too am a Catholic. My leader came with soldiers to our home on the outskirts of Prague and butchered my parents while we were saying the family rosary." The gist of the story of course is that the guard rediscovers his faith in the devotion.[27]

On the more global scale we find in the post war era the world divided by the iron curtain. The fear of communism looms large in the experience of many of the immigrants. The totalitarianism implied by communism results in the victimization of the Christian church in Eastern Europe and Russia. At Barrie, prayers were offered for the oppressed church around the world. This January 1949 announcement encapsulates the church's view, "Sunday, January 30 will be set aside as a day of prayer for all captives of persecution especially for Cardinal Mindszenty and Archbishop Stepinec. There will be a holy hour in all churches on that day. All the faithful are urged to receive Holy Communion, assist at devotions and to combine prayer and almsgiving in invoking divine assistance for the sufferers, a change of mind and heart in the persecutors and an amelioration of the conditions which constitute a threat to peace and the security of church and state in so many lands."[28]

The rise of communism was the impetus for encouraging of a second devotional revolution. Centred in Marian spirituality, the church sought to create a

---

25. Ibid., December 23, 1956.
26. Ibid., December 8, 1968.
27. SMPA, Year Book, 1950.
28. SMPA, Announcement Books, January 23, 1949.

consistent response to the threat of communism. The devotion to Our Lady of Fatima arose after the Second World War to a status that was not experienced before. In 1945, the practice of the first Saturday being dedicated to Our Lady of Fatima developed. The core of the devotion is prayer for the conversion of Russia and all sinners."[29]

There was a strongly held belief that godless communism was the heart and soul of so much which was leading to the rapid secularization of society. As the Second World War was winding down in Europe and the iron curtain was being drawn between east and west the anxiety about communism was being felt at home as well. The Holy Name Society gathered at St. Catherine's in July of 1945 to participate in a forum on the question, "Should all Strikes be Illegal?"[30]

In 1949, following a holy hour, the Knights of Columbus were hosting 'a smoker' at which Fr. Lawlor would deliver an address on communism.[31] The Parent Teacher Association in 1951 had a presentation on Education in Estonia in peace time and under the communists.[32]

It was noted in the report of the CWL in 1953 that sixty-four members of the league were registered for emergency civil defense.[33]

It was the era of the cold war, of fears of invasion and of practiced air raid drills.

The age of increasing secularization was in part responded to through a new and significant emphasis on the rosary. This was a pastoral response to materialism which in its most insidious form is understood as communism but it is also the call for a strong sense of community among Catholics and an emphasis on the Catholic family. The rally cry of the age coined by Fr. Patrick Peyton was, "The family that prays together, stays together."

This strong emphasis was found in the call to the Rosary Crusade Rally at the Martyrs' Shrine in May of 1950. In addition to buses the parishioners are informed, "It is expected that a cavalcade of motor cars will form, with parishioners joining in along the route. All who have cars should join the cavalcade."

The emphasis of the rosary is seen in this call to the rally, "My dear people, you have a very special appointment with the Mother of God on May 24 at 2:45 at the Martyrs' Shrine, at the family prayer rally to be held then. Mary

---

29. Ibid., August 19, 1945.
30. Ibid., July 15, 1945.
31. Ibid., January 30, 1949.
32. Ibid., April 22, 1951.
33. SMPA, Year Book, 1953, p. 39.

has her great chance to win you and your family and all your neighbours back to the practice of family prayer. Not only do I beg you to attend yourself with your whole family, bringing even children in arms, but in the name of Our Lady of the Rosary I beg you to invite and bring all other families that you can influence, Catholic and non-Catholic. The rally will begin on time and will not exceed one and one quarter hour."[34]

In addition to rallies, pledges were solicited of the parishioner, through the work of the Holy Name Society. This included a door to door canvas of the parish to seek the pledge of parishioners to say the rosary. "The pledges are to be signed by all members of the family who can write or print their names. Country people, or others who are roomers or any family who may be at one of the earlier masses may sign in the vestibule after mass today."[35]

The pledge became an ongoing feature of Catholicism, with an annual renewal of the pledge at the end of mass. All the faithful would stand as a body and repeat after the priest, "I solemnly renew my pledge to say the daily family rosary, that my heavenly mother may guard and protect my home."[36]

The emphasis on the rosary found its way into the concerns about international peace and became the essential prayer for peace during the time of the Cold War. The parish joined the universal church in this campaign in the fall of 1959 as this announcement proclaimed, "On Tuesday of this week, the eve of the Feast of the Holy Rosary there will be a continuous recitation of the Rosary in the church beginning after 7:30 a.m. mass and concluding with Benediction in the evening. Our Holy Father, John the XXIII, has asked the whole church to say the Rosary during October for peace and concord among nations. We ask all who can to come to the church Tuesday for a period of 20 minutes. This will be a wonderful day of prayer."[37]

An Evolving Liturgy.

Creating some standards at baptism seem to have been a concern in the 1950's. The 1953 Parish Year Book reminds parishioners that there are baptisms each Sunday at 2:00 p.m. and there must be two Catholic Sponsors and at least one of the parents present.[38]

34. SMPA, Announcement Books, May 14, 1950.
35. Ibid., May 28, 1950.
36. Ibid., October 5, 1952.
37. Ibid., October 4, 1959.
38. SMPA, St. Mary's Annual Year Book, 1953, "Calendar."

The 1959 bulletin announcement states, "The canon law of the church says that infants must be baptized 'as soon as possible' after birth, usually considered to be within two weeks. It is a grave sin to delay baptism for a long time, since there is a danger that the infant could die without being baptized. The church also requires that the child should be given a saint's name, not some fashionable pagan name."[39]

By 1948 First Communion had arrived at Sunday mass. Parents were reminded they should attend with their children.[40]

The church found itself in a rapidly evolving culture. The evolving experience of the church was perhaps most concretely seen in the evolution of the liturgy. What had seemed permanent, had in fact always evolved, and was evolving in surprising ways.

The fast before communion had been for many generations from midnight till the time of mass. Mass was limited to morning celebrations. In March of 1956, the parishioners are informed that the fast is now to be three hours before communion, that water is always permissible and non alcoholic liquids up to an hour before receiving.[41] In December of 1964 the faithful were informed the pre communion fast would now to be one hour.[42]

Rules which at one time were absolutely written in stone, such as all masses were before noon hour was being considered as open for discussion. In 1956 Msgr. Clair contacted Fr. Fulton, the chancellor of the diocese, seeking permission, which not many years before would not have been entertained. "The Knights of Columbus have been accustomed to holding their annual ceremony for the deceased each year on November 4. They have asked me to find out if permission could be granted for an evening mass and communion on that day. Do you think that the occasion is sufficient reason? If so, it would not be too much of an inconvenience for us. Permission would also be needed to hold mass in the auditorium."[43]

Within six months the practice of evening mass became normative.[44]

A shift was also coming in the role of the laity at mass, from those who hear

---

39. SMPA, St. Mary's Announcement Books, May 16, 1948.

40. SMPA, Bulletin, April 26, 1959.

41. Ibid., March 18, 1956. In the March 31, 1946 bulletin the question the instruction corner was whether it was permissible to smoke before receiving communion. The answer was yes. Was it permissible to brush your teeth? The answer was yes as long as you did not swallow anything.

42. Ibid., December 6, 1964.

43. ARCAT, St. Mary's Files, Clair to Fulton, June 21, 1956.

44. Sisters of St. Joseph Toronto Archives, Annals for Barrie, March 1, 1957.

mass to those who participate. In the spring of 1959 the people of St. Mary's were informed that there would be a dialogue mass according to the decree from Rome on the following Friday. The goal of the initiative was to invite the faithful to join in the responses which to this point had been predominantly the task of the altar servers.[45]

In 1962, the Second Vatican Council began a process of reflection on the place of the church in the modern world. In the process of exploration, liturgical life came under particular scrutiny, which resulted in profound changes in the way that mass was celebrated. For some, these changes were a profound break with past.

In January of 1963, the parishioners were invited to an event called the Mass in Slow Motion, an instructional effort to inform people about the meaning of the liturgical actions and to encourage reasonable participation in mass.[46]

Four years later the bulletin focused on congregational singing, especially at the high mass. The congregants who can sing are encouraged to attend and assist in supporting those who are less able. Practices had been offered during the previous year.[47]

The role of collectors gave way to the formation of an usher's club in 1947. The function of the ushers as their name implies was chiefly to make sure people were seated at mass. They were to dissuade people from standing at the back of the church.[48]

When the new liturgy was introduced in Barrie in February of 1965 men were invited to take on the role of lectors and commentators.[49] The gist of the appeal was that this was a moment that called for dedicated men. A radio announcer was engaged to assist with the training. Commentators essentially in the time after the change in liturgy invited people to follow along in English and encouraged participation.[50] The events which were unfolding were not isolated but part of an ongoing reflection on the life of the church.

The bulletin in July of 1965 included words ascribed to Pope Paul VI in regards the new liturgy, "First, it is inevitable that there should be at the outset

---

45. SMPA, Announcement Books, April 5, 1959.

46. SMPA, Bulletin, January 27, 1963.

47. Ibid., November 17, 1963. It is interesting that the same notice reminds people that they should be in their pews about three minutes before the time the mass is to begin so they may sing the processional hymn. The hymn is not seen as part of the mass which begins with the prayers at the time scheduled for mass.

48. Ibid., August 17, 1947.

49. Ibid., February & March 1965.

50. Ibid., March 14, 1965.

some confusions and some trouble. It is in the nature of a practical as well as of a spiritual reform of set religious habits, piously observed, to cause some agitation, not always pleasant to everyone . . . it should not be believed that after a while we shall again become quiet and devoted or lazy as of old. No; the new order will have to be different and will have to prevent and shake the passivity of the faithful who are present at Holy Mass. Before, it was enough to attend; now it is necessary to participate. Before, presence was enough; now attention and action are necessary, before, some could doze or perhaps even chat; now they must listen and pray."[51]

By 1967 when the Christian Family Movement invited the parishioners to a folk mass, it was to be celebrated in the hall, rather than the church, and they felt it necessary to qualify what it was they hoped to achieve. "They would like to invite all who are interested to join this celebration. This is not a membership gimmick. The C. F. M. has not been part of such a mass before and they believe that a number of parishioners would be very much interested in experiencing this form of participation ."[52]

The sixties with its many impulses to reform and redefinition often seemed to be striving to respond to an anxiety of deterioration in the life of the church. In 1967, it was announced that the Sanctuary Society Investiture Ceremony would take place. For many years before and after this restless time, the Sanctuary Society was known as the altar servers.[53]

The place of children at mass had over the years provided its challenges. In previous decades children had been restricted to certain masses which were called nursery masses. The building of the parish hall at St. Joseph's High School in the early fifties provided a venue in which children could be babysat during mass.[54]

The Sisters of St. Joseph in 1958 are pleased that the poor weather has been at bay for First Communion Sunday. The children, they note, sat with their parents for First Communion.[55]

The role of Eucharist was being constantly explored and redefined in the post war era. The Paulist Fathers were invited to Barrie to conduct a pulpit dialogue in the church in 1953.[56]

---

51. Ibid., July 4, 1965.
52. Ibid., November 5, 1967.
53. Ibid., February 26, 1967.
54. Ibid., October 4, 1951.
55. Sisters of St. Joseph Toronto Archives, Annals of Barrie, May 25, 1958.
56. SMPA, Bulletin, October 11, 1953.

The New Order Will Have to be Different

The perception of the liturgy was changing. The members of the various societies of the parish were reminded that when having a Communion Sunday, "that in order to gain indulgences of your society, it is necessary that all members join the group, sit together in church and receive communion together. You cannot gain the spiritual benefits of your society if you occupy seats elsewhere in church."[57]

The problem was deeper than just enforcing discipline on the Holy Name Society or the Catholic Women's League. It reflected an individual independence that was perhaps a source of anxiety if it was not addressed. It was the beginning of the end for many of the parish organizations which were lost in the shuffle of renewal.

The understanding of roles was changing as well. A 1948 announcement reflects the princely aspect of a bishop's role. "The Sacrament of Confirmation will be administered this afternoon at 3:30 by His Eminence James Cardinal McGuigan. The church will be about three quarters filled with those to be confirmed and their sponsors. (More than 200 in all). If you are not able to get in, we advise you to wait and come back because the Cardinal wishes to meet everyone. After Benediction he will be at the sanctuary gates. We ask you to go up two by two. When you take his hand genuflect and kiss his ring. Return by the side aisles."[58]

One was to see in the years ahead a constantly evolving change in this area of church life. Marriages which were once witnessed in the rectory if one of the parties was Protestant were now celebrated in the church. Catholics no longer sought the permission of their pastor to attend the weddings or funerals of a Protestant friend or neighbour.

The bulletin in the winter of 1969 reiterated the regulations for marriage which in light of later practice seem extraordinary. If the marriage was interfaith, three months' notice was to be given, and if both were Catholic they should give at least six weeks notice. It was emphasized that no wedding would be celebrated at St. Mary's after noon hour.[59]

In 1960, optional marriage instruction classes were offered.[60] By 1967, a ten-week program was being undertaken at St. John Vianney Parish. The cost for the ten weeks was four dollars.[61]

---

57. Ibid., November 16, 1958.
58. SMPA, Announcement Books, May 16, 1948.
59. SMPA, Bulletin, February 9, 1969.
60. Ibid., October 7, 1960.
61. Ibid., April 9, 1967.

Spiritual Formation.

The post war era saw signs of the faithful taking a new direction in their own spiritual lives as well. The bulletin in June of 1949 reminded the parishioners, "Sometimes, it is advisable for people to make a retreat and break the tentacles of the world. Men are directed to Mary Lake, and women to the Catholic Women's Retreat Association."[62]

This was an interesting shift in spirituality. To this point in St. Mary's there would have been many who stepped out of their daily routine, but the removal from the every day would have been to pilgrimage. The site of pilgrimage for almost all people in the Barrie area would have been the Martyrs' Shrine. The other spiritual diversions would have happened in the parish through missions and forty hour devotions.

By the winter of 1965, the Catholic Women's League was calling on its members to attend spiritual workshops which were to provide them with a better understanding of lay spirituality. "The lay apostle should carry the banner of Christ, and this she will do if she is fortified and strengthened spiritually."[63]

Another change that reflected deeply on Catholic identity was announced in the parish bulletin on October 23, 1966, "It is to be noted that the law of abstinence from meat has been done away with by the Church. Nevertheless, we are warned of the importance of doing penance. It is probable that more merit is gained by voluntary abstinence from meat or other acts of penance, than could be gained by penance performed in obedience to law. Fridays are still days of voluntary penances in honor of Our Lord's death on Good Friday."[64]

The bulletin was a forum a few weeks later when the issue of discontinuance of Friday abstinence was discussed again reminding the faithful that the change was about calling all to a deeper sense of personal penance rather than one that was imposed.[65]

The optimism of the sixties flowed over into ideas related to family life. The Legion of Mary offered to provide Advent Wreaths for homes in 1961 at a cost of 15 cents.[66] The rigour of the family rosary was giving way and we find the following suggestion for parish families getting ready for Christmas, "Plan a family ceremony for blessing the tree on Christmas Day. Work it out so that

62. Ibid., June 26, 1949.
63. Ibid., January 31, 1965.
64. Ibid., October 23, 1966.
65. Ibid., November 13, 1966.
66. Ibid., December 3, 1961.

everyone takes part. Psalm 95, the Magnificat, The Gospel of Luke, 2:6-20, and a hymn or two are possible elements in such a ceremony. The father of the family might compose a suitable prayer."[67]

Building in the Mid Century.

In the spring of 1950, plans to build a parish hall began to come together. A call went out on April 9 of that year for all interested parties to attend a meeting at the high school the following Tuesday. By May 14, it was announced that, "St. Joseph's Auditorium Building Fund to date amounts to more than $2,000. A great deal more is required to meet our objective in order that we may start to build. This is the last week of the campaign. There is a box at the back of the church where donations may be placed."

By July the enthusiasm had increased, "As you will see by the thermometer on the bulletin board the auditorium fund is rising like the temperature out doors. The committee is still receiving donations. Every dollar collected now will decrease our debt. Place your offering in the box in the church vestibule after mass. Tenders for the building will be arranged this week and the work will begin at once."[68]

The undertaking met with great success. By September 10 it was announced to the parish that the cornerstone will be laid the following Thursday. The parishioners were reminded that if they could not attend the ceremonies, they should listen to the news broadcast on CKBB at 7:30 p.m.[69] The formal opening of the hall took place on March 18, 1951 in the presence of Cardinal McGuigan.[70]

The hall which was constructed on the west side of Mulcaster, where at the time of writing it still stands, was attached to St. Joseph's High School. It fulfilled a dual purpose of providing additional space for the school as well as a gathering place for the parish. The lower floor included a gymnasium and the upper floor, a hall. On the most practical of levels it provided washrooms for those who were attending church.[71]

In 1952, the Knights of Columbus undertook to clear more ground for the cemetery to expand beyond the eight acres that were already being used.

By 1953, there was a recognition that the rates paid for plots in the cem-

67. Ibid., December 18, 1966.
68. Ibid., July 9, 1950.
69. Ibid., September 10, 1950.
70. Ibid., March 18, 1951.
71. SMPA, Year Book, 1953, p.9.

etery were too low and income was insufficient. A ten grave plot was increased to $80.00 with an additional $100.00 requested for perpetual care. Those who opted not to have perpetual care were asked to pay two dollars a year and were not permitted to put grave markers on the graves.

The most significant improvement to the cemetery in the period after the war was the building of a vault at the cemetery under the initiative of the Knights of Columbus which was undertaken in the spring and summer of 1954.[72]

In 1953, the yearbook of St. Mary's announced that Dean Clair had purchased ten lots south of Shear Park. The lots were bounded by Baldwin and Innisfil Street. Sixty percent of the land was in town limits and 40 percent was in Innisfil Township.[73] This was to be the site of St. John Vianney Parish which opened in 1957 with Fr. Peter Rosettis as pastor.

He began with two masses in the new parish, one at Allandale and one at Bell Ewart.

Parish Life.

The post war era was a time of changing dynamics of parish life. In 1946, the Knights of Columbus sponsored a "Get Acquainted Night" so all could become acquainted with old and new members of the parish.[74]

The Knights with their strong commitment to the larger community initiated a number of fundraising endeavours, including furnishing a room at the hospital in 1961. In 1965, the Knights were active in supporting a low rental housing effort on the part of the city.[75]

From 1912 until 1950, the Knights met at the Dunlop Street location. Throughout the 1950's they used the new parish hall on Mulcaster Street. In 1961, the Knights bought their hall at the top of Berczy Street.

In 1947, the Catholic Women's League hosted the annual convention of the C. W. L. for the Archdiocese of Toronto at Barrie. The parish announcements of the day are emphatic in noting that men are welcome at the banquet and the league members should invite their husbands.[76]

In 1946, the Holy Name Society had initiated the task of building a rink in the basement of St. Joseph's High School. It was to be transported to the spot

72. SMPA, Bulletin, December 18, 1966.
73. SMPA, Year Book 1953, p. 37.
74. SMPA, Announcement Book, February 2, 1946.
75. SMPA, *A Century of Service.*
76. SMPA, Announcement Book, September 21, 1947.

at the elementary school where it was to be assembled. Levelling the ground was seen as a particular problem in making the rink.[77]

Sports were a natural segue into matters of faith as a February 1, 1953 undertaking indicates, "Next Sunday after the 9:30 mass, the Holy Name Society will sponsor a communion breakfast for the men and boys of the parish in St. Joseph's Auditorium. The guest speaker at the breakfast will be Rev. Hugh Mallon, CSB of St. Michael's Junior "A" Memorial Cup hockey champions. His guest will be Mr. Les Costello, former hockey star of the same team and later with the Toronto Maples Leafs and at present studying for the priesthood in St. Augustine's Seminary. Also in attendance as guests will be the five Catholic hockey players from the Barrie Flyers Club. For this occasion we expect as many men and boys as possible to attend. The committee in charge has gone all out in preparing for a large gathering of men and boys. Do not disappoint them.[78]

The provision of recreational facilities, though not a first priority of the parish once again appeared to come and go. In June 1952, the executive of the Tennis Club announced that the newly renovated tennis courts at the rear of the church were being officially opened. Fees for a year membership was three dollars.[79]

In the spring of 1963, a parish library was formed and actively encouraged the community to be informed of their Catholic faith through reading.[80] The library sought to have a diverse number of titles, some strictly devotional while others were recommended because they were controversial.[81]

The Holy Name Society made tremendous efforts to develop a hockey program and organize competitions with other Catholic parishes. The youth of the parish played baseball against other churches, including Emmanuel Baptist and First Baptist in the late fifties.[82] In 1965, the Knights of Columbus took on the organization of touch football for the Catholic youth of the city.[83]

It is unclear when the Catholic Family Movement was formed but it was active and involved in many projects throughout the 1960's. Formed to be a support system for Catholic parents, it found itself involved in a number of

---

77. Ibid., November and ff, 1946.

78. Ibid., February, 1, 1953. Fr. Les Costello served The Diocese of Timmins until his death in 2002.

79. Ibid., June 29, 1952.

80. SMPA, Bulletin, April 18, 1965.

81. Ibid., July 1965.

82. Ibid.,June 7, 1959.

83. Ibid., September 5, 1965.

Third World endeavours. They also welcomed new families into the parish.

The Holy Name Society which had in many ways been the dominant men's organization in the parish created endless mandates for themselves which were only loosely connected. They were involved in organizing hockey, showing movies on Sundays, as well as overseeing a number of liturgical responsibilities.

January 1967, saw an endeavour on the part of the Holy Name Society to renew its program. The announcement of the time stated, "The Holy Name Society is undergoing a complete renewal program. Substantial changes have taken place in the overall structure of the Society which will enable men of the parish to play more important roles, not only within the church, but within the community as well . . . This is an excellent opportunity for young men of the parish to receive training in self development and leadership ability."[84] By March of that year they were announcing that the Holy Name Society would be called the St. Mary's Laymen's Association.

The CYO which existed in the parish though, like in so many places, confronting the great challenge of engaging youth in participation seems to have slipped from the scene sometime in the mid-sixties to be replaced at St. Mary's by the St. Dominic Savio Club. This organization was particularly directed at young adults, eighteen to twenty-five.[85] Within the year this seems to have been superceded by the Youth Corps.[86]

Education.

The twin effects of a vibrant economy and the burgeoning population created by the baby boom saw education become an issue constantly in the forefront of public discussion. In Barrie, the growing population made education a pressing issue.

The initiatives for development in education found their impetus in the midst of war. Cardinal McGuigan began pastoral visits to the parishes of the diocese to promote Catholic education in 1943.

The parishioners of Barrie were told of his plan to visit in early May. It was related to the people that, "The Archbishop is very anxious to address a series of meetings throughout the archdiocese to give a final impetus to the campaign for establishment of a fund to erect high schools and recreational centres

84. Ibid., January 29, 1967.
85. Ibid., October 16, 1966.
86. Ibid., September 24, 1967.

throughout the archdiocese. His Grace will address a deanery meeting in the K. of C. Hall, Barrie on Wednesday, May 5 at 8 p.m. A general invitation is extended to both men and women, boys and girls of high school age to attend this meeting."[87]

The endeavour in relation to St. Mary's was not the success that Dean Clair would have hoped as his pulpit announcement indicated, "The Archbishop came to Barrie on the evening of May 5, 1943, to deliver a talk on education. About thirty members of the Barrie parish thought it worth their while to attend. Yet priests and people came here from all parishes in the deanery. We can partly make up for the rebuff by sending in a large Spiritual Bouquet for his Grace's 25th anniversary. To date only 30 have been handed in. We wonder if it is the same 30. Everyone in the parish can offer up communions, visits, beads and ejaculations.[88]

The goal was to create a financial environment which would extend the support of publicly funded Catholic schools. The challenge to the provincial government was crucial but also reminders to the faithful about their responsibilities in supporting Catholic education and in making sure that the support through taxation was received. The pastor reminded the people of the parish in September of 1944 that, "It is the obligation of everyone who lives in two self-contained rooms to report their address, even if not called on, so taxes may be allocated to separate schools."[89]

Another tact which developed as the Second World War drew to a close was the formation of the Parent Teacher Association for St. Mary's School. The purpose of the organization was for the advancement of the material needs of the school.[90] It was noted they were striving to secure a piano, in good condition, for the grade seven and eight classes as well as a couch and pair of blankets and an electric hot plate for the nurse's room at the school.[91]

At the end of the war we find that two new initiatives are being introduced in Catholic education in Barrie. In the same year both kindergarten and secondary education were introduced. Announcements in August 1946, show the extent of those new initiatives. "Schools open September 3. Parents who have children four or five years of age who wish them to attend kindergarten should notify the sister as soon as possible. Quite a number have also signed up for

87. SMPA, Announcement Books, April 25, 1943.
88. Ibid., May 16, 1943.
89. Ibid., September 17, 1944.
90. Ibid., Feb 13, 1944.
91. Ibid., October 8, 1944.

grade nine, but there is room for a few more. It is our intention to teach household science to the girls and manual training or shop work to the boys."[92]

Both the high school and kindergarten were housed in the recently vacated convent. The building constructed in 1882 was proving to be too large for the needs of the sisters and they purchased the residence at the corner of Berczy and Eugenia. That September, St. Mary's School opened with 140 students, St. Joseph's with twelve and the kindergarten with 12.[93]

Quick renovations were done over the summer to create a classroom for the incoming grade nines. It appears that through these first years each grade had a dedicated classroom, as well as a shop for manual training created by Dean Clair in the basement.

The new parish hall was built as an addition to the high school in 1950 providing better space for physical education. Four classrooms were added to the school in 1958.

The initiation of kindergarten and high school both in the same year reflected a tremendous confidence in the community's ability to create effective institutions.

This confidence was not misplaced as the announcement of May 18, 1947 shows. "Kindergarten is a great success. Parents are pleased. The numbers are small, since most are going into primary in St. Mary's School in September. All parents who may send children to kindergarten in September should make registration at once of those who are four or five years old . . . In making registration please state whether you are able to pay anything for tuition."[94]

The growth of high school was also noted at the same time. "There will be no fees next September. Parents have the same obligation to send children to nine and ten as they had to the other grades. Since costs must be met with taxation, you will be given a chance to make a donation in place of taxation. Envelopes will be given out every month to those who would like to contribute any amount however small."[95]

These new endeavours placed a demand on the parish. "Some time ago we placed envelopes in the church vestibule marked, "For education in place of taxation." Evidently most people did not take these very seriously. We have placed them in the pews today. We hope that every wage earner will at least give something to this collection. It is for the promotion of education in this parish and to keep our own schools going. Last Sunday we announced the

92. Ibid., Aug. 26, 1946.
93. Sisters of St. Joseph Toronto Archives, Annals of Barrie, September 3, 1946.
94. SMPA, Announcement Books, May 18, 1947.
95. Ibid.

collection for St. John's Industrial School and St. Mary's Training School. The parish donated $125.00 to help erring boys and girls. Surely we can get that much at least to help the good boys and girls of our own parish get a Catholic Education."[96]

The financial burden on the parents was however quickly alleviated when the school board agreed to take over the expenses related to both kindergarten and high school in August 1947.[97]

By 1949, the numbers of students were becoming an issue, first at the secondary school where students from outside the parish were turned away.[98] The high school had not only the kindergarten students but the overflow from the elementary schools as well.[99]

The school built in 1894 was quickly becoming redundant, because of the burgeoning population and the changing understanding of education. The initial course of action was to consider putting an addition on the old school, but this was shelved rather promptly in favour of a new school.[100]

In the fall of 1951, the new St. Mary's School opened. It was located behind the old school which had faced onto McDonald Street.[101] The old school continued to be used for another fifteen years, finally being torn down in 1966 to make way for the new ten room addition on St. Mary's School.[102]

By 1952 there were 72 students[103] in the high school. An event to raise funds also assured the community that St. Joseph's High School was on the cutting edge of athletic pursuits as the announcement suggested. "On Saturday, February 9, at 8:30 p. m. St. Joseph's High School is presenting, "High School Follies," the proceeds of which will be used for the purchase of sports equipment for the auditorium. There will be a demonstration of badminton and volleyball, by the pupils of the school. This will be followed by round and square dancing and refreshments for all. Also, there will be bridge and euchre in the committee room of the auditorium for all who may be interested. Will some people please bring playing cards? Admission is 50 cents."[104]

Much of what needed to be done was carried out by volunteer labour, in-

---

96. Ibid., June 25, 1947.
97. Ibid., August 3, 1947.
98. Ibid., September. 4, 1949.
99. Sisters of St. Joseph Toronto Archives, *Barrie Annals*. 1949.
100. Ibid., April 16, 1950.
101. Ibid., September 30, 1951.
102. Ibid., Bulletin, February 20, 1966.
103. Sisters of St. Joseph Toronto Archives, September 4, 1952.
104. SMPA, Announcement Books, February. 3, 1952.
105. Ibid., August 25, 1952.

cluding building sidewalks for the high school in 1952.[105]

Increased population was an ever growing problem within the city and district. On May 8, 1955, a letter was included with the bulletin, asking people in and near Allandale to send in the included form which was seeking to ascertain the need for a school in Allandale.[106] It would be more than two years until this initiative bore concrete results.

The growth in the schools was not strictly the result of population growth in the town but reflected an active pursuit of students. The announcements for June 10, 1956, included what can be only understood as a singularly uncompromising message, "Registrations for St. Mary's School are on Wednesday afternoon from 1:30 to 4:00. Only 24 pupils were registered on the previous date. In the year 1950 more than 100 babies were baptized and should be school age now. Parents have an obligation of sending children to Catholic schools. This is an obligation under pain of mortal sin.[107]"

The parish announced January 27, 1957, "Registration for the new separate school in Allandale was announced in last week's bulletin. Several families have already registered their children. It is important that the township residents within three miles, as the crow flies, register immediately.[108]

By the end of August, clear directions were being given to families on the matter of school attendance, "Schools open next week, September 3. The following will attend St. Mary's School: All pupils in Barrie north of John Street and those from Vespra and Oro Townships. The following will attend St. John's School: All pupils in Barrie on and to the south of John Street and those attending from Innisfil and Essa Township. Should some pupils in Barrie on the north side of John Street wish to attend St. John's School it may be arranged. It is also possible that some in Vespra Township may find it more convenient to attend St. John's School since part of Vespra is nearer the school site. St. Mary's School is expected to be at capacity and can only accept pupils from its designated area."[109]

By 1958 another announcement was being made regarding education in St. Mary's Parish. "The board trustees of the Roman Catholic Separate Schools have announced that a new grade school will be built on the north side of Steele Street, near Nelson Street to relieve the serious over crowding of our two parish schools. Construction will be started as soon as possible, and it is

106. Ibid., May 8, 1955.
107. Ibid., June 10, 1956.
108. Ibid., January. 27, 1957.
109. Ibid., August 25, 1957.

anticipated that the building will be ready for classes by October. Registration held last week, for the September term showed a considerable increase over the previous years. As the two schools of the parish were much too crowded, this additional increase made it obligatory to provide more accommodation. The new school will have four rooms similar to the Allandale school."[110]

The ever greater complexity that education was creating led to a more systematic way of undertaking education. In December 1965, for the first time Catholic Separate School Trustees were elected under a provincial mandate.[111] It was a time of sincere struggle for financial equity for Catholic schools in a most reluctant environment. The parish was active through presentations, pulpit talks and public campaigning to keep Catholic education on the front line of debate. In 1968 rumours about the high school closing were sufficiently strong that an announcement was put in the bulletin to assure the parish that this was not true.[112] These rumours may have been in part a reflection of confusion in a period of change. In 1968 the government mandated regional school boards. The Barrie area was originally served by the Combined Roman Catholic Separate School Board.[113] The late sixties were marked by a consistent political campaign promoting the cause of Catholic education. Frequently, parishioners were encouraged to write their M. P. P. to express their advocacy of a fully funded Catholic education system.

The late sixties saw the formation of Lay Advisory Councils for the promotion of equitable funding of Catholic education. This was a province wide endeavour and was actively pursued by the parishioners of St. Mary's.[114]

Although transportation improved and Msgr. Clair was an adamant advocate for Catholic education it is clear that for many rural children summer school religious education was still the option. In the summer of 1953 the summer school at Bell Ewart had forty-four students and the school at Barrie that summer had one hundred and eleven students.[115] These summer schools continued every summer in recognition of the fact that rural children did not have the opportunity to attend separate schools. The Sisters of St. Joseph were put into service teaching the classes.[116]

110. Ibid., June 15, 1958.
111. Ibid., December 12, 1965.
112. Ibid., January 28, 1968.
113. Ibid., April 28, 1968.
114. Ibid., January 26, 1969.
115. Sisters of St Joseph Toronto Archives, June 29, 1953.
116. SMPA, Year Book, 1953, p. 29.

Msgr. Clair.

Msgr. Clair looms over the parish of St. Mary's in the mid-twentieth century. The marks of his ministry were steadiness and a stalwart disposition. Cardinal McGuigan noted when Clair was raised to the status of monsignor in 1955 that he was, "quiet in speech and unostentatious in manner."[117] Though this was said as a compliment there seems to have been, in Cardinal McGuigan's mind, a certain diffidence in regards to Monsignor Clair. To be fair, Cardinal McGuigan was never a man with a strong check on his emotions. He had risen quickly in the church becoming an archbishop before the age of forty. He was valued for his ability to take on a difficult task and turn it around. He at the same time was abrasive if things were not as he expected them, as the following letter suggests.

The Loyalty Campaign of 1957 was undertaken as a diocesan wide initiative to raise funds for needed educational and church facilities in areas of particular growth. It is unclear if the perception was to be purposely put forward that for those parishes where the campaign was not a success that they in some way were disloyal.

The Cardinal's directions to Msgr. Clair were as follows, "I do not know when the Loyalty Dinner is, but please have nobody talk about the pastor or the parish. It has been one of the deadest parishes in the diocese. Let us forget the past and look to the future. The chairman should have something to say, constructive and inspiring. I do not think that the custom of introducing the head table guests is necessary. However, if it is done let it be done quickly. One sentence from two or three lay people is sufficient. The people who count are the clergy; Monsignor Clair should make a short speech and Father Rosettis should also make one. If you want me to go, I will have something to say. That will be plenty perhaps too much for poor, dead old Barrie . . . What is necessary is that the clergy carefully supervise the director, and I am going to watch over your shoulders to see that everything is O. K.

Pray that you may get everybody on their toes and get them excited for once in their lives over Holy Mother Church."[118]

The intemperance of the communication suggests to a large extent an unawareness of the progress that had been made and was being made by the parish. Msgr. Clair was never a self promoter. Taciturn to a fault, tempered by a deep sense of responsibility to his pastorate, this could of course be perceived

---

117. SMPA, News cuttings, Examiner, February 18, 1955.

118. SMPA, Correspondence, McGuigan to Clair.

the Cardinal that Msgr. Clair was a plodder. It is worth noting that by the end of the year pledges in Barrie were in excess of $160,000; St. John's Parish, barely a year old, pledged $52,000 and St. Mary's over $110.00.[119]

SISTERS OF ST. JOSEPH.

The post war era, as has been noted, was a time of great expansion in education. For religious communities, the post war era was to be one of extraordinary change and challenge.

The sisters in 1946 decided to relocate. The convent on Mulcaster because of the size did not serve the community well. As the Annals of the Sisters of St. Joseph noted five of the cells in the convent had no heat at all.[120] The move was not far, basically up the hill to 83 Berczy Street, at the corner of Eugenia. The purchase included a number of lots along Berczy and Eugenia. The potential of the lots was the consideration of starting a girls' school.[121] At the back of the property, facing Eugenia was a garage which was fitted out as a studio to teach music.

A footnote found in the annals of the community on moving to Berczy Street recalled that the bronze figure of Autumn on the newel post in the front hall was replaced with a more conservative crystal globe. "The scantily clothed lady will offer her fruits and foliage in a more appropriate setting."[122]

From its foundation in 1946, St. Joseph's High School for many years was solely under the direction of the Sisters of St. Joseph. The first lay teacher was hired in 1955.[123]

Change in the world and the lively discussion going on at the Second Vatican Council impacted the life of the sisters. They purchased a portable television in 1963. Convents began to acquire cars for their transportation later in the decade.

The period of renewal in the church saw the move to provide habits for religious which were more practical and to reflect more the spirit of their mission which was to work in the world. To have worn the large cumbersome habit of the Sisters of St Joseph and to see change on the horizon was for many welcome, but also somewhat intimidating. For the Sisters of St. Joseph that change came in May and June of 1963. At the beginning of May the Annalist

---

119. SMPA, Announcement Books, December 28, 1957.
120. Sisters of St. Joseph, Toronto, Annals. June 1,1946.
121. Ibid., 1946.
122. Ibid., February 9, 1952.
123. Ibid., June 29, 1955.

notes that they are belting and cutting sleeves in preparation for the new look deadline of June. The deadline was met as it is related on June 1 that they had appeared in their new type of cinctures after a few weeks of hooking and eyeing and measuring.[124]

Over time the lots along Berczy were sold off, but the ones along Eugenia were retained.[125] In 1968 there was discussion of building a new convent on Eugenia Street behind the building in use. The proposal was taken as far as having initial plans drawn up.[126] These plans were quickly shelved while the church found itself in the midst of a radical transformation of religious life. Numbers in all orders were dropping at a significant rate.

Redemptoristines.

The Redemptoristines, as their name would suggest are part of the large Redemptorist movement within the Catholic Church. The spiritual life of the order had a particular emphasis focused on the redemption received through Christ. The Redemptoristines came to Canada from Chudleigh, England in 1947. The timing of their arrival in Canada was not accidental. During the Second World War the Redemptorist order provided many priests to serve as military chaplains. While in England, they connected with the houses of the Redemptorist tradition, including the convent at Chudleigh. The order was invited to Canada by the visiting Canadians.

They first set down roots on St. George Street in Toronto. The first few years saw the arrival of 25 postulants into the community which made it impossible to stay in the St. George Street house.

In May 1951, the parish welcomed into its midst the Redemptoristine Sisters who established their monastery at the corner of Dundonald and Amelia Street on the estate that had been previously owned by the Sparham Family. An addition was put on the building and in May of 1952 the monastery bell was blessed which would call the sisters to their office of prayer each day. The parish pitched in to promote this effort by initiating a food shower to help the sisters to get established in their new home.[127] The northern region of the Catholic Women's League made the Redemptoristines their main project in the early 1950's.[128]

---

124. Ibid., May & June 1963.
125. Ibid., November 1966 & September 1967.
126. Ibid., 1968.
127. SMPA, Announcement Books, May 11, 1952.
128. SMPA, Year Book, 1953, page 39.

The New Order Will Have to be Different

In the archives of the order there are some interesting records regarding the establishment of the community in Barrie.

The owner of the house, Mr. Sparham, drove to Toronto to pick up the sisters to have them tour the house. The tour lead to the conclusion, "that it was a most satisfactory spot for a monastery. It stands on a height overlooking Lake Simcoe. The Town of Barrie is below it at the foot of the hill, but not readily visible from the house and the grounds."[129]

Once the purchase was agreed to, a post Christmas tour for the whole community was arranged which included lunch as guests of the Sisters of St. Joseph, a tour of the future monastery, travel north to see the Martyrs' Shrine though it was closed for the winter and a return by way of Uptergrove to stop in on Mrs. McIsaac, "the stigmatist whom every Friday from 6 till 9 p. m. endures extensive suffering." She was, in fact, not home and they were met by her husband who asked for their continued prayers for his family.[130]

The Mother Superior visited Barrie on a number of occasions after the property was purchased. On one trip the Ovendon School, at the bottom of the Dundonald Street hill, was the destination. The school was closing and the sisters were seeking the kitchen appliances for the monastery kitchen.

She also made her way to the mayor's office to be assured that the widening of Amelia Street would not result in the destruction of trees which were essential to create a private monastic space.

The diarist on May 7th, the day of their move noted that after school got out the Sisters of St. Joseph dropped by to welcome them to Barrie. The diarist concludes the day's entry with the words, "However it was good to be here, the silence is beyond description . . . as Fr. Daly aptly expressed it, 'God Alone'. This is the place he had chosen for us from all eternity."[131] The idea of enclosure expressed well the ministry of the Redemptoristines which was first and essentially prayer and separation from the world. As the title of their promotional pamphlet from the 1950's expressed it, "Forgotten in Christ."[132]

When the sisters first came to Barrie they did not have a formal enclosure as there was much to be done in renovating the monastery to meet their needs as well as the construction of the new wing.

Formal enclosure was delayed for about fifteen months. The greatest source of intrusion was through the main entrance off of Dundonald Street The in-

129. Redemptorist Archives, Redemptoristine Files, Diary, December 17, 1950.
130. Ibid., December 28, 1950.
131. Ibid., Diary, May 7, 1951.
132. Ibid., Promotional Booklets.

truders were children. As the diarist notes, "Recreation this evening included every child in the neighborhood. They were in such high spirits and tumbling about in our midst at such a speed we had to put our work away for fear of impaling one on knitting needles . . . our recreation resembled a nursery more than a contemplative community."[133]

The affection in which children were held was very much in evidence. The diarist records a small incident observed; "two little boys on the way to school took a shortcut through the convent grounds and passed through the narrow gap between the hedge and cloister corridor. The younger one seemed to be hanging back his eyes fixed on the windows. The older boy kept urging him and finally asked him what he was scared of? The younger boy with his eyes still fixed on the convent windows as he backed hurriedly through the gap and kept right on going, said 'nuns' in exactly the same sort of tone he might have used to say 'bears'."[134]

The relationship developed with the neighbourhood children before the formal enclosure was recognized as having other values. As the diary of the monastery notes, "This we do know, the whole hearted acceptance and devotion (of the children) spread wonderful good will for us in the town, and dispelled many a misinformed prejudice that Protestant minds may have harboured in the past about cloistered convents."[135]

To sustain their community of prayer, the sisters made cassocks which were not only worn by the Redemptorist priests, but most priests at the time. They also augmented their income by encouraging devotion to the Infant of Prague and the sale of statues of the same. They also promoted a devotion they called Our Lady's Lamp Association. This devotional undertaking called on the faithful to pay to keep a lamp in front of the image of Our Lady of Perpetual Help burning in perpetuity. The donation was not only for the lamp but for the prayers of the Redemptoristine community for a particular need.

When Cardinal McGuigan had made a brief visit in 1951 he had stated that he would come to put on the enclosure, but not too tightly as he felt that cloistered nuns should adapt to the times.[136]

The Cardinal may have been implying that some of the traditions and practices of the Redemptoristines should be reconsidered. Their habit consisted of a red tunic over which there was placed a blue mantle. They wore a white veil

---

133. Ibid., Diary, August 1, 1951.

134. Ibid., March 27, 1952.

135. Ibid., October 31, 1951.

136. Ibid., May 16, 1951.

with a second veil of black over top. Their footwear was sandals. This habit was altered for certain types of work.

The formal enclosure took place on September 1, 1952 at which time the parish held a reception in connection with the rites. Fr. Ehman, the Provincial of the Toronto Province, preached at the enclosure. His sermon was recorded and telecast on CKBB radio the following weekend. It was left to Monsignor Clair to lock the enclosure gate and pass the key through to the Mother Superior beginning the formal years of the cloister in Barrie.[137]

The monastic life as experienced by the Redemptoristines was organized around prayer, especially around praying the psalms or office at the prescribed times of the day. These would normally be sung in Gregorian Chant.

The Redemptoristines with their particular focus on redemption had rituals that were uniquely their own. On the twenty fifth of each month an image of the Christ child was given a place of honor and Christmas themes in prayers and songs became part of the day. On the first Friday of each month the focus was on Calvary and rituals included a procession with objects representative of the crucifixion of Christ, like a crown of thorns, nails and hammer.

These dramatic acts of faith and pageantry which seem obscure in a secular environment were in fact not that foreign to the religious milieu in which the order evolved. The idea of dying to the world was very much part of the call of the monastic nun who on entering the cloister leaves the world behind.[138]

By 1957 there were thirty-two sisters in the Barrie monastery. In December of 1957, the sisters made a foundation in Esopus, New York and further a community was formed in Ligouri, Missouri in April of 1960. The final foundation to grow out of Barrie was at Redhead, New South Wales in Australia in March of 1965.

The community was constantly plagued with having access to priests. Redemptorists and Jesuits both offered what services they could. St. Mary's priests looked after the sacramental needs of the community on weekdays.

The changes in the church in the 1960's had impacted religious communities in a particularly profound way. The expectations and anticipation of change were reflected in a comment made by the Mother Superior to one of the Redemptorist priests who had an advisory role in the community. "Recently I heard that you are under the impression that we are dyed in the wool conservatives. Nothing could be more false. In fact, all but a few of the older

---

137. Ibid., Edmonton and Toronto, Notes on the Redemptoristines in Barrie, Sr. Joan Calver, O. S. S. R.

138. Ibid., *Redemtoristines*, recruitment booklet, p. 22 ff.

members are all rarin-to-go liberals, perhaps too much so."[139]

The monastery had, by the number of foundations it created in other places in the world, proven to be very successful but there were problems that were presenting themselves. The building which was very old seems to have not been as adaptable as first hoped.

Making cassocks and ornate vestments had been a big part of their livelihood. With the renewal in the church the demand dried up. To adapt, the sisters began to make gowns for first communion and confirmation and to rent them to parishes. Since they wished to tap into the market in upstate New York as well as Ontario they believed a more central location would be desirable.

The parish bulletin of September 16, 1966 announced that later that afternoon all parishioners were invited to the chapel of the Redemptoristines for a folk mass which would be their thank you to the people of the parish.[140] In October1966, they moved to Keswick, to what had been the Redemptorist novitiate. This arrangement provided a short term solution, though eventually the community found accommodation with the Sisters of St. Joseph for a period of time before opening a new monastery in Fort Erie.

A caring relationship with the Sisters of St. Joseph had been forged in Barrie. The Annals of the Sisters of St. Joseph note early in the time of Redemptoristines' presence in Barrie, "A basket of apples and a bag of turnips went from us to the Redemptoristines today. Not a glamorous gift but a more than welcome one to our sisters on the hill."[141] At the time of their departure for Keswick, the Annals of the Sisters of St. Joseph stated simply, "we will miss them and their brown bread."[142]

Building the Third St. Mary's Church.

On November 8, 1965, Fr. John O'Meara of the diocesan building committee wrote to Monsignor Fulton Chancellor of the Archdiocese of Toronto. His letter stated, "Monsginor Clair met with the Committee at their last meeting and following a lengthy discussion of the expansion in the Barrie area the Committee recommends the following:

1) That a new church be built in the centre of the town to accommodate

139. Ibid., Correspondence, Sr. Mary Angela to Fr. G.T. O'Reilly, February 16, 1964.
140. SMPA, bulletin, September 18, 1966.
141. Sisters of St. Joseph Toronto Archives, Annals of Barrie, February 4, 1952.
142. Ibid., September 1966.

800 persons.

2) A new rectory be built at the same time and that serious consideration be given to the building of a parish hall too.

3) That the properties of the Redemptoristine Sisters be considered as an alternative site and that this question of the site be resolved as soon as possible.[143]

The letter of November 8 was given approval on November 10th and Msgr. Clair wrote to the procurator of the Redemptorist Fathers on November 12th, 1965, "Far be it for me to hasten the departure of the good sisters. Their prayers have been an asset to us from the start. However, if their property is to be sold it would make an excellent site for a church. If this parish could purchase the property, is it not possible that we could go ahead with the building of the new church next summer?"[144]

The church on Mulcaster Street which was almost a hundred years old could accommodate three hundred people. The brick was soft and the idea of an addition was not seen as feasible, as well the problem of parking which had been an ongoing struggle at the Mulcaster site.[145]

By April 1967, the *Barrie Examiner* took note of the new initiative. The initial plan in accordance with best practices of the time imagined a church and hall which would be separated by a dividing wall which could be removed to provide overflow seating in the hall.[146] These original ideas were speculative as the commitment to build was not announced in the parish bulletin until July 16, 1967. Only then were drawings undertaken with conviction.[147]

The same paper noted on May 24, 1969, that Fr. Stan Blackwell the Associate Pastor of St. Mary's said the last mass in the church built in 1872 and after transferred the sacrament to the new church.[148]

The property had its own interesting history before the arrival of the Redemptoristines. The lot overlooking Kempenfelt Bay had been the home of Herbert Sparham, a jeweller, who called his home Barrandale Hall. The house which the Sisters moved into had been built by Mrs. Loring on the property which had been owned by her daughter Elizabeth and her husband William O'Brien. It was during this time that the home was known as Inchiquin. For much of its life the original house had been a high quality rental property.

143. SMPA, Correspondence, O'Meara to Fulton, November 8, 1965.
144. Ibid., Clair to Callaghan, November 12, 1965.
145. SMPA, New Church file, Notes from Joe Whelan, November 11, 1999.
146. *Barrie Examiner*, April 3, 1967.
147. SMPA, Bulletin, July 16, 1967.
148. Ibid., May 24, 1969.

Through the years the property was owned after the O'Briens by Judge Charles Hughson and for many years by Hugh Calderwood.[149]

Local architects, Nesbitt and Davis, were hired to oversee the project. The building committee offered its first opportunity for companies to tender for the building of the new church in February 1968.[150] The initial tenders were too high and the process was repeated after some alterations to the plan were undertaken.[151]

In May the new tenders came in within budget and the work began almost immediately.[152] By July it was reported that all was progressing well with the walls of the rectory almost to the first floor level.[153]

The winter issue of "Canadian Catholic Institutions" that year featured a cover story on the new St. Mary's including some numbers of interest. The cost for construction of the whole complex was $600,000. The square foot cost of the church was $25.00, and of the rectory $16.00, and the hall $15.00.[154]

By February 1969, the site on Mulcaster St. was for sale.[155] The sale of the property did not move ahead as would have been hoped and the old church, stood at the corner of Mulcaster and McDonald for a period of time. In the fall of 1971, a fire was set in the old church and petty vandalism further affected the building.

On May 11, 1969, the bulletin included the schedule of mass times for the new church in which we see a reduction of masses because of the larger building. The same announcement reminded the parishioners that hearing aids would be available in every fifth pew. Communion would be received standing. At the same time a losing battle was begun to remind the faithful that all were to enter the church by the main doors rather than the side door especially in the winter months.[156]

The church was blessed by Archbishop Pocock on May 26, 1969.[157] One day previously, Msgr. Clair had celebrated mass in the new St. Mary's.[158]

---

149. SMPA, *Barrie Examiner*, undated clipping. Letter November 15, 1976 Graham, Wilson and Green to Msgr. Clair.

150. SMPA, Announcement Books, February. 11, 1968.

151. Ibid., March 3, 1968.

152. Ibid., May 19, 1968.

153. Ibid., July 28, 1968.

154. SMPA, New Church file, Canadian Catholic Institutions, "S*t. Mary's Church and Rectory*, page 12-16.

155. Ibid., February 9, 1969.

156. Ibid., May 11, 1969.

157. Ibid., May 18, 1969

The move demanded other practical considerations. In August 1969 the Simcoe County Health Unit gave permission for the disinterment of Fr. Egan who was buried beside the old church and his reburial at St. Mary's Cemetery.[159]

Eventually the Province of Ontario purchased the property because of its proximity to the courthouse for parking. This transaction was settled in August of 1971.[160]

158. SMPA, New Church File, Notes from Joe Whelan, November. 11, 1999.

159. SMPA, Letter Armbrust to Clair, August 27, 1969. There could be no reference found to the disinterment of Fr. James O'Donoghue who was buried under the altar during the construction of the church in the 1870's.

159. Ibid., New Church File, Letter Gray to Wall August 25, 1971.

The Devout and Active Participation by the Faithful

At the end of the nineteen sixties, St. Mary's Parish moved into a new building. The new church provided almost three times the seating, as well as parking off the street for a significant number of cars. For some, the move was traumatic. The old church was deeply connected to personal histories. After a century of having the Catholic church as a significant feature on the city's skyline, the new building seemed hidden from view, having been built out of the downtown core.

The Amelia Street location was on the edge of what was popularly called Vatican Hill. The perception was that Catholic families had congregated in a significant way on the streets behind the old church and to the north of where the new building was located.

The transition to the new site happened over time. One of the concluding tasks was noted in the bulletin in May of 1971, two years after the new church was opened. "In the lounge room in the lobby of our church you have most likely seen the Pieta. This was brought up from the old church last week. Its present setting is not necessarily permanent. From all of our numerous parishioners we should be able to come up with some good ideas about what to do with it. Should we leave it where it is? Should we put it in the church? If so, where? Should we destroy it? Please submit your ideas in writing."[1]

In the fall of the same year, a committee of the parish advisory council recommended that the statue be removed and replaced with a more contemporary image of Mary.[2] This, of course, in the end did not happen.

During the early sixties the Second Vatican Council had embraced renewal. This undertaking veered between the dramatically optimistic and the problematic and controversial. In the last three decades of the twentieth century the parish was deeply influenced by the movements of renewal. These movements were seeking to bring transformative experiences into the lives of parishioners on a personal level and in relation to the larger community.

---

1. SMPA, Bulletin, May 30, 1971.
2. SMPA, Parish Council Minutes, October 5, 1972.

After the thirty one year pastorate of Msgr. Clair the parish was served by a number of men over the next forty years. Fr. Jim Hayes had a rather short tenure on Msgr. Clair's retirement, followed by Fr. Charles Reeves. During his pastorate economic concerns in relation to education and the parish cemetery were addressed. Fr. Len O'Malley supported many efforts of faith enrichment. Fr. John Hawkshaw served the parish and was instrumental in putting the addition on the church and establishing the seniors building. Fr. John Vella brought to his service a concern for the care of individuals and the enrichment of community of life. Fr. Ambrose Sheehy invited the community into a deeper prayer life. Fr. Frank McDevitt served the parish during the period of the sesquicentennial.

Parish Organizations.

In the period after the war there was a void left by the loss of almost all organizations that focused on spiritual formation. By the end of the seventies, only three organizations, in each case with a strong community service component had survived. These were the Catholic Women's League, the Knights of Columbus and the St. Vincent de Paul Society.

Gone was the Sodality of the Blessed Virgin, the Holy Name Society, the Christian Mothers and the Altar Society as a spiritual entity. The League of the Sacred Heart was still in existence, but the demands of membership were minimal. Members were directed to pray for a monthly intention and to pick up their monthly magazine.

Older organizations would soon confront competition from different forms of ministry which did not require membership in an organization. These ministries were much more specific in their mandate and flexible in their understanding of belonging.

Part of the Catholic Women's League's strength was found in the work that they had undertaken in the parish in the decades before. The parish bazaar was a significant annual event leading up to Christmas. In the sixties and the seventies much of the time of the C. W. L. was spent in leadership training.

On the national level, the Catholic Women's League continued to raise concerns about public issues. These issues often reflected concerns regarding family life, an advocacy for the poor and the protection of life.

By the turn of the century, the Catholic Women's League wandered into a national controversy which impacted the League in the parish. In March of 2000, the League's national body endorsed a country wide protest called the Women's March Against Poverty which included organizations across the political and social spectrum. The source of contention was the fear that marching with organizations that were actively pro-abortion was creating the wrong impression. Though the issue was played out on the national stage and locally with emotion and debate, in the end, the march went forward with League participation and with the continuation of League work at the parish level.

In 1973, the Knights of Columbus renovated their property at the corner of Berczy and Codrington and in 1990 put on an extensive addition to create a hall, providing them with exceptional facilities.[3] Throughout the period they actively endorsed athletic and other endeavours for youth. This, at times, included Squires, the youth wing of the Knights. One initiative which did not succeed was the Squires of Mary which would have been a parallel group for girls.[4]

The Knights supported many community efforts. Grants of 10,000 dollars were common as in the case of relief after the Barrie Tornado (1984) and improving the track for St. Joseph's High School (1987). These commitments kept the Knights in the public eye and encouraged them to create some steady sources of income, for their work, such as the sale of Christmas trees which began in 1959.[5]

In the early 1970's, the St. Vincent de Paul Store moved into its facilities on Dunlop Street. By 1996, they were operating a second store in the Letitia Street Plaza.[6]

On a diocesan level the organization supported initiatives which would aid the poor and distressed in a more permanent way. This was reflected in Barrie in the opening and maintenance of a half way house for recovering addicts in May of 2002.[7] The proceeds from the store were the source of funds to initiate this effort.

Overtime the changing economic realities, changes in shopping habits with introduction of large box stores, provided more and more challenge for the viability of the St. Vincent de Paul Store. In addition, the city put in place fees at the city dump which encouraged people to find alternative destinations for their discard. Far too often it was the drop boxes for groups like the Society. St. Vincent de Paul found itself stuck with huge amounts of waste for which they needed to pay disposal fees. The store on Letitia Street was short lived. The store on Dunlop Street closed in 2008.

---

3. SMPA, *A Century of Service.*
4. SMPA, Bulletin, November 1, 1998.
5. SMPA, *A Century of Service.*
6. SMPA, Bulletin, February 18, 1996.
7. Ibid., May 26, 2002.

Laity and Liturgy.

Near the end of 1969, the parish bulletin reported, "After about five years of experimentation throughout the world, the method of celebrating the Sacrifice of the Mass has been finalized. Officially, as of November 30, the First Sunday of Advent, Mass will be offered in the same way (substantially) throughout the world. The rites have been simplified. Duplications are to be eliminated. The "Prayer of the Faithful" has already been restored. A Penitential Act for the reconciliation of the people is added at the opening of the Mass. The Sacred Scripture Readings, Epistle and Gospel read at Mass will be put on a three-year cycle instead of the one year cycle now used, exposing us to the riches of more of the scriptures. Furthermore, on Sunday and the great feasts an additional reading either from the Old Testament or the Acts of the Apostles will precede the Epistle . . .

It should be possible, therefore, sometime during the next year or so to procure a new missal that will remain useful for many years. The purpose of the revision, of course, is that the intrinsic nature and purpose of its various parts, as also the connection between them can be clearly manifested and that the devout and active participation by the faithful can be the more easily accomplished."[8]

The understanding of the sacraments in light of church renewal was reinforced at St. Mary's in the summer of 1969 when the people were reminded that anointing was not a sacrament of death, but of healing. Anyone who was seriously ill should receive the sacrament.[9]

This was followed a week later with a teaching on how to go to confession and a discussion of baptism, reminding the congregation that sponsors are to be practicing Catholics of a reasonable age.[10] Near the end of 1969 it was noted that non-Catholic Christians could stand as a Christian witness at a baptism as long as the distinction of witness and sponsor was maintained.[11]

Throughout the seventies, a lot of time and effort was put into the preparation of families for baptism. Couples went into the homes of those seeking baptism for their children to discuss the sacrament and encourage them in the desire for the sacrament. We find by the beginning of the eighties, St. Mary's, like most parishes, had baptism teams that lead times of reflection in anticipa-

8. Ibid., November 23, 1969.
9. Ibid., July 27, 1969.
10. Ibid., August 3, 1969.
11. Ibid., December 14, 1969.

tion of the sacrament. As the information booklet of 1979 states, "Baptism is a community affair because it is the initiation of a member into the community of faith."[12]

Marriage preparation became a requirement in March of 1977. Before this time, though programs were offered, there was not a clear expectation in regard to participation.[13]

The initiative was undertaken to center the sacraments more emphatically in the parish community and to emphasize the role of parents in the process. This evolution was clearly seen throughout the seventies when first communicants were acknowledged by the parish after the child had made communion, first, with their parents.

Enrolment for sacraments of initiation became an important gesture which was part of church life in Barrie from 1989 on.[14] In a letter to parents in 1992, Fr. Hawkshaw framed the issue. "Because a child is in grade two, they do not automatically make their first communion. In consultation with the parish council and other priests and bishops, we designed a program for first communion. The sacraments are special and belong to the church, not the school, so we ask the school to teach lessons on first communion and first confession, but the children, with their parents, come to the church for an interview, and if they show faith and good will, they receive their first communion with their family, making it a parish and family affair. In this way we hope to show that the parents must accept the promise they made at baptism to bring their child up in the practice of the faith."[15]

Throughout the seventies the preparation for confirmation began to include retreat days which gathered in all candidates for the sacrament.

In the early church, adults who wished to be Catholic would go through a process of initiation. This ministry was restored to the church during the renewal and became a part of parish life, most often identified as R. C. I. A.: Rite of Christian Initiation of Adults.

In December of 1969, the fast before communion was drawn back to one hour.[16]

Saturday evening mass, at seven, began in June of 1971. It was quickly embraced by a large part of the community.[17]

---

12. SMPA, St. Mary's Parish Information Booklet, 1979, page 3.
13. SMPA, Bulletin, March 6, 1977.
14. Ibid., October 22, 1989.
15. SMPA, Correspondence, Hawkshaw to Parishioners, October 23, 1992.
16. SMPA, Bulletin, December 21, 1969.
17. SMPA, "*The Last 25 Years at St. Mary's.*"

The role of music at mass was an ongoing concern. The senior choir was disbanded to be reorganized in 1979. The issue seemed to be finding enough singers to make a choir viable. The problem was sufficiently pervasive that one suggested solution was the formation of a choir for St. Mary's and St. John's which would serve the parishes week about.[18]

The choral tradition in the parish found its footing sufficiently to participate in the music at the Martyrs' Shrine when Pope John Paul II visited in the fall of 1984.

In the parish, the organ which had been installed in the old church in1914 and moved to the new church in 1968 was renovated in 1985.[19]

At St. Mary's, embracing "folk" music at mass was a slow and well-discussed undertaking. It was originally experienced as a special occasion, as in March of 1969, when a folk mass was held at St. Mary's with the choir from St. Augustine's Seminary.[20] The Parish Advisory Council explored the possibility of having folk masses as part of the liturgical life at St. Mary's. In 1971 a folk mass a month was offered. The parish initiated singing practices on a weekday evening for the whole congregation to prepare for these masses.[21] By the new year, folk masses were becoming a regular feature of Sunday morning.[22]

By the summer of 1972, the folk masses had moved to Saturday night as the regular music for that liturgy.[23]

A strong social theme throughout the later part of the century was the place of women in society. The changing role of women and evolving understanding was reflected in the bulletin announcement in 1971 which stated, "We are appealing to the men and boys of the parish, and possibly the women and girls too, to come on Tuesday evening to assist with raking the yard. The following week they acknowledged the men, boys and girls who assisted with the task.[24]

The ministry of lector which men had undertaken at mass was extended to women at the beginning of the new year of 1975.[25] It had first appeared on the agenda of the parish advisory council in 1971.[26]

In the fall of 1979 a shift came in the liturgy when girls were welcomed to

---

18. SMPA, Parish Council Minutes, September 4, 1979.
19. SMPA, Blessing and Dedication of the Organ, March 3, 1985.
20. SMPA, Bulletin, May 2, 1969.
21. Ibid., June 13, 1971.
22. Ibid., February 13, 1972.
23. Ibid., May 7, 1972.
24. Ibid., May 16 & 23, 1971.
25. Ibid., January 5, 1975.
26. SMPA, Parish Council Minutes, October 5, 1971.

serve at the altar. No announcement was made in the bulletin to invite potential servers. They just began to appear on the altar servers' schedule.[27] They disappeared off the schedule in 1991 for a number of years and their role was reestablished at mid-decade.

Shortly after the opening of the new church, the parish undertook a communal celebration of penance. Efforts were made to reassure the community that this liturgy would centre on shared scripture and prayer and would conclude with individual confession.[28]

By 1975, the parish was offering conference style confession on a weekly basis. Since the confessionals were not spacious enough to do this comfortably, the opportunity for conference style confession was celebrated in the sacristy.[29]

Eleven years later, permission was sought for the celebration of reconciliation by the third rite, often called general absolution.[30] Permission was given on occasion, but over the subsequent years, the practice, though always popular with the faithful, was not encouraged and fell out of practice.

The new St. Mary's was built without a communion rail. The faithful would come to communion and line up at the perimeter of the sanctuary and the priests would move back and forth giving the sacrament. This proved highly problematic in that it lead to a rather chaotic time at communion with no very defined rows or process, described by the pastor of the time as 'the stampede.' The liturgical report of 1971 suggested the priest remain stationary and the faithful approach him.[31]

Changes in the liturgy were not easily embraced by all. After communion being received on the tongue in a kneeling position at the communion rail with hands under the cloth that covered the rail, through a quick evolution communion, by 1970, was received standing, more often than not in a processional line, with the option of receiving on the tongue or the hand. Fr. James Hayes wrote to the chancellor, Fr. Leonard Wall, in June of 1970, "The Dean and I received the excrescence from the Liturgical Committee today and agree that in a combined total of 76 years of giving communion almost every Sunday, neither of us has ever observed anyone well enough to go to mass who couldn't extend his tongue. Who are these dreamers?"[32]

---

27. SMPA, Bulletin, October. 14, 1979.
28. Ibid., July 20, 1969.
29. Ibid., April 27, 1975.
30. SMPA, Correspondence, Boissonneau to O'Malley, March 10, 1980.
31. SMPA, Parish Council Liturgical Report, Fall 1971.
32. ARCAT, *St. Mary's Files*, Hayes to Wall, June 23, 1970.

A year later the faithful were reminded that communion in the hand was not a novelty, rather a return to a traditional practice. In the same announcement the faithful were cautioned against a false sense of unworthiness when going to communion.[33]

In December of 1978, the parish council, first discussed lay assistance with the distribution of communion.[34] In November of 1979, the practice of lay people serving as extra ordinary ministers of communion was introduced.[35]

In the fall of 1981, the parishioners were invited to send their children to participate in Children's Liturgy which ran parallel to the Liturgy of the Word at mass.[36]

The evolving role of the people perhaps came to its fullest realization with the reinstatement of the permanent diaconite. After a number of years of training, Joe Duncan and George Wilson were ordained early in 1978. They were joined in the diaconite by Ron MacLellan five years later.[37]

The arrival of the mass in the language of the people created a new pastoral need which was addressed in Barrie in a number of ways over the years. At various times in various places Sunday mass was celebrated in French, Polish and Korean.

In 1987, Ukranian Catholic ministry began in the City of Barrie under the patronage of St. Olga. The first liturgy was celebrated at St. Mary's on October 18, 1987.[38] Initially, the community met at St. Mary's, but for many years, made the chapel of the separate school board offices their home until they purchased a church building on Parkside Drive in 2007. The church was blessed and put under the patronage of the Exaltation of the Holy Cross.

Some of those who found the "changes" problematic for intellectual or theological reasons continued to embrace the Latin mass. The Latin mass was celebrated in various places throughout the area, including Phelpston and for many years in Schomberg. The same anxieties motivated the foundation of Catholics United for the Faith, generally called C. U. F., which was concerned with the weakened understanding of the faith which was developing in religious instruction.

---

33. SMPA. Bulletin, November 19, 1978.
34. SMPA, Parish Council Minutes, December 5, 1978.
35. SMPA, Bulletin, November 18, 1979.
36. Ibid., October 4, 1981.
37. SMPA, "*The Last 25 years at St. Mary's*".
38. SMPA, Parish Council Minutes, October 4, 1987, Bulletin October 11, 1987.

Active Participation by the Faithful

The Need for Community.

There had in every era been those who were weak in practice. From the seventies on, there was an escalation in those less willing to participate in Sunday Eucharist and other public expressions of faith. One theory was that the rapid change in many of the exterior expressions of faith, suggested that all things were open for change and essentially many came to see personal responsibility in a much more self defined context. In others words, the individual came to believe their own choices were paramount rather than the expectations of the church.

The ministry of the church became more concerned with meeting the individual in their own experience. This had always been the case with youth and youth ministry. It was now the thrust of the church to respond to all types of needs.

The registration form of the parish in 1980, invited those registering to identify their marital status as: single, married, separated or divorced.[39] This was a significant shift in Catholic sensibility which had struggled with an authentic response to marriage failure over the years.

In the fall of 1975, the Parish Advisory Council offered coffee after mass on Saturday evenings and on Sunday after the noon mass.[40]

In the late 1970's, an effort was made to create family weekends in the parish. It optimistically promised, "Free from outside distractions, the members of each family focus on their relationships with one another. As the weekend develops, parents and children, brothers and sisters, communicate with increasing trust and openness. By Sunday afternoon, the oneness that each family arrived with has deepened into a new sense of mutual understanding, acceptance and love."[41]

The role of scripture in personal life was evolving in Catholic communities in general. Reflection on the Gospel of St. Luke was offered over several weeks in the fall of 1975 with a presenter coming from Toronto each week. Bible reflection evolved into a Bible study lead by the parishioners themselves with printed help such as the Journey program.[42]

"We the Parish" was introduced in the fall of 1978. The purpose of the four evenings was to assist the parishioners to locate their experience of church

39. SMPA, Bulletin, January 6, 1980.
40. SMPA, Bulletin, September 7, 1975.
41. SMPA, Parish Booklet, p. 10., 1978.
42. SMPA, Bulletin, November 2, 1975.

in the context of community and to deepen the individual parishioner's sense of responsibility for parish life. The core idea was the family. Parishioners were encouraged to be sensitized to isolation and to promote the warmth, security and acceptance that family implies.[43]

The need for community was reflected in a 1984 initiative of the C. W. L. to form a widows' group. The main focus of the group was social and the creation of a forum for widows. The work of the widows' group continued well into the 1990's.[44]

In the early 1990's, an evangelization committee called "Welcome Home" was formed to "reach out more and more to others, who felt alienated from the church. This initiative was to be part of a ministry of selfless concern."[45]

Around the same time the parish initiated a program of evangelization for those who may be new in the parish, those seeking sacraments for their children, and those who may be transitory, particularly students.[46] These programs had been preceded and would be followed by other programs of outreach to Catholics who were away from the church.

In 1993, a visitation ministry was started to reach out to new registrants in the parish through home visits. The visitors carried with them a loaf of homemade bread as a gesture of welcome.[47]

In 1994, a play group was initiated for parents who were at home with young children.[48] Parenting was an ongoing concern of the church. Evenings for parents were offered in 1982, with the hope that they could put the 'spark' back into parenting.[49]

The church had long been the host of children's organizations such as Brownies and Cubs. Twelve step programs at various times accessed church facilities.

A bereavement group was formed in 1997, "to provide a sense of community and caring for parishioners experiencing grief due to death."[50]

During the mid 1990's the focus of parish life became very centered in the communitarian aspect of church life. An initiative was undertaken to create small Christian communities which would gather weekly, discuss scripture and

---

43. Ibid., October 15, 1978.
44. SMPA, *News from the Pews*, May 1, 1994.
45. SMPA, *News from the Pews*, May 29, 1993.
46. SMPA, Evangelization Committee Minutes, April 1993.
47. SMPA, *News From The Pews*, November 28, 1993.
48. Ibid., February 13, 1994.
49. Ibid., January 31, 1982.
50. SMPA, *News from the Pews*, September 21 1997.

celebrate on a more personal level the journey of faith.[51]

TRANSFORMING SOCIETY.

From the beginning of its history, the church in Canada had been connected with the works of charity and justice. The church's work in education, health care and social service sustained Canadian society when the response from government was muted. Over time government moved education, health care and social services into their realm. Models of cooperation between the church and government existed, but with the passing decades the role of the church was ever more muted in the models of care.

Shortly after the opening of the church on Amelia Street, Jean Vanier visited the parish holding a number of ecumenical events and connecting with facilities for those with intellectual challenges in the region.[52]

The church's impulse for community care expressed itself in a number of ways throughout the latter part of the twentieth century at St. Mary's.

In August of 1971, a John Bosco Home, at 68 Mary Street, was opened. This original effort had twelve beds for hard to place teenaged boys. Homes were located in various places in Ontario. St. Mary's was closely aligned with this work.[53]

In the fall of 1978, an initiative was undertaken to explore the social needs of the local community. Catholic Charities of Simcoe County was formed to meet the identified needs.[54] By April of 1979, the organization instigated the creation of Catholic Family Services. Over the next several months the proposal for a Catholic Family Life Centre of Simcoe South was formed. On September 4, 1979, the family center opened to provide services.

The initiative included a strong media effort to inform and educate the public about the work of the centre. The first director, Sheila Wallace, communicated to the *Barrie Banner* in September 1980, "the agency may assist a woman who was being physically abused by her husband or a young man coming to terms with his homosexuality."[55] Originally located on Dunlop Street, the office provided counselling and support for individuals and families without denominational consideration. In subsequent years the Catholic Family Life Centre created a number of programs focused on the enhancement of the

51. SMPA, Bulletin, April 9, 1995.
52. Ibid., July 20, 1969.
53. Ibid., August 22, 1971.
54. Ibid., October 1, 1978.
55. SMPA, Catholic Family Life File, *Barrie Banner*, Sept 10, 1980.

role of grandparents in families, to assist with curbing violence and with the encouragement of pro active parenting.[56]

An initial meeting regarding the possibility of St. Mary's sponsoring refugees took place in July 1979.[57] There had been a groundswell of concern arising from the plight of Vietnamese refugees which was now showing itself in the move to action as expressed in the bulletin that October.[58] By January it was announced that a family of ten would arrive soon. The children of the family were from twenty-eight to eleven years old.[59] The first five members of the family arrived on April 3. Those of school age were integrated into parish schools.[60]

In the fall of 1982, the parish committed itself to sponsoring Polish refugees.[61] In the case of the Polish couples that were sponsored they quickly assimilated into life in Toronto where they knew people from their home country.

At various times the parish found itself involved in a public campaign of resistance to trends in society.

Sunday shopping became an issue in the late 1980's and the parish encouraged parishioners to add their voice to the concern in light of challenges placed on families who were depending on commerce for employment.[62]

The Catholic Women's League embraced the white ribbon campaign in 1989 to express opposition to pornography. The faithful were invited to wear a white ribbon publicly for a week and then send it to their member of parliament to express their concern about the proliferation of pornography in society.[63]

C. O. M. E. was initiated by the archdiocese in 1979 to bring a spiritual dimension to the elderly who were living alone and those who were housebound.[64]

In 1982, a coalition of churches in Barrie took the initiative to form a food bank. The directors of the food bank were drawn from the many churches in town. The food bank was relocated on George Street in the spring of 1989.[65]

---

56. SMPA, Bulletin, November 7, 1982 and June 26, 1983.
57. SMPA, Parish Council Minutes, JULY 4, 1979.
58. SMPA, Bulletin, October 28, 1979.
59. Ibid., January 20, 1980.
60. Ibid., April 27, 1980.
61. Ibid., October 10, 1982.
62. Ibid., April 17, 1988.
63. Ibid., October 29, 1989.
64. Ibid., September 9, 1979.
65. Ibid., March 19, 1989.

Active Participation by the Faithful

Discussion about abortion started to appear in parish bulletins in the late 1960's. Over the subsequent years the work of various campaigns strove to make the issue of 'right to life' more clearly understood. Some efforts were educative while others were political. Feelings on both sides of the debate often led to less and less opportunity for useful dialogue.[66] Throughout these years, the confidence in political action was believed to be sufficient to assert the 'right to life.' The bulletin leading to the 1972 provincial election confidently encouraged, "Have your candidate declare himself publicly on the abortion issue."[67]

The spring of 1979, saw the initiation of Birthright which was organized to assist women who had challenging pregnancies. Crossing denominational lines and remaining apolitical, Birthright offered personal support for individuals.[68] The pro life cause expressed itself under numerous permutations, including a diocesan effort called Options for Life[69] in 1991 and the introduction of Life Chain, a public protest, in 1992.[70]

In May of 1986, it was reported that Hospice York was coming to Barrie to make a presentation about the work of the hospice movement.[71] Over the next couple of years the hospice movement took root in Barrie. By April of 1989, they were seeking space for an office and were ready to train volunteers.[72] The Royal Victoria Hospital had taken up the care of the dying through palliative care in 1981. Hospice sought to move this work from the hospital to less clinical surroundings.[73]

The parish bulletin discussed the Out of the Cold ministry in November of 1997. This ministry to serve those who were on the street, was instituted in Barrie with a number of churches hosting the work. St. Mary's parishioners were actively involved in this effort and in 2001 St. Mary's became a host parish.[74]

In 1993, the Collective Kitchen which allowed people in a communal endeavour to create meals in an economical fashion was instigated at St. Mary's.[75]

---

66. Ibid., January 3, 1971.
67. Ibid., October 22, 1972.
68. Ibid., March 25, 1979.
69. Ibid., May 5, 1991.
70. Ibid., September 27, 1992.
71. Ibid., May 25, 1986.
72. Ibid., April 2 & 9, 1989.
73. Ibid., November 1, 1981.
74. Ibid., November 2, 1987.
75. SMPA, *News from the Pews*, February 28, 1993.

Though much of the effort on the part of Barrie citizens and St. Mary's parishioners were centred on local problems, the parish, in 1981, formed a Development and Peace Group to look at international issues. Development and Peace was formed in the late sixties by the Bishops of Canada to reflect the growing awareness of global responsibility of all Christians.[76] As the years passed, Development and Peace was present in the parish at various times with various levels of effectiveness. Share Lent began in the 1960's for third world development and support of the seminary and was replaced by Share Life in 1977.[77]

In 1993, the parish sought to initiate a Crisis Support Committee. The initiative was to be present to the families who were facing serious illness or dealing with a death in their families. The announcements reflected well the sensibility of the time, "through the caring and sharing of parishioners a committee will be formed to offer help."[78]

The ecumenical movement which flowered in the 1960's, over the subsequent decades was carried along by some strongly motivated individuals, but on the whole never bore the fruit that the church anticipated.

There were efforts such as Friendship Sunday in the early seventies. This event had replaced the shut-in mass of the late sixties and it brought together the infirmed and aged of many faiths in one celebration at St. Mary's.[79]

The Barrie Prayer Breakfast was initiated in 1976. This in a formal way offered an opportunity for Christians to come together and affirm their common belief in prayer and community. It among the many ecumenical endeavours, was to prove to be the most successful.

There were events that crossed denominational boundaries of an evangelical nature though they often occurred in what seemed like isolation. The Barrie Alive event, in October of 1981, as well as efforts related to the Billy Graham Rally were a case in point.[80]

There were moments which were singular in their variation from the normal flow of the movement. One of these was the ordination of twenty-three United Church of Canada ministers at St. Mary's Church on May 27, 1980. The use of the space was indicated by the anticipated size of the congregation.[81]

---

76. SMPA, Bulletin, March 15 1981.
77. Ibid., March and April 1977.
78. Ibid., May 29, 1993.
79. Ibid., May 30, 1971.
80. Ibid., October 18, 1981.
81. SMPA, Program for Ordination, May 27, 1980.

Active Participation by the Faithful

The fruit of the ecumenical movement was realized in a greater civility between religious denominations and a willingness to dialogue on common goals. This common ground had perhaps been best expressed in the service of the poor as seen in the formation of the Barrie Food Bank and the Out of the Cold Movement which had particular dependence on the support of the local churches.

New Initiatives.

In January of 1971, the idea of a "parish advisory board" was first brought to the attention of the people.[82] It was reported in February that twenty nine people attended a meeting to discuss the undertaking with twelve in attendance agreeing to serve as a steering committee.[83] By the end of February, the steering committee was ready to present a proposal to the parish.

By May, the parish advisory council had been established with fourteen members.

The parish advisory council reflected the ideals of lay enthusiasm well. At the meeting in September of 1971, members discussed the folk mass which was now being celebrated at certain times, coffee breaks after mass, wide open parish advisory meetings, creation of a social committee, education on receiving communion in the hand, encouraging more enthusiasm on the part of lectors and acquisition of new hymn books.[84]

In the early days the parish council involved elections. Over time, it became normative that candidates were acclaimed and a new method of formation of a parish council was created, involving the appointment of members of every ministry. With the burgeoning number of ministries this proved to be unwieldy which lead to the creation of a parish council by appointment with consideration of broad representation.

It was promulgated that all parishes were required to have a parish finance council which was to be comprised of interested lay people as well as the pastor. The first finance council was duly appointed at St. Mary's in 1987.[85]

From the early nineties the parish council discussed the value in creating a parish library. In 1992, they were not convinced of the value. However, a

82. Ibid., January 31, 1971. It was not until 1975 that the term parish council came into use.

83. Ibid., February 7, 1971.

84. SMPA, Parish Council Minutes, Sept 7, 1971.

85. SMPA, Bulletin, December 27, 1987.

86. Ibid., May 24, 1998.

library was to become a reality in May of 1998,[86] providing a focus for the principle of ongoing learning as part of the life of the Catholic.

The challenge of communications was driven as much by technology as by need. The constantly changing ability to communicate lead to ever more expectations. The parish produced bulletin was superceded by a professionally produced bulletin in the late 1990's. A first parish website appeared in April of 2000.[87] The access to the televised mass for "shut-ins" was first offered on Sundays but was soon available daily and then twice daily for parishioners.

Property Matters.

The parish carried a significant debt in relation to the new church. Early in the seventies property owned by the church in the area of Cundles Road and Ferris Lane was sold. This had been purchased with a view to providing land for a school. This significantly defrayed the principal on the debt, which when moving into the new church was a half a million dollars.

In 1987 the Steele Street property beside St. Monica's School was sold. This property was part of an original gift from the Spearin Family which was given when the need for a second elementary school in the parish was recognized. In the early seventies this property had been, for a period, considered as a potential site for a nursing home. It was sold and the proceeds were applied to the cost of putting an addition on the church.[88]

The ever growing parish demanded a need for space both inside and out. Fifty seven parking spaces were added in 1978.[89]

Beginning in 1986, the parish considered the addition of meeting rooms to the church. The first proposal offered two meetings rooms and over time this plan was altered to allow for the creation of three meeting rooms as well as additional washrooms.[90] This project was undertaken in the fall and winter of 1987 and 1988.[91] The new addition was blessed and officially opened on May 18, 1988. The three rooms were originally put under the patronage of the Sacred Heart, Mary and the Holy Family. They eventually became known as room one, two and three.

Early in 1987, the diocese had entered into an agreement with the province to create more affordable housing for seniors.

87. Ibid., April 9, 2000.
88. SMPA, Parish Council Minutes, February 27, 1987.
89. SMPA, Bulletin, October 29, 1978.
90. SMPA, Parish Council Minutes, October 27, 1986.
91. SMPA, Correspondence, Hawkshaw to Blackwell, May 2, 1988.

In February of 1989, the diocese presented a plan to the parish council for the creation of a seniors' building on the church property. At this meeting the two chief concerns that would challenge the project were identified. The first was the parishioners' concern with parking being negatively impacted and the second the neighbourhood's concern with increased traffic.[92] Some of the parish discontent related to the focus group who would be served by the project. There were those who felt that the care of the frail and physically limited would be a better use of resources and space.

As to location, many felt that the cemetery lands fronting Anne Street would provide an adequate site for the project.

At the end of December, 1989, the plan for a four-storey seniors' residence was brought before the city council.[93] Heated discussion through the month of February often pitted councillors against each other. When approval came to a vote, the City of Barrie voted against the project.[94] The issue came to a head on January 7, 1991, when the Ontario Municipal Board, overturned the city council's decision to prevent construction. With the O. M. B. decision a local citizens group then went to the divisional court where in July of 1991 their case was lost and the project finally moved forward.[95] The groundbreaking occurred on March 1, 1992 and the building was officially opened on September 19, 1993.[96]

The parish was informed that applications for tenants were being accepted in September of 1991.[97]

During the tenure of Fr. Charles Reeves, Catholic Cemeteries of the Archdiocese took on responsibility for St. Mary's Cemetery. There was still a large tract of land fronting on both Sunnidale and Anne Street. In 1972, the Separate School Board had approached the diocese regarding the land fronting Anne Street, wanting to be considered if the land was to be sold. This initiative was discouraged at the time. Many years later the land was sold as the site for the French Catholic high school, Nouvelle Alliance.

In 1987, Catholic Cemeteries committed themselves to a more proactive management of the cemetery which led to the renovation of the upper level of the vault for offices. At the same time permanent on site staff were employed for the management and maintenance of the property.

---

92. SMPA, Minutes of Parish Council, February 21, 1989.
93. BPL, *Barrie Examiner*, December 20, 1989, p. 2.
94. SMPA, Bulletin, February 25, 1990.
95. Ibid., May 19, 1991.
96. Ibid., February 23, 1992.
97. Ibid., September 1, 1991.

In 2012, the cemetery undertook the clearing of more land. The cemetery was eleven acres, with the addition of the additional cleared land it increased to twenty acres.

Transformative Movements.

The September 1977, parish council noted that members had been approached about meetings and seminars in relation to charismatic renewal.[98] Charismatic prayer was present in the life of St. Mary's by the summer of 1978. The invitation in the June 1978 bulletin invited people to come out, assuring them that outward expressions of fervour were not required, that all were welcome. It was hoped that there would be a Life in the Spirit Seminar available later in the year to better orient people to the charismatic renewal.[99]

The charismatic team from St. Joseph's Hospital was invited to come and to take the lead in a healing mass at St. Mary's in the fall of 1977. The mass was to assist with healing of both a spiritual and a physical nature.[100] The focus of the ministry was in part to gather people in prayer but also to intervene on their behalf through intercessory prayer. Fr. Stan Blackwell who spent a significant part of his ministry in Simcoe County was highly identified with the charismatic renewal as a healing ministry. As the note on charismatic prayer in the 1979 annual booklet stated, "Everyone is invited to come and pray and to be prayed over."[101]

At the parish council meeting in October 1977, presentations were made by Marriage Encounter, Cursillo and charismatic renewal. It was promised that Genesis II and COR would make presentations at an upcoming meeting. This reflected the significant movement in the church to lay based organizations taking the lead in faith formation.[102]

Cursillo was initiated in Spain in 1949, and reached the Archdiocese of Toronto in 1963. Cursillo, which was an ongoing formation process which began with a weekend retreat, which consisted of teaching, emphasizing the role of baptism in the Christian life and the need to be responsive to the call to conversion throughout life. One interesting feature of the Cursillo movement was the requirement that husbands participate in Cursillo before wives. The thought being that if the work was to be successful the full willingness of

98. SMPA, Parish Council Minutes, September 18, 1977.
99. SMPA, Bulletin, June 25, 1998.
100. SMPA, Parish Council Minutes, October 23, 1977.
101. SMPA, Parish Booklet, 1979, p. 6.
102. SMPA, Parish Council Minutes, October 23, 1977.

men to participate must be considered first. It is an interesting reflection on the evolving experience of church life that in 1979, Cursillo promoted as part of its attractiveness that, "There are no long periods of silence and there is very little solitude."[103]

In the spring of 1977, the bulletin announced that there would be a Cursillo weekend in Toronto and that there were local men who could be contacted for more information regarding "this opportunity to enrich your personal life."[104] By the early 1980's the movement was present in Barrie, with weekend retreats taking place in schools.[105]

The Cursillo movement with its strong emphasis on personal conversion grew and adapted the values of the movement to create COR; a movement for youth; Marriage Encounter; which celebrated marriage; and Retrouvaille; which sought to heal struggling marriages.

The 1970's saw the burgeoning of Marriage Encounter in the church in Canada. First promoted at St. Mary's in the spring of 1975, throughout this period the Marriage Encounter movement was extremely active.

Early in 1979, the parish was introduced to Retrouvaille.[106]

At the end of February 1977, a call went out for young people to attend a COR weekend in Toronto.[107] Later that year COR was offered in Penetanguishene.[108] The first COR weekend occurred in Barrie in April of 1978, with two weekends occurring each year until February of 1987. Throughout the early seventies, outreach to youth, through youth groups and other initiatives took on endless permutations.

In February of 1987, the New Beginnings team came to Barrie to explain and promote their work of spiritual care of those whose marriages had ended.[109] The initiative for this work grew out of the ministry of the Sisters of St. Joseph.

The vocations to priesthood and religious life in the church during the 1950's had reached astounding numbers. With the coming of the sixties there was a radical decline in the number of people responding to the call to serve in the church and large numbers of priests and professed religious were leaving their calling. The easiest analysis suggested that somehow the changes them-

---

103. SMPA, Parish Booklet, 1979, p. 8-9.
104. SMPA, Bulletin, May 8, 1977.
105. Ibid., September 26, 1981.
106. Ibid., January 7, 1979.
107. Ibid., February 27, 1977.
108. Ibid., October 2, 1977.
109. Ibid., February 15, 1987.

selves had brought about the drop in vocations.

One initiative to encourage vocations that found its way into the parish was called VIVA. (Ventures in Vocation Awareness) This event at Springwater Park on Vocation Sunday took the form of a family picnic at which a significant number of religious were present to interact with those in attendance.[110]

During the early 1980's, the archdiocese facilitated a number of initiatives to encourage vocations. These initiatives reached into the life of the parish and offered an opportunity for thoughtful discussion on the priesthood and other forms of vocational life.

Education.

In the fall of 1969, the provincial Liberals came out in support of full funding of Catholic education till the end of grade thirteen. The initiative was endorsed also by the NDP. In November of 1969, the Barrie Examiner, also endorsed the effort to bring about what they described as, "the channelling of benevolence where it has been pledged in the first place."[111] The ongoing discussion was highlighted with a number of public actions including an Equality Sunday early in 1970 in which church going Catholics petitioned their legislators at Queen's Park.[112]

St. Joseph's High School, from its founding in 1946, proved to be a successful institution, but one which placed great financial demands on the parish. For those grades that were not subsidized by the province the support had come from the parish. An effort was undertaken to encourage greater financial support of other Simcoe County parishes in the early seventies. Many parishes were responsive, but others could simply not undertake the effort.

In January of 1971, a meeting was planned for parishioners to consider the course of action for the future. By this period, the parish was committing $60,000 annually for the maintenance of the secondary school for grade nine to twelve. The funding by the government ended after grade ten. It was suggested that if no provincial funding was forthcoming, the high school should be closed in June of 1972.[113]

Instead in 1972, the economic demands led to a decision to discontinue the Grade 11 and 12 classes at St. Joseph's High School.[114]

---

110. Ibid., May 29, 1977.
111. Ibid., November 16, 1969.
112. Ibid., February 22, 1969.
113. Ibid., January 24, 1971.
114. SMPA, School Files, Memorandum re: St. Joseph's High School, January 10, 1972.

At this time St. Joseph's became a junior high school, including classes for grade eights from St. John's and St. Mary's. All grade sevens from both schools attended St. Mary's. It lightened the pressure for space on St. John's School which was experiencing serious over crowding.[115]

In 1975, the proposal was put forward that a new junior high school should be built in Barrie.[116] The proposal met with little success.

In June of 1978, another push was made to move out of the site on Mulcaster and build a new school which would be able to accommodate grade eleven and twelve.[117] A committee was struck to explore the possibility of extending Catholic education to grade 13.[118] What came to be called the St. Joseph's Private High School Board undertook its work with determination. By November of 1981, they were able to report to St. Mary's Parish that they were confident that the numbers existed to merit a Catholic High School to Grade 13. They had the general commitment of a good number of households to support the effort and were in the process of creating a charitable foundation.[119] In 1983, the St. Joseph's Private School Board announced that the new St. Joseph's had more than thirty grade elevens and more than sixty grade nines signed up for the coming year. Tuition for the school would be four hundred and fifty dollars a year though no one would be turned away.[120]

Fund raising and site selection committees were formed. By May the interested parties were forming an alumnus of St. Joseph's graduates to promote the new school.[121]

Catholic secondary education continued to move forward. Plans were put in place to build a new high school on what was at the time, the perimeter of the city on Cundles Road East. In the fall of 1985, the opening of the school coincided with the change of government policy allowing for the full funding of separate schools to the end of grade thirteen. The change was to radically transform Catholic secondary education as the schools were fully accessible not only to Catholic families, but by agreement were to welcome any non-Catholics who may opt for the system at the secondary level. This lead to continuous growth at St. Joseph's High School over the next number of years.

---

115 ISMPA, School Files, Memorandum, Bolger to Parents of Grade 7 And 8 students, 1972.

116. SMPA, Bulletin, May 11, 1975.

117. Ibid., June 11, 1978.

118. Ibid., June 18, 1978.

119. Ibid., November 8, 1981, tip in bulletin.

120. Ibid., March 13, 1983.

121. Ibid., May 1, 1983.

The growing population brought about a demand for elementary schools. In 1976, Monsignor Clair School at Livingstone and Cundles was opened. There was subsequently the addition of St. Marguerite D'Youville in 1993, The Good Shepherd in 1998, and Sr. Catherine Donnelly welcomed students in 2003.

St. Mary's, the oldest school in the Simcoe Muskoka Separate School Board made a radical transformation when the sixth building to carry that name was opened in April of 1992. Its relocation from the city core to the north west corner of the city allowed the continuation of the school as a vital entity in a changing city.

Junior kindergarten was introduced in 1980 extending the reach of Catholic education one year earlier in most families.

The role of French education was quickly unfolding in tandem with funded Catholic secondary education.[122] In the fall of 1982, the parish bulletin was used to solicit interest in a bilingual program of education. By 1983, kindergarten in both official languages was being offered at St. Monica's.[123] In 1987, the St. Monica's facility was shared with Ecole Frere Andre a unilingual French elementary school.[124] Frere Andre opened its own building beside St. Joseph's High School in May of 1990.[125] In the initial stages, the schools for French speaking education were understood to be under the pastoral care of the parish. Over time various approaches were undertaken to provide pastoral care in these schools which fell outside the jurisdiction of the Parish of St. Mary's.

The parish was reaching its apex as far as size in 2002. That year the parish had eighty-eight classrooms of students in grade one through eight.[126] By 2012 there were sixty four classes serving the same grades. Processes were well in place to explore the consolidation of the students and schools.

The Religious within our Midst.

The Sisters of St. Joseph continued to serve the church in Barrie, though the focus on teaching became less pronounced. Secondary teaching was discontinued in 1971, and elementary teaching in 1977.

For the sisters, the changing vocation numbers and discernment of the role of the religious led to changes at the convent on Berczy Street. In the early

122 Ibid., November 14, 1982.
123. Ibid., February 27, 1983.
124. Ibid., March 7, 1987.
125. SMPA, Parish Council Minutes, May 9 1990.
126. SMPA, Bulletin, March 30, 2002.

seventies, the convent became the novitiate, welcoming prospective candidates for the order. The mandate of the community to be in solidarity with those in need led to the creation of Maranatha House in 1977.[127] Under the auspices of the sisters, this facility located in the convent was a home for young girls until 1980.[128]

With the changing purpose of the house on Berczy Street, in 1976, the sisters moved their community house to 130 Cundles Road East[129] This initiative was short lived as the sisters decided after one hundred and eighteen years to leave Barrie. The last entry in the Annals of the sisters in Barrie states that they literally washed themselves right out of the house. They left and closed the convent on Cundles Road East at 5:45 on July 5, 1977.[130]

For a period, a Sister of the Good Shepherd, Clare Peckham, was resident in Barrie. She served as chair of the parish council and seems to have served the parish in various capacities. She left the area in 1977.[131]

In May of 1971, the bulletin of the parish stated that a member of the Grey Sisters of the Immaculate Conception of Pembroke would be in the parish that summer taking a course at Eastview Secondary and was seeking room and board. This is the first note regarding a relationship between the Grey Sisters and the parish which was to last for forty years.[132]

Various members of the Grey Sisters came to Barrie and lived, at times, in community on Strabane Avenue. At other times sisters lived individually and worked in education.

The pastor included a note in the bulletin in October 1993 which stated in part, "I am glad to be able to give you some good news. Sr. Marjorie Casey, whom many of you know, has agreed to come on the parish staff." Marjorie Casey who had for many years worked for the separate school board as family life coordinator, also served as choir director at the parish. For fifteen years she served as a pastoral minister in the parish.[133] Sister Marjorie Casey was to serve the parish until 2010 when she returned to the Grey Sisters Motherhouse in Pembroke.

Sr. Mary Rose Marrin, a member of the Sisters of St. Joseph, came to St. Mary's in 2007 to begin a ministry with maturing adults. Her time of service,

---

127 SMPA, Bulletin, January 30, 1977.

128. SMPA, Correspondence, Lemire to O'Malley, October 6, 1980.

129. SMPA., Bulletin, April-September 1976.

130. Ibid., July 5, 1977.

131. SMPA, Parish Council Correspondence, June 2 1977.

132. SMPA, Bulletin, May 23, 1971.

133. Ibid., October 3, 1993.

laid the groundwork for this effort, creating foundations that would permit the continuation of the ministry. The thrust of the work was to engage those in the second half of life, in ministry and to assist them through varied activities to deepen their sense of self awareness of their role in the life of the church. With the completion of Sr. Mary Rose's term of service in 2012 and her return to Toronto, Simcoe County for the first time since the mid nineteenth century had no women religious serving any Catholic institution of the county.

The Beginning of a New Millennium.

With the coming of the year 2000 the parish continued to seek ways to best express the aspirations of the faithful. A few months before the turn of the century the parish embraced the discipline of Eucharistic Adoration. The practice of personal prayer before the Blessed Sacrament was under the auspices of the Holy Cross Committee for Adoration. Each evening was to end with Benediction.[134] Over the next many years adoration continued, though the format and oversight was simplified.

The ecumenical movement called Alpha set down roots in the parish seeking to engage those whose faith was not well articulated.[135] Alpha was present in most Christian denominations and continued to be a positive force for Christian life over many years, though its life in St. Mary's was shorter.

The changing climate in relation to physical security of vulnerable people lead to the introduction of the Ministry Affirmation in 2003. Through this effort those who were to have significant contact with children or the frail aged were to seek a security check from the police and be screened for their ministry.[136]

World Youth Day was planned for Toronto and the role of the parish in recruiting billets and encouraging the interest of the young people in the event was an active consideration throughout the year, leading up to the event in 2002.

In 2001, Holy Spirit Parish was officially launched to serve the south west corner of the city and the Town of Essa. The congregation gathered first at St. Bernadette and later St. Joan of Arc School for Sunday worship.[137] Just before

134 Ibid., November 14, 1999.

135. Ibid., March 16, 2003.

136. Ibid., March 9, 2003.

137. Ibid., September 21, 2001.

Christmas 2012, Holy Spirit Parish began the celebration of Eucharist in their church on Essa Road. Barrie's second Catholic parish, St. John Vianney, by this time had been in their permanent church just over twenty years.[138]

In 2005, the parish marked its sesquicentennial. This year centered its celebrations on the theme taken from the Magnificat, "His mercy is from age to age."[139] Central to these celebrations was the commitment made to the Royal Victoria Hospital that through fundraising a gift of one hundred and fifty thousand dollars be made for cancer care. The motto that was chosen for this parish campaign was, "Bringing Care Closer to Home."

In 2010 and 2011, the church underwent a renovation which included the installation of stained glass windows and new lighting. Several of the initiatives which were part of the renovation sought to make the church brighter and emphasize the church's role as sacred space. The area around the entrance was redesigned to offer a greater sense of welcome and the bell which had been displayed outside the main doors since 1968 was hung and reactivated.

Initially, all lay ministers who came to work at St. Mary's were members of religious orders. As the numbers of religious decreased, the services of competent lay people were called upon. Colleen Evans, Robin Parkes, Mickie Oakes and Mary Perry White all came to work at St. Mary's as pastoral associates bringing their expertise from previous work to specific areas of concern in the parish.

The needs of refugees spurred the parish to action once again. Over the early years of new century families were welcomed from Afghanistan and Iraq.

And so current events and sociology slowly become history. The parish is in constant dialogue with the community around it and energized by the longing to know the possibilities of faith. With change and renewal there is still at the core of the parish the sure and certain hope that faith matters and makes a difference.

---

138. Ibid,. December 10, 1989: The church had been blessed December 17, 1989.
139. Ibid., March 27, 2005.

Bibliography

Beaudoin, Marc, *Glancing Over our Shoulders*, Knights of Colulmbus, Barrie, 1997.

Boddy, Samuel, *Samuel Ardagh, A Brief Memoir*, Blueberry Hills, 2003.

Boland, Edgar, *From the Pioneers to the Seventies, A History of the Diocese of Peterborough*, Maxwell Review, Peterborough, 1976.

Brown, Jennifer S. H., *Strangers in Blood*, UBC Press, Vancouver, 1980.

Clarke, Brian, *Piety and Nationalism*, McGill-Queen's University Press, Kingston, 1993.

Connolly, S. J., *Priests and People in Pre-Famine Ireland*, Four Courts Press, Dublin, 2001.

Cotton, Larry D., *Whiskey and Wickedness*, Vol. 1, Barrie, 1815-1885, Larry D. Cotton Associates, Barrie, 2004.

Fay, Terence, *A History of Canadian Catholics*, McGill-Queens University Press, Kingston, 2002.

Flynn, Lt. Col. L. J., *Built on a Rock, The Story of the Roman Catholic Church in Kingston*, 1826-1976, Brown and Martin, Kingston, 1976.

Hunter, Andrew F., *The History of Simcoe County*, The Historical Committee of Simcoe County, Barrie, 1948. (reprint)

Kelly,Edward, *The Story of St. Paul's Parish*, Toronto, 1822-1922, Centenary Committee, Toronto, 1923.

Ladell, John, *They Left Their Mark*, Dundurn Press, Toronto, 1993.

Lovell, Clint, *The Boys of Barrie*, RNU Press, Barrie, 2009.

MacDougall, Florence, et al., *The History of Barrie Collegiate Institute*, Barrie, 1943.

McDevitt, Francis V., *Father Gordon's Register*, 1830-1833, Halton-Peel Genealogical Society, 1995.

McGowan, Mark, *Michael Power*, McGill & Queen's University Press, Kingston, 2005.

McGowan, Mark, *The Waning of the Green*, McGill-Queen's University Press, Kingston, 1999.

Moir, John, *Church and Society*, Archdiocese of Toronto, 1991.

Murdoch et al., *Beautiful Barrie*, DBS Heritage Consulting and Communications, Barrie, 2005.

Power, Michael, *A Promise Fulfilled*, Ontario Catholics School Trustees, Toronto 2002.

Scollard, Robert, *They Honoured the Vestments of Holiness, A Calendar of the Deceased Bishops, Priests, and Deacons of the Archdiocese of Toronto, 1792-1990*, Archdiocese of Toronto, Toronto, 1990.

Smith, Donald B., *Sacred Feathers*, University of Toronto Press, Toronto, 1987.

Taves, Ann, *The Household of Faith*, Notre Dame Press, Indiana, 1986.

Trinity Anglican Church, *Sesqui-centennial of Trinity Anglican Church 1835-1985*, Barrie, 1985

The Archives and Libraries Used and the Main Records Researched.
Each Archive or Library is preceded by the abbreviation used in footnotes.

AHCH: All Hallows College Library
Dublin, Ireland
All Hallows Reports
Correspondence with the Diocese of Toronto

ARCAT: Archives of the Catholic Archdiocese of Toronto
The St. Mary's Parish Files
Sacramental Records of St. Anne's, Penetanguishene
Sacramental Records of St. John's, Newmarket

AO: Archives of Ontario
Upper Canada Sundries
Gowan Papers

BPL: Barrie Public Library
Barrie Advance
Barrie Examiner

SMPA: St. Mary's Parish Archives
History of Barrie Mission (1832-1944)
Registrum Memoriale of St. Mary's Parish
Announcement Books
Parish Bulletins
Various Committee meeting Notes.

MTRL:Metro Toronto Reference Library
Baldwin Room
Anderson Papers
O'Brien Papers

SCA: Simcoe County Archives
Gowan Letter Books
Francis Steeven's Diary
Hunter Papers

Index

A

B

C

Index

M

N

O

P

Q

R

S

CPSIA information can be obtained at www.ICGtesting.com
Printed in the USA
LVOW112328030613

336734LV00002B/9/P

9 780987 778451